COOKING
WITH WILD BERRIES & FRUITS
OF THE ROCKY MOUNTAIN STATES

by Teresa Marrone

Adventure Publications, Inc.
Cambridge, MN

ACKNOWLEDGMENTS

Huge thanks to Chris and Neil Swanson, and also Joe Musich, for help with the recipe testing. Thanks to Bernis Ingvaldson at Honeyberry USA for her help and advice with the sweetberries. Finally, a big thanks to Bruce Bohnenstingl for help with the wine recipe, and for being willing to eat the results of my recipe testing without complaint.

Cover and book design by Jonathan Norberg

Cover photo: Utah serviceberry by Teresa Marrone

Edited by Dan Downing

10 9 8 7 6 5 4 3 2 1

Copyright 2012 by Teresa Marrone
Published by Adventure Publications, Inc.
820 Cleveland Street South
Cambridge, Minnesota 55008
1-800-678-7006
www.adventurepublications.net

ISBN: 978-1-59193-291-8

TABLE OF CONTENTS

INTRODUCTION

Wild berries and fruits are everywhere, once you learn to look for them. You'll find raspberries growing in the shrubby areas around the playground, elderberries on the edges of cattail swamps, and hawthorns growing in forest remnants that have been kept as buffers around office parks. Some species, like apricots, blackberries and raspberries, look just like commercially available fruits, although in the wild they are usually smaller. Others have never been commercialized, and so will be unfamiliar at first.

This book celebrates edible wild berries and fruits. It includes information and recipes for over 50 species that are found in our area. Here you'll find recipes for sauces, baked goods, and other foods made with these delicious wild fruits. (For more information on identifying these plants please see the companion book, *Wild Berries & Fruits Field Guide of the Rocky Mountain States*.)

One thing to keep in mind is that wild fruits are much less consistent than domestic fruits, which have been bred for specific flavor characteristics (as well as the ability to withstand the rigors of packing and shipping). When working with wild fruits, it may be necessary to adjust the amount of sugar, for example, if the fruit you've picked isn't as sweet as it might be. If you use wild berries in recipes calling for the same type of domestic berry you may need to adjust quantities; wild berries are typically smaller and pack more closely together, so a cup of wild blueberries weighs more than a cup of domestic blueberries.

Another very important thing to remember is that wild fruits have not been thoroughly tested for possible adverse reactions in sensitive individuals. Some foods—both wild and domestic—simply don't agree with everyone. When you're sampling a wild fruit for the first time, eat only a small portion to make sure that you won't have a problem.

It is also worth stressing that before eating something which you've harvested from the wild, you must be *absolutely certain* that the plant has been identified properly. Further, it's important to realize that even if the fruit of a plant is edible, the leaves and other parts may make you sick if you eat them. Some fruits are mildly toxic when underripe; others have pits or seeds that contain harmful substances, and so require specific preparation. This book attempts to alert the reader to possible problems, but it's still a good practice to get assistance from a knowledgeable forager before harvesting or preparing unfamiliar wild foods.

How This Book Is Organized

Fruits are listed in alphabetical order, by their common name. In several cases, similar fruits have been grouped because they are interchangeable in recipes; for example, huckleberries and blueberries are in one section.

Each species includes a bit of general information about the plant, including any harvesting tips that might be particularly helpful. If the fruit is commonly juiced, instructions are included with this general information. You'll learn how to successfully preserve your harvest by freezing, if appropriate. Recipes for each species are included; and at the end of each species, there's a list of recipes elsewhere in the book that use that particular fruit, as well as some quick ideas for using the fruit.

After the individual species, there are two recipes that use mixed fruits, as well as six recipes using juice or syrup from virtually any of the fruits in this book. Following this are instructions on how to make jelly and jam; each species includes measurements for making jelly and jam (when appropriate), but rather than repeating the same instructions multiple times, the specific instructions are written on pgs. 176–179. The book concludes with general information that pertains to many different fruits, such as instructions on dehydrating berries and fruits, making fruit leather, and instructions for sterilizing jars and canning.

You'll also find useful tips throughout the book. These explain things like how to make a lattice-top pie crust, zesting lemons and other citrus fruits, and how to make a quick home-made balsamic vinaigrette. These tips apply to a number of recipes in the book and will make cooking easier.

ABOUT ALTITUDE VARIATIONS

As anyone who lives in the Rocky Mountain states knows, altitude can have a dramatic effect on cooking. Cakes and other baked goods are particularly affected; baking recipes in most cookbooks that work great in, say, Omaha may produce unexpected results (or fail completely) if prepared without adjustment in the high-elevation parts of our area.

To some extent, all baking recipes prepared by home cooks are subject to varying results based on a number of factors. Home ovens are often not calibrated accurately; many are 10 degrees off or even more. Surprisingly, measuring cups and spoons are not all as accurate as they should be, either; in a 2011 test by the staff at *Cook's Illustrated* magazine, it was discovered that some commonly available 1-cup measures were off by as much as 2 tablespoons, an amount that can have a fairly big effect on the final results of a recipe. Most home cooks have learned to make minor adjustments to recipes, adding a little more milk if the batter seems too dry, for example, or baking a little longer than the recipe says. Altitude adjustments, however, are often beyond this simple sort of trial-and-error adjustment so many cooks are used to.

The fundamental issue is that air pressure drops as the altitude, or elevation, goes up. Even the simplest of kitchen tasks, boiling water, is greatly affected by air pressure because water boils when it has the same pressure as the surrounding air, so when the air pressure drops, so does the boiling point. Rather than boiling at 212°F (which is the most common number used when discussing boiling point at sea level), water on the officially "mile-high" Capitol steps in Denver would boil at 202°F . . . in theory. You may wonder why this can't this be pinned down exactly. In reality, the actual boiling point of water is affected by many subtle things, including microclimates, daily barometric pressure and mineral content of the water.

Altitude plays havoc with the action of leaveners like baking powder, baking soda and yeast. Leaveners work by creating gas bubbles in the food; as air pressure drops, the gas bubbles meet less resistance so they expand more quickly and vigorously. As a result, a cake may rise dramatically midway through baking, then collapse before it is baked through.

Liquids evaporate more quickly at higher elevations, and the dry mountain air in much of our region also means that pantry staples such as flour have less moisture in them (ever notice that an opened box of crackers stays fresh longer in the mountains than it would in, say, Omaha?).

Many high-altitude bakers are accustomed to simple recipe adjustments, such as adding a little more flour to a muffin recipe. The science behind this is that the flour helps strengthen the batter, enabling it to support the more powerful leavening action. Experienced cooks may also increase the oven temperature slightly, which helps the risen muffins "set" before they have a chance to collapse. But additional liquid is also often needed, and that seems counterintuitive; why add more flour *and* more liquid? Well, the liquid is helping compensate for the more rapid evaporation (and also the lower moisture in the flour), and also for the higher oven temperature often used at high elevations. If the muffin batter dries out too quickly, the concentrations of sugar and butter rise, leading to dense, heavy muffins. So, we must also sometimes reduce sugar, and possibly fat … suddenly, this is becoming extremely complicated!

To help you avoid these hit-or-miss experiments, the recipes in this book have been standardized for the approximate altitude of the area's largest city, Denver, which is officially at one mile above sea level: 5,280 feet. If changes to ingredient measurements, baking temperatures or procedures are required at other altitudes, adjustments are included as footnotes; a band at the top of the recipe reminds you that the recipe has been adjusted for 5,000 feet and that you may need to make adjustments based on the altitude of your kitchen. These adjustments are primarily in recipes for baked goods, and include suggested changes at altitudes below 5,000 feet; at 7,500 feet; and at 10,000 feet. So if you are baking in Boise, Idaho (elevation 2,858) you'd make the adjustments noted for altitudes below 5,000 feet; if you're baking in Gunnison, Colorado (elevation 7,673), you'd need to look at the adjustments for 7,500 feet.

Even with all these suggested adjustments, you may have to make your own slight adjustments to get a dish to come out just right in your own situation, on that particular day—just as cooks do even at low elevation. If a recipe states that a cake should bake for 35 to 40 minutes but a wooden pick inserted in the center does not come out clean after 40 minutes (even though the recipe instructions say that it should), continue baking it, checking it again in a few minutes. If the cake (or other food) is browning too quickly but is not yet done, prevent scorching by draping a piece of foil loosely over the top during the last 5 or 10 minutes of baking.

Here are a few additional tips for cooking at high elevations.

- Pie crusts are particularly prone to scorching around the edges before the filling is cooked through. Shield the crust edge during the last 10 minutes of baking with strips of foil, shaped to fit loosely around the edge of the pie plate and to cover the edge of the crust.

- Spices such as cinnamon may need to be increased slightly at altitudes above 7,500 feet.

- When making jelly, fudge or other foods that require cooking the mixture to a certain number of degrees above boiling, always measure the boiling point of water in your kitchen, *on that day*, before beginning, then add the recipe's "degrees above boiling point" to the number you measured. Jelly, for example, should be cooked to 8 degrees above boiling, so if your thermometer measures boiling water at 202°F, cook the jelly to 210°F. Use the *same thermometer* to test both the boiling water and the temperature of the mixture you're cooking.

- Baked goods such as cakes, bars and gooey rolls tend to stick to the baking pans more at higher elevations. Grease and flour your baking dishes well; above 7,500 feet you may also wish to line the bottom of a baking dish with a piece of waxed paper that has been cut to fit.

- When making cakes, quick breads and muffins at altitudes of 7,500 feet and higher, it's sometimes necessary to use a larger pan to allow for increased expansion. For example, substitute a 9x9-inch dish in a recipe that calls for an 8x8-inch dish; use a slightly larger loaf pan for quick breads; put less batter in each muffin cup so you make 8 muffins rather than the 6 indicated in the recipe.

- Meats and vegetables may take a bit longer to cook at high altitude, whether you're grilling, frying, baking, boiling or cooking in a slow cooker.

- Canning in a boiling-water bath requires altitude adjustments; see the chart on pg. 183.

For additional information about cooking at high altitudes, consult the Extension Service in your area. I also recommend *Pie in the Sky: Successful Baking at High Altitudes* by Susan G. Purdy (see Bibliography, pg. 184) as a helpful guide and useful resource. Now, let's get cooking!

APPLES and CRABAPPLES (*Malus* spp.)

Apples aren't native to the United States, but they may be found in the wild as escapees from cultivation, "planted" by birds or, perhaps, by a picnicker who tossed an apple core into the woods. You might also find apple trees that are remnants of an abandoned orchard, or those that grow on old homestead sites. Typically, these feral apples are smaller than commercially grown varieties and are often misshapen and blotchy. However, they are great for eating or cooking; simply cut away and discard any damaged or wormy portions.

Wild apples in our area may have reddish skins just like the apples you buy in the grocery store. They may also be yellow with a reddish tinge, or even solid yellow. Numerous varieties of crabapple have been planted in yards and parks, and may occasionally be found in the wild in our region. In addition, a native wild crabapple (*Peraphyllum ramosissimum*) is found in some of the warmer, drier parts of our region such as the Four Corners area. Although size, shape and color vary dramatically among crabapples, all are edible, although the native variety is somewhat bitter and has large seeds. Larger fruits, ¾ inch across or more, work best for making purée, or for cutting up to use in recipes; tiny crabapples have a lot of seeds in comparison to the amount of flesh, and it's next to impossible to remove the seeds without destroying the fruit. However, tiny crabapples can be used to make juice; the high proportion of skin makes the juice a particularly deep pink color. Large crabapples can be used to make juice also, but since they are more versatile, you may wish to save them for recipes that call for cut-up fruit.

Apples and crabapples, especially those that are slightly underripe, are rich in natural pectin; the juice can be used to make jelly without the commercial pectin needed for most jellies. Even though the juice may look a bit cloudy, the jelly will be clear as long as you don't squeeze the fruit during juicing. Apples also make excellent leather (pg. 182).

To prepare apple or crabapple juice, cut fruits in half (or into quarters or eighths if large), removing stems and blossom ends; if fruit has soft spots or bugs, cut away and discard the affected portions. Place in non-aluminum pot; add water to cover the fruit completely. Heat to boiling over high heat. Reduce heat so mixture is simmering, then cover and simmer without stirring until the fruit is very soft, 20 to 25 minutes. Transfer the mixture to a strainer lined with doubled, dampened cheesecloth and let it drip for 30 minutes; if you're making jelly, don't squeeze the fruit or the jelly will be cloudy. After the liquid has dripped away, set it aside and squeeze the fruit into a different container; you can use this cloudy juice as a beverage or for cooking. Yield varies quite a bit, because apples and crabapples vary so much in size; in general, you'll get 2 cups of juice per pound of crabapples, or about 2½ cups per pound of apples.

If you have a fruit press, you can use it to make fresh apple cider from apples or crabapples. You may want to mix in some regular cider apples with the wild fruits, to balance the flavor. Home-pressed cider is a delicious beverage on its own, and can also be fermented to make an outstanding wine or hard apple cider. For more information on making apple wine or hard cider, consult a book on home winemaking such as *First Steps in Winemaking* by C.J.J. Berry or *The American Cider Book* by Vrest Orton.

Apple or Crabapple Jelly (no added pectin)
About 3 half-pints per 2 pounds of fruit

Crabapple or apple jelly has a pleasant flavor; if red-skinned crabapples are used, it will also have a lovely pink color.

Apple or crabapple juice

1 teaspoon lemon juice for each cup of juice

²/₃ cup sugar for each cup of juice

Because this recipe does not use commercial pectin, it's more flexible; you can make as little as 2 pints, or as much as 5 pints, depending on how much fruit you've got. When preparing the juice, use a mix of ripe and slightly underripe fruit for the best flavor and texture. Please read "Jelly Instructions for Fruits with Natural Pectin" on pgs. 177–178 to learn about testing for doneness.

Measure the juice; for each 2 cups of juice, prepare 3 half-pint canning jars, bands and new lids as directed on pg. 183. Place measured juice and lemon juice in a non-aluminum pot that holds at least four times the amount of juice you're using. For each cup of juice, measure ²/₃ cup of sugar; set it aside. Heat juice to boiling over medium-high heat. Add sugar and cook, stirring constantly, until sugar dissolves. Increase heat to high and cook, skimming off any foam and stirring frequently, until jelly passes one or more of the doneness tests on pgs. 177–178; this typically takes 10 to 15 minutes, but will take longer at higher elevations.

Once the jelly is done, skim any foam off the surface and pour the jelly, while still hot, into the prepared canning jars; seal with prepared lids and bands. Process in a boiling-water bath for 15 minutes at 5,000 feet, or at the recommended time for your elevation (see pg. 183); if you prefer, you can store the jelly in the refrigerator where it will keep for a month or longer.

Variation: Add a handful of fresh mint leaves to the apples or crabapples when preparing the juice, for a delightful Apple- or Crabapple-Mint Jelly.

Make some extra jelly when apples or crabapples are in season, to use as holiday gifts. Cut a square of colorful fabric, large enough to cover the top of the canning jar; wrap it over the lid and tie in place with some pretty ribbon.

Apple Filling

About ½ cup; easily increased

Cinnamon and brown sugar give a wonderful flavor to this easy filling.

1 cup cored, chopped apples
1½ tablespoons lemon juice
1½ tablespoons (packed) brown sugar
⅛ teaspoon cinnamon

In small, heavy-bottomed non-aluminum saucepan, combine apples and lemon juice. Cover and cook over medium heat, stirring frequently, until fruit is tender, about 5 minutes. Stir in brown sugar and cinnamon; cook for about a minute longer to dissolve sugar. Cool before using.

Use this to prepare Easy Bear Claws (pg. 81), Fruit-Striped Cookie Fingers (pg. 126), or Fruit-Filled Muffins (pg. 155). Refrigerate extra filling, and use to top oatmeal or toast.

Crabapplejack

One fifth-sized bottle

Traditional applejack is a brandy that has been distilled from apple juice. Here's an easy way to make apple-flavored brandy.

2 cups small crabapples
1 fifth brandy
½ cup sugar, or to taste

You'll need a glass jar that holds at least 40 ounces, with a mouth wide enough to insert the crabapples; juice is often sold in these types of bottles. Wash it very well, then fill it with boiling water and let stand for at least 5 minutes.

Wash crabapples very well; remove stems and blossom ends. Drain water from bottle; add crabapples and brandy. Cap bottle, and place in a cupboard or other dark location that is room temperature or slightly cooler. Let steep for 8 to 10 weeks, gently shaking the bottle once or twice a week.

After the 8- to 10-week period, strain out and discard crabapples. Filter the brandy through a funnel lined with a paper coffee filter into a clean bottle; add sugar. Return the bottle to the cupboard, and let mellow for a few weeks before serving.

Apple-Ginger-Cardamom Jam (no added pectin)
5 half-pints

Sparkling, bright red and tangy, this jam is a favorite of all who try it.

2 pounds apples

1 piece peeled fresh gingerroot, about 1 inch by 3 inches or slightly larger

3 ⅓ cups sugar

2 cups water

2 tablespoons freshly squeezed lemon juice

¾ teaspoon cardamom seeds (from about 15 cardamom pods)

Prepare 5 half-pint canning jars, bands and new lids as directed on pg. 183. Cut apples into small pieces, removing and discarding cores. Place apples in heavy-bottomed non-aluminum pan. Grate gingerroot and add to pan along with remaining ingredients.

Heat to boiling over medium-high heat, stirring frequently. Reduce heat so mixture is bubbling at a moderate pace and cook, stirring frequently, until thickened, 45 minutes to 1 hour; a small scoop of jam should jell as described in Green Gooseberry Jam on pg. 57. Ladle into prepared jars, leaving ½ inch headspace. Seal with prepared lids and bands. Process in a boiling-water bath for 20 minutes at 5,000 feet, or at the recommended time for your elevation (see pg. 183); if you prefer, you can store the jam in the refrigerator where it will keep for a month or longer.

Other recipes in this book featuring wild apples:
Easy Chokecherry Applesauce, pg. 37
Fruits of the Forest Pie, pg. 168
Six Recipes Using Wild Fruit Juice or Syrup, pgs. 170–174
Wild Berry or Fruit Syrup, pg. 175
Wild Berry or Fruit Leather, pg. 182
As a substitute in Blackberry-Apple Crisp, pg. 21
As a substitute in Pear Butter, pg. 106
As a substitute in Rose Hip-Apple Jelly, pg. 131

Quick ideas for using apples:
Apple juice mixes well with other wild fruit juices for making jelly.

APRICOTS and PEACHES (*Prunus* spp.)

While not common in our area, apricots (*Prunus armeniaca*) and peaches (*P. persica*) are occasionally found growing wild; some are remnants of old orchards, while others may have drifted into the wild from commercial fruit-growing operations. The fruits tend to be quite a bit smaller than orchard-grown fruits, and the skin might be more pale in color. Like many wild fruits, eating quality varies quite a bit from tree to tree. Some are sweet and delicious, and taste even better than store-bought fruits; use these in the same way that you would use commercially grown fruits. Others are not as sweet or may have a slightly bitter quality. If you've found peaches like this, try the Sweet-Sour Pickled Peaches recipe on pg. 14. The Sweet and Sour Sauce on pg. 13 and the Apricot or Peach Salsa on pg. 15 would both work well with either apricots or peaches that are not perfectly sweet; these are also great recipes if the fruits you've found are slightly blemished, because you can simply cut away the damaged parts and cut up the rest of the fruit for the recipes. Finally, apricots or peaches make good leather (pg. 182).

Apricot or Peach Filling

About ½ cup; easily increased

½ teaspoon water

¼ teaspoon cornstarch

¾ cup finely chopped apricots or peaches, peeled before chopping

1 tablespoon sugar, or as needed according to the sweetness of the fruit

½ teaspoon lemon juice

¼ teaspoon vanilla extract

In small bowl, blend together water and cornstarch; set aside. In small, heavy-bottomed saucepan, combine chopped peaches, 1 tablespoon sugar, the lemon juice and vanilla. Heat to boiling over medium-high heat, then cook, stirring frequently, until fruit is soft and is beginning to break up; this will take 5 to 10 minutes. Taste, and add additional sugar if necessary; cook for a minute longer, stirring constantly to dissolve the sugar. Add cornstarch mixture, stirring constantly; cook for 1 to 2 minutes longer, or until thick. Cool before using.

Use this to prepare Easy Bear Claws (pg. 81), Fruit-Striped Cookie Fingers (pg. 126), or Fruit-Filled Muffins (pg. 155). Refrigerate extra filling, and use to top oatmeal or toast.

Sweet and Sour Sauce

About 1 cup

This is a nice variation on the classic sweet and sour sauce that usually contains pineapples. Serve it with egg rolls, either warm, just after making, or cold, after it has been in the refrigerator. It also works well as a base for sweet and sour pork. This comes together quickly, so have all your ingredients prepped and ready to go before you start cooking.

2 tablespoons cold water

2 teaspoons cornstarch

½ to ¾ teaspoon dry mustard powder (use the larger amount for a slightly spicier sauce)

½ cup finely diced onion (¼-inch dice)

2 teaspoons vegetable oil

1 clove garlic, minced or pressed

1 teaspoon finely minced fresh gingerroot

¾ cup finely diced apricots or peaches (¼-inch dice; peeled before dicing)

⅓ cup dry sherry

⅓ cup unseasoned rice vinegar

¼ cup ketchup

¼ cup (packed) golden brown sugar

In small bowl, stir together the water, cornstarch and dry mustard; set aside. In medium non-aluminum saucepan, sauté onion in oil over medium heat until just beginning to soften, 2 to 3 minutes; do not let it brown. Add garlic and gingerroot; cook, stirring constantly, for about 15 seconds. Add apricots and sherry; increase heat to high and cook for about 1 minute, stirring several times. Stir in vinegar, ketchup and brown sugar. Cook until mixture just begins to boil, then adjust heat and cook at a gentle boil for about 5 minutes. Stir the cornstarch mixture quickly, then add to mixture in saucepan, stirring constantly. Cook until mixture returns to a gentle boil, then cook for about 2 minutes, stirring constantly. Remove from heat and set aside to cool slightly before serving; serve warm or cold. Store in refrigerator.

To peel apricots or peaches, drop a few into a saucepan of boiling water. Let cook for about 1 minute, then remove with a slotted spoon and hold under cold running water for about 30 seconds. The skins will slip right off.

Sweet-Sour Pickled Peaches

Per pint; easily increased

Serve these as a side dish with ham and other smoked meats; I've also read that some people enjoy them on cucumber sandwiches. Try it and see what you think!

About 2 pounds wild peaches

1½ cups sugar

¾ cup apple cider vinegar

⅓ cup water

4 whole cloves

1 whole cinnamon stick

Sterilize a wide-mouth one-pint canning jar, band and new lid according to the instructions on pg. 183; let the jar sit in the hot water until needed. Peel the peaches by placing them, a few at a time, into a saucepan of boiling water for about a minute; remove with a slotted spoon and slip the skins off under cold, running water. Slice into wedges that are ½ inch thick on the outside edge, cutting along the pit as necessary to free the slice; also cut away and discard any damaged areas. Cut enough slices to fill the pint jar completely, plus a few extra (the slices pack more tightly when they've been cooked for a bit).

In non-aluminum saucepan, combine sugar, vinegar, water, cloves and cinnamon stick. Heat to boiling over medium-high heat, then cook, stirring constantly, until sugar dissolves. Add peach slices; adjust heat so mixture is simmering and cook until peaches are tender but not mushy, 5 to 10 minutes. Use a slotted spoon to transfer the peaches to the prepared jar; also slip the cinnamon stick and cloves into the jar. Pour the vinegar mixture over the peaches, filling to ½ inch from the top; discard excess vinegar mixture. Seal jar and set aside until cool. Refrigerate for at least a week to allow flavors to blend before serving; keep refrigerated.

Note: You could also can the peaches, especially if you're preparing more than one pint. If you'll be canning the peaches, cook them a bit less, so they're just barely tender; they will get additional cooking during the canning process. Process in a boiling-water bath for 20 minutes at 5,000 feet, or at the recommended time for jam at your elevation (see pg. 183).

Aluminum and Non-Aluminum Cookware

Citrus juices, such as lemon or lime juice, are obviously high in acid, but even wild fruit juices have some acid. Aluminum reacts with acid to create undesirable flavors; the acid also dissolves minute particles of aluminum into the food, which may be a health concern. Many recipes in this book call for the use of non-aluminum cookware. Stainless steel and Pyrex are good choices; this type of cookware is sometimes called "non-reactive" because it doesn't react with acids.

Apricot or Peach Salsa

About 1¼ cups

This is delicious with fish tacos or pork carnitas, and makes a wonderful accompaniment to spicy black beans or any type of refried beans. It is also good with grilled chicken or fish.

2 tablespoons freshly squeezed lime juice

2 teaspoons honey

½ to ¾ teaspoon ancho chile powder (see tip below)

1 clove garlic, minced or pressed

1 cup diced apricots or peaches (¼-inch dice), peeled before dicing (see tip on pg. 13 for peeling instructions)

¼ cup finely diced red onion (⅛-inch dice)

¼ cup finely diced red bell pepper (⅛- to ³⁄₁₆-inch dice)

1 tablespoon finely chopped cilantro

½ teaspoon coarse (kosher) salt

In medium mixing bowl, whisk together lime juice, honey, chile powder and garlic until well blended. Add remaining ingredients; mix well. Taste for seasoning and add more salt, pepper, honey or lime juice to make the salsa the way you prefer it. Cover and refrigerate for a few hours before serving, to allow the flavors to mellow and blend together.

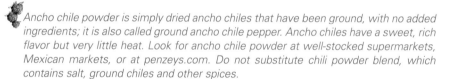

Ancho chile powder is simply dried ancho chiles that have been ground, with no added ingredients; it is also called ground ancho chile pepper. Ancho chiles have a sweet, rich flavor but very little heat. Look for ancho chile powder at well-stocked supermarkets, Mexican markets, or at penzeys.com. Do not substitute chili powder blend, which contains salt, ground chiles and other spices.

Other recipes in this book featuring apricots or peaches:
Wild Berry or Fruit Leather, pg. 182

BARBERRIES (*Berberis* spp.)

Two types of barberry are found in our area: the native Colorado barberry (*Berberis fendleri*) and common barberry (*B. vulgaris*), a cultivated plant that has become naturalized. Both produce similar edible fruits. Common barberry has been used for centuries as a spice and in cooked dishes in central Asia, the Mideast, Africa and Europe. Common barberry plants were brought to the U.S. in Colonial days, but have been the target of eradication programs because the plants are an alternate host for a rust disease that kills wheat.

You'll have to keep a sharp eye out for thorns when picking barberries; the plants are loaded with them. The thorns grow at leaf axils; unfortunately, the fruiting stalks grow from the same place. If you concentrate on picking fruits that are towards the ends of the clusters, you will not get pricked as much. Better still, use a small scissors to snip off the entire cluster, then pull the berries off the stemlets at home.

Unlike some cultivated barberry species, fruits of Colorado and common barberry grow in long clusters, which make it a little easier to avoid the thorns when you're picking the fruits.

Be sure to pick only fully ripe, red fruits; underripe fruits are too tart and may be bitter. The berries remain on the plants for a long time after ripening, and can be harvested in fall or even winter; some foragers believe that the fruits get sweeter after a frost, but I can't verify that. Like many wild berries, quality can vary from plant to plant even after the fruit is ripe; if the fruits are too bitter from a particular bush, pass it by.

Barberries are tart, somewhat similar in flavor to sour cherries; like sour cherries, barberries can be delicious when properly prepared. They can be juiced alone or in combination with apples or other fruits to make jelly or wine. Barberries have small seeds that are noticeable but not objectionable; however, some people prefer to cook the fruit and strain it to remove the seeds. Barberries dehydrate well (see pgs. 180–181), and commercially dried common barberries (called *zereshk*) are available in specialty markets, particularly those catering to Mideastern clientele. You can also freeze barberries in a single layer on a baking sheet, then pack into freezer containers; they will soften when thawed but will still work fine for cooking.

To prepare barberry purée or juice, measure the fruit and place in a non-aluminum pot. For purée, add ½ cup water per quart of fruit; for juice, add 1 cup water per quart of fruit. Crush the fruit with a potato masher. Heat to boiling, then crush the fruit again. Reduce the heat; cover and simmer for about 15 minutes. **For purée,** process the cooked fruit through a cone-shaped colander or food mill, then discard the seeds and skins. **For juice,** transfer the mixture to a strainer lined with doubled, dampened cheesecloth and let it drip for 30 minutes; if you're making jelly, don't squeeze the fruit or the jelly will be cloudy. Processed this way, a quart of fruit will yield about 1¼ cups of purée, or about 2 cups of juice.

Barberries contain berberine, a compound with medicinal uses. The roots contain the highest concentration, but the berries do have some as well. Berberine is used by herbalists to lower cholesterol, improve the immune system, reduce blood pressure and treat diabetes, among other things. It is unlikely that you'd eat enough foraged barberries to get a therapeutic dose, but if you take medications for heart disease or diabetes, you may want to discuss barberries with your doctor. Also, barberries may cause stomach upset in some people.

Persian Barberry Rice

6 servings

This classic Persian dish is called zereshk *polow (barberry pilaf). My version is based on a recipe from my Persian friend, Yas. This dish is traditionally served with roasted chicken.*

1½ cups basmati rice (do not substitute other types)
A pinch of saffron threads
¼ teaspoon plus 2 tablespoons sugar, divided
2 tablespoons plain yogurt (not fat-free)
1 tablespoon vegetable oil
Ground cumin, to taste (¼ to ½ teaspoon)
2 tablespoons butter
1 medium onion, halved and thinly sliced
1 cup fresh barberries (or ¾ cup dried; see tip on pg. 18)

Rinse the rice by placing it in a bowl and covering it with cold water, then swirling it with your fingers until the water is cloudy. Pour off the water and repeat four times. Heat a large pot of water to boiling, adding a bit of salt as though cooking pasta. Add the drained rice. Cook for 6 to 10 minutes or until just tender but not mushy, stirring several times near the beginning. While the rice is cooking, combine the saffron and ¼ teaspoon of the sugar in a mortar. Crush with pestle and place in a small bowl; add ½ cup hot water and set aside. When rice is tender, drain in a wire-mesh strainer and rinse with cold water.

In small bowl, stir together the yogurt, half of the saffron water, and ½ cup of the cooked rice. Add the oil to a heavy-bottomed saucepan. Spread the yogurt mixture evenly in the saucepan. Spoon one-third of the drained rice over the yogurt mixture; sprinkle with cumin. Spoon half of the remaining rice into the saucepan; sprinkle again with cumin. Spoon remaining rice into saucepan. Use the handle of a wooden spoon to poke several holes into the rice mixture, going just through the plain rice but not into the yogurt mixture. Cover and cook for 10 minutes over medium heat (this begins the formation of the crust, which is called *tah dig* and is a hallmark of this dish). After 10 minutes, drizzle the remaining saffron water evenly over the rice. Place two paper towels on top of the saucepan, then cover tightly with the lid; moisten the corners of the paper towels and fold them up against the lid. Reduce heat to low and cook for 45 minutes.

While the rice steams, prepare the barberry mixture. In large skillet, melt the butter over medium heat. Add the onion and sauté for about 15 minutes, or until golden and very tender. Reduce the heat to medium-low. Add the barberries and remaining 2 tablespoons of sugar; cook for about 1 minute, stirring constantly. Remove from heat and set aside.

When the rice has steamed for 45 minutes, place the saucepan on a thick, damp towel and let it stand for 5 minutes to loosen the crust. Spoon about one-third of the loose rice (not the crust) onto a serving platter; top with one-third of the barberry mixture. Repeat with remaining loose rice and barberries. Slightly break up the crust from the bottom of the saucepan and place on top. Serve immediately.

Barberry-Apple Jelly (no added pectin) 3 or 4 half-pints

This makes a lovely, rose-colored jelly that has an intriguing, slightly tangy flavor. Try it with a toasted bagel that has been slathered with cream cheese.

1½ pounds apples

1½ to 2 cups fresh barberries

2½ cups water

2½ cups sugar

Apples and barberries both have natural pectin, so you don't need to add commercial pectin. Before starting, please read "Jelly Instructions for Fruits with Natural Pectin" on pgs. 177–178 to learn about testing for doneness.

Cut apples into quarters; remove and discard stems and blossom ends. Cut apples into ½-inch chunks. In medium (4-quart) non-aluminum soup pot, combine apples, barberries and water. Heat to boiling, then reduce heat and simmer for 10 minutes. Crush fruits with a potato masher, then simmer for 5 minutes longer. Transfer the mixture to a strainer lined with doubled, dampened cheesecloth and let it drip for 30 minutes; don't squeeze the fruit or the jelly will be cloudy. While the fruit is dripping, prepare 4 half-pint canning jars, bands and new lids as directed on pg. 183. Wash the pot so you can use it to prepare the jelly.

When the mixture has dripped for 30 minutes, discard the contents of the strainer (unless you want to squeeze it to use as a juice, but you won't get much of it and what you do get will already be fairly thick and somewhat cloudy). Return the strained juice to the cleaned pot. Heat juice to boiling over medium-high heat. Add sugar and cook, stirring constantly, until sugar dissolves. Increase heat to high and cook, skimming off any foam and stirring frequently, until jelly passes one or more of the doneness tests on pgs. 177–178; this typically takes 10 to 15 minutes, but will take longer at higher elevations.

Once the jelly is done, skim any foam off the surface and pour the jelly, while still hot, into the prepared canning jars; seal with prepared lids and bands. Process in a boiling-water bath for 15 minutes at 5,000 feet, or at the recommended time for your elevation (see pg. 183); if you prefer, you can store the jelly in the refrigerator where it will keep for a month or longer.

If you're working with dried barberries in a recipe that calls for fresh ones, soak them in water for about 15 minutes. Drain well, blot dry and proceed with the recipe. (If you happen to buy imported dried barberries—called zereshk, *and generally from Iran— from a specialty store, they also need to be rinsed several times after soaking, to remove sand and grit that is often found on the commercially grown fruits.)*

Barberry-Pear Chutney

About 2 half-pints

Serve this mellow chutney as an accompaniment to a cheese platter; it is particularly good with aged Cheddar. It also works well with grilled meats, sausage or poultry.

½ cup diced red onion

2½ teaspoons vegetable oil

¼ teaspoon minced fresh gingerroot

Half of a small hot red pepper, minced

1½ cups apple juice

1 cup fresh barberries (or ¾ cup dried; see tip on pg. 18)

⅓ cup chopped pecans

¼ cup honey

1 teaspoon mustard seeds

½ teaspoon salt

¼ teaspoon freshly ground black pepper

1 slightly underripe purchased pear (8 ounces), peeled, cored and diced (¼-inch dice); or equivalent in wild pears

In a heavy-bottomed non-aluminum saucepan, sauté onion in oil over medium heat until tender, 3 to 5 minutes. Add gingerroot and hot pepper; sauté for about a minute longer. Add remaining ingredients. Heat until mixture just begins to boil, then reduce heat and simmer, stirring occasionally, until most of the liquid has cooked away and the mixture is nicely thick, 35 to 50 minutes longer. Transfer to clean jars and store in the refrigerator.

Other recipes in this book featuring barberries:
Six Recipes Using Wild Fruit Juice or Syrup, pgs. 170–174
Wild Berry or Fruit Syrup, pg. 175
Dehydrating Wild Berries and Fruits, pgs. 180–181
As a substitute in Refrigerator Cookies with Dried Goji Berries, pg. 51

Quick ideas for using barberries:
Add a handful of barberries to the apples when making an apple pie; the tart barberries are an excellent complement to the sweetened apples.
Add a handful of barberries to chokecherries or other fruits when making juice.
Some foragers stew barberries with spices and other fruits to make jam, compote or sauce.
Scatter a few barberries over a spinach salad.
Substitute barberries for the elderberries in the Elderberry-Sumac Jelly on pg. 49.

BLACKBERRIES (*Rubus* spp.)

The Himalayan blackberry (*Rubus armeniacus*) and the other blackberry varieties found in our area are the wild versions of the familiar fruit found in the supermarket. Himalayan blackberries are large, non-native shrubs that grow with abandon in the Pacific Northwest; they are less common in our area but may still be found in the wild, particularly in northern Idaho but also scattered in all other states of our region except Wyoming. Himalayan blackberry fruits are as large as the blackberries found in the store. The other two wild blackberries in our area have much smaller fruits, typically ½ inch long or smaller. Cutleaf blackberry (*R. laciniatus*) is a tall shrub like Himalayan blackberry; trailing blackberry (*R. ursinus*) is a ground-hugging, sprawling shrub.

Himalayan blackberry is originally from Asia, and was introduced to the U.S. as a fruit crop in the late 1800s. It proved to be too aggressive and has taken over many areas in the Pacific Northwest; in spite of its delicious fruits, many people despise it for its thorny, aggressive nature.

Luckily, fruits from any of these blackberry plants can be used in the same way, although for some recipes, the larger Himalayan berries will need to be cut in half.

One thing that these fruits have in common are seeds . . . lots and lots of them. They're harder than seeds found in raspberries, and can make jam or desserts seem almost crunchy. Some people prefer to strain cooked or crushed blackberries to remove the seeds. For most dishes, I like the texture that the whole or lightly crushed fruits provide. (See pg. 25 for a jam recipe that is a compromise; half of the seeds are strained out, while the rest of the fruit provides texture to the jam.)

To prepare purée or juice, measure the fruit and place in a non-aluminum pot. For purée, add ½ cup water per quart of fruit; for juice, add 1 cup water per quart of fruit. Gently crush the fruit with a potato masher to start the juices flowing. Heat to boiling, then reduce the heat; cover and simmer for about 10 minutes. **For seedless purée,** process the cooked fruit through a food mill, then discard the seeds; if you don't mind the seeds, the purée is ready after cooking. **For juice,** transfer the mixture to a strainer lined with doubled, dampened cheesecloth and let it drip for 30 minutes; if you're making jelly, don't squeeze the fruit or the jelly will be cloudy. After the clear liquid has dripped away, set it aside and squeeze the fruit into a different container; you can use this slightly cloudy juice as a beverage or for cooking. Processed this way, a quart of fruit will yield about 1½ cups of purée, or about 2 cups of juice.

Blackberries can be frozen for later use in jam, pies and other cooked desserts. Simply lay them on a baking sheet in a single layer and freeze; when the berries are solid, pack them into plastic bags or freezer containers for storage. Some foragers also prepare fruit leather from strained, seedless blackberry purée (see pg. 182 for information on making fruit leather).

Blackberry-Apple Crisp

The combination of blackberries and apples makes a wonderful crisp—the color is lovely, and the mix of tart and sweet is just right. Serve with a scoop of vanilla ice cream.

2 large cooking apples such as Granny Smith, Fireside or McIntosh

2 cups fresh or previously frozen blackberries (about 10 ounces), cut in half before measuring if large

2 teaspoons cornstarch

½ cup all-purpose flour

½ cup (packed) golden brown sugar

½ teaspoon cinnamon

¼ teaspoon nutmeg

4 tablespoons (half of a stick) cold butter, cut into pieces

¼ cup quick-cooking rolled oats (not instant)

Position rack in center of oven; heat to 375°F. Spray 8x8-inch baking dish generously with nonstick spray. Peel and core apples, then chop them coarsely in food processor or by hand; place in prepared dish. Add blackberries and cornstarch; stir gently to mix. Set aside.

In mixing bowl, combine flour, brown sugar, cinnamon and nutmeg; stir to mix. Add butter; blend with your fingertips (or a fork) until the mixture is the texture of very coarse sand, with a few pea-sized pieces of butter remaining. Stir in rolled oats. Sprinkle the mixture evenly over the fruit. Bake until topping is golden brown and filling bubbles, 35 to 45 minutes. Let cool on wire rack at least 15 minutes before serving; serve warm or at room temperature.

Substitutions: Huckleberries, bilberries, blueberries, serviceberries or raspberries may be substituted for the blackberries in this simple crisp. Wild apples may be substituted for the purchased apples.

When making the topping for a crisp, don't over-mix or make it too fine. It's easiest to sprinkle when it's still got some coarse bits in it, and it comes out with a better texture than if it is well blended.

Wild Berry Vinegar

1 quart

Use in salad dressings or in marinades for poultry, meat or fish. This makes a lovely gift.

1 pint blackberries, raspberries, dewberries, strawberries, elderberries, squashberries or highbush cranberries

1 quart white wine vinegar

You'll need a glass bottle that holds at least 2 quarts for this, with a mouth wide enough to insert the berries; juice is often sold in these types of bottles. Wash it very well, then fill it with boiling water and let stand for at least 5 minutes.

Drain water from bottle; add berries. In medium saucepan, heat vinegar over low heat until it just begins to steam; don't let vinegar boil. Pour warm vinegar over berries in bottle. Let stand until cooled to room temperature, then seal bottle and shake gently. Set bottle in dark, cool place for 1 week, shaking occasionally. Strain through a sieve lined with a paper coffee filter into clean 1-quart measuring cup with a spout; discard berries. Pour vinegar into a clean bottle. It will keep, at room temperature, for at least 6 months.

For a more decorative presentation, spear a few fresh berries and a curl of lemon zest on a wooden skewer; place skewer in the storage bottle before adding strained, finished vinegar to the bottle. (Be sure to wash the lemon well before making the zest curl.)

Blackberry Sidecar

Per serving

This is a strong drink, so try it when you don't have anywhere to drive!

2 ounces gin

1 ounce triple sec liqueur

1 tablespoon blackberry syrup (pg. 175)

1 tablespoon lime juice

2 or 3 fresh blackberries for garnish, optional

Combine gin, triple sec, blackberry syrup and lime juice in a shaker filled with crushed ice. Cover and shake well. Strain into a chilled cocktail glass; garnish with fresh blackberries. Call a cab.

Blackberry Filling

About ½ cup; easily increased

This filling is dark, thick, glossy and totally luscious.

½ teaspoon water

½ teaspoon cornstarch

6 ounces fresh or previously frozen blackberries (about 1¼ cups),
cut in half if large

1 tablespoon grated apple

1½ tablespoons sugar

In small bowl, blend together water and cornstarch; set aside. In small, heavy-bottomed non-aluminum saucepan, combine blackberries, apple and sugar. Crush fruit gently with a potato masher to start juices flowing. Heat to boiling over medium-high heat, then cook, stirring frequently, until mixture is no longer runny; this will take 9 to 11 minutes. Add cornstarch mixture, stirring constantly; cook for about 1 minute longer, or until thick. Cool completely before using.

Use this to prepare Easy Bear Claws (pg. 81), Fruit-Striped Cookie Fingers (pg. 126), or Fruit-Filled Muffins (pg. 155). Refrigerate extra filling, and use to top oatmeal or toast.

Smooth Blackberry Sauce

About 1 cup

This type of sauce is sometimes called a coulis. *It's excellent when used to top ice cream, French toast or cooked cereal. For an elegant dessert, spoon a puddle of the sauce onto individual dessert plates, then top with a piece of cheesecake or a poached pear.*

1 cup strained, seedless blackberry purée

¼ to ½ cup sugar

⅛ teaspoon finely grated lemon zest (colored rind only,
with none of the white pith; see "Zesting Citrus Fruits," pg. 35)

In small, heavy-bottomed non-aluminum saucepan, combine purée, ¼ cup sugar, and the lemon zest. Heat over medium-high heat, stirring constantly, until boiling. Cook, stirring constantly, until purée has thickened to a sauce-like consistency. Taste, and add additional sugar if needed; if you do add more sugar, cook the sauce for another few minutes, stirring constantly, to dissolve the sugar. Cool before using.

Blackberry Freezer Jam

4 half-pints

The fruit is not cooked when preparing this easy jam; it has a fresh, vibrant flavor.

1 quart blackberries, cut in half before measuring if large

1³⁄₄ cups sugar

**Two-thirds of a 1.75-ounce box powdered pectin
(see pg. 176 for information on dividing pectin)**

²⁄₃ cup water

Prepare 4 half-pint canning jars, bands and new lids as described on pg. 183 or have clean plastic freezer containers ready (see tip on pg. 140). Crush fruit with a potato masher in a mixing bowl, or chop to medium consistency in food processor (don't over-process; jam should have small fruit chunks in it). Measure 1³⁄₄ cups crushed or chopped fruit; use any leftover fruit to top ice cream or cook in other recipes. Place measured fruit and the sugar in a large ceramic or Pyrex mixing bowl. Stir well; set aside for 10 minutes, stirring several times with a wooden spoon.

When fruit has rested for 10 minutes, prepare pectin. In small non-aluminum saucepan, combine pectin and water; stir well (mixture may be lumpy). Heat to a full, rolling boil over high heat, stirring constantly. Cook at a rolling boil for 1 minute, stirring constantly. Pour pectin mixture into fruit in bowl. Stir constantly with a wooden spoon until sugar is completely dissolved and no longer grainy, about 3 minutes; a few grains may remain, but the mixture should no longer look cloudy (or the jam will be cloudy).

Pour into prepared jars or containers, leaving ½ inch headspace; cover with clean lids. Let stand at room temperature for 24 hours; the jam should set (it may be softer than regular jam, especially at first; that's okay). If jam is not set, refrigerate for several days until set before using or freezing. Use within 3 weeks, or freeze until needed; thaw frozen jam in refrigerator.

Blackberry Jelly

4 half-pints

2³⁄₄ cups blackberry juice

2 tablespoons lemon juice

Two-thirds of a 1.75-ounce box powdered pectin

½ teaspoon butter, optional (helps reduce foaming)

3½ cups sugar

Prepare and process as directed in Jelly Instructions (using pectin), pgs. 176–177.

Smoother Blackberry Jam

4 half-pints

Blackberry jam has a wonderful, deep flavor, but some find it too seedy to enjoy. This recipe removes about half of the seeds; this leaves enough whole berries for a good texture.

5 cups fresh blackberries, cut in half before measuring if large

2 tablespoons lemon juice

**Half of a 1.75-ounce package powdered pectin
   (see pg. 176 for information on dividing pectin)**

3¼ cups sugar

Place blackberries in mixing bowl; crush with potato masher. Transfer half of the crushed berries to a wire-mesh strainer set over another mixing bowl; press through with wooden spoon to strain seeds. Measure strained blackberries; add crushed blackberries to equal 2½ cups. Transfer measured fruit to 3-quart (or larger) heavy-bottomed non-aluminum pot (reserve any remaining fruit to top ice cream). Prepare and process as directed in Jam Instructions (using pectin), pg. 179.

Other recipes in this book featuring blackberries:

Mahonia-Blackberry Turnovers, pg. 95
Rice Pudding with Wild Berries, pg. 103
Fruits of the Forest Pie, pg. 168
Brambleberry Cream Sauce, pg. 169
Six Recipes Using Wild Fruit Juice or Syrup, pgs. 170–174
Wild Berry or Fruit Syrup, pg. 175
Wild Berry or Fruit Leather, pg. 182
As a substitute in Strawberry Smoothie, pg. 156

Quick ideas for using blackberries:

When making apple pie, reduce the amount of apples by 1 cup and add a cup
   of fresh or previously frozen blackberries.

BUFFALOBERRIES (*Shepherdia argentea*)

First, a word of advice to the forager: Make sure that you are picking silver buffaloberries, not the similar, related russet buffaloberries (*Shepherdia canadensis*; also called Canada buffaloberries). The plants are similar, and the fruits may *look* the same … but they sure don't *cook* the same! Russet buffaloberries are sweet when you first start chewing, but quickly turn intensely bitter as you continue to chew; they won't work for any of the recipes in this section. To distinguish between the two plants, remember that silver buffaloberry plants are thorny, with leaves that are silvery-green on top and silvery-gray below; russet buffaloberries have no thorns, and their leaves are dark green on top, gray-green below with brownish scales or spots. Silver buffaloberry fruits are generally sweet-tart and tasty even when raw, although some may have a slight bit of bitterness.

When foraging buffaloberries, taste one or two before filling your bucket. If the plant is a russet buffaloberry, you'll most likely spit the berry out because it has such a bitter aftertaste. Silver buffaloberries are sweet, without that terrible bitterness.

Once you've identified the shrub properly, the work begins, because silver buffaloberry's thorns make picking somewhat difficult. The best way to pick buffaloberries is to spread a clean tarp under the branches and jostle the shrub (use a stick if you can, to avoid having to grab onto those thorny branches). The berries often grow thickly on the plant, so you should have no trouble shaking off a good quantity in a short amount of time. Some foragers report that buffaloberries are sweeter after a frost, but I can't verify this.

Buffaloberries are very juicy, with small seeds that are noticeable but not objectionable; however, some people prefer to cook the fruit and strain it to remove the seeds. To prepare seedless buffaloberry purée or juice, measure the fruit and place in a non-aluminum pot. For purée, add ¼ cup water per quart of fruit; for juice, add ½ cup water per quart of fruit. Crush the fruit with a potato masher. Heat to boiling, then crush the fruit again. Reduce the heat; cover and simmer for about 15 minutes. **For purée,** process the cooked fruit through a cone-shaped colander or food mill, then discard the seeds and skins. **For juice,** transfer the mixture to a strainer lined with doubled, dampened cheesecloth and let it drip for 30 minutes; if you're making jelly, don't squeeze the fruit or the jelly will be cloudy. Processed this way, a quart of fruit will yield about 1¼ cups of purée, or about 2 cups of juice. Note that buffaloberries contain saponin, a substance that foams and makes the juice look milky or cloudy (it also is responsible for the bitterness which is particularly intense in russet buffaloberries; evidently they have a lot more saponin than do silver buffaloberries). The cloudiness disappears when the juice is cooked and sweetened for jelly or other uses. (According to data from the U.S.D.A., saponin is absorbed poorly by the body, and thorough cooking breaks it down.)

Buffaloberry purée can be used to make fruit leather (pg. 182); whole buffaloberries can also be dehydrated (see pgs. 180–181). They freeze fairly well, although they may flatten upon thawing, releasing a lot of juice. To freeze buffaloberries, follow the instructions for freezing currants on pg. 38.

Grilled Bananas with Buffaloberry Sauce   4 servings

Here's a fun way to introduce family and friends to buffaloberries. The grilled bananas are a great complement to the bright red, sweet-tart buffaloberry sauce.

<u>Buffaloberry sauce:</u>

½ cup fresh silver buffaloberries

½ cup orange juice

3 tablespoons sugar

1 tablespoon minute tapioca

2 ripe but not over-soft bananas, unpeeled, rinsed and dried

1½ teaspoons sugar

¼ teaspoon nutmeg

2 teaspoons vegetable oil (approximate)

1 pint vanilla ice cream

Prepare the sauce: In small, non-aluminum saucepan, combine buffaloberries, orange juice and sugar. Cook over medium heat, stirring frequently, until berries "pop." Increase heat slightly and cook at a gentle boil for about 5 minutes, stirring occasionally. Stir in tapioca; cook, stirring constantly, until thickened and glossy, 2 to 3 minutes. Remove from heat and set aside. (Sauce can sit at room temperature for an hour before using; re-warm slightly if it has cooled down completely. If prepared further in advance, cover and refrigerate until needed, then re-warm slightly before using.)

When you're ready to finish the dish, prepare grill for medium heat; use a grill brush or a crumpled piece of foil to clean the grate. Cut the stems off the bananas and slice the unpeeled bananas into two shorter halves, then halve each lengthwise; you will have eight skin-on quarters. In a small bowl, mix the sugar and nutmeg; sprinkle over the cut side of the bananas and let stand for about 5 minutes.

Oil the grill grate (dip a paper towel in some oil and use a tongs to rub it over the hot grate). Arrange banana pieces, cut side down, on grate. Cover the grill and cook for about 2 minutes; fruit should be nicely marked (if it is not, re-cover grill and check again in a minute or so). Flip the banana pieces gently with tongs, re-cover the grill, and cook for about 5 minutes, or until the banana skin starts to separate from the cut edges. Transfer to a plate and let cool for a few minutes, then carefully peel each banana piece and arrange two pieces, grilled side up, on a dessert plate. Top with a scoop of vanilla ice cream; divide the buffaloberry sauce evenly over the ice cream. Serve immediately.

Substitution: Use red currants or raspberries in place of the buffaloberries.

Buffaloberry Salsa

About 1½ cups

This fresh salsa is just a little different than the usual tomato salsa.

1 cup fresh silver buffaloberries
¼ cup water
½ cup diced red onion
Half of a small jalapeño pepper, seeded and minced
3 tablespoons freshly squeezed lime juice
¾ teaspoon salt
¾ cup diced grape tomatoes or cherry tomatoes (diced before measuring)
¼ cup chopped cilantro leaves (medium-coarse texture)
2 teaspoons sugar, or as needed
⅛ teaspoon ground cumin
Freshly ground black pepper to taste

In small saucepan, combine buffaloberries and water. Heat to boiling, then reduce heat and boil gently for 5 minutes, stirring occasionally. Set aside to cool. While berries are cooling, stir together onion, jalapeño, lime juice and salt in a non-aluminum bowl; set aside for 30 minutes.

When berries are cool and onions have marinated, add berries with their juices, tomatoes, cilantro, sugar, cumin and black pepper to bowl with onions. Stir to mix well. Let stand for at least 15 minutes to allow flavors to blend; taste and add a little more sugar if needed.

 Marinating red onions in a little vinegar helps set their color, and also tames a bit of the onion bite. Try it with sliced white onions, too, especially when you're going to use them raw as a garnish on tacos or salads.

Buffaloberry Jelly

4 half-pints

This pleasantly tart jelly has a rich, deep golden-orange color.

2½ cups silver buffaloberry juice
2 tablespoons lemon juice
Half of a 1.75-ounce box powdered pectin
½ teaspoon butter, optional (helps reduce foaming)
2¾ cups sugar

Prepare and process as directed in Jelly Instructions (using pectin), pgs. 176–177.

Spiced Buffaloberry Spread

3 half-pints

This is a cross between a jelly and a jam, since it is made with whole fruits that are strained to remove the seeds. Orange juice and spices add a wonderful flavor to this pretty spread.

3 cups fresh silver buffaloberries

¾ cup freshly squeezed orange juice

1 cinnamon stick

½ teaspoon vanilla extract

¼ teaspoon nutmeg

2 cups sugar

**Half of a 1.75-ounce package powdered pectin
(see pg. 176 for information on dividing pectin)**

Prepare 4 half-pint canning jars, bands and new lids as described on pg. 183. In non-aluminum saucepan, combine buffaloberries and orange juice; mash well with a potato masher. Add cinnamon stick, vanilla and nutmeg. Heat to boiling over high heat. Cover and reduce heat; simmer for 10 minutes, stirring several times. Remove and discard cinnamon stick. Transfer mixture to a food mill and process into a medium (4-quart) non-aluminum soup pot. Discard seeds and skins from food mill.

Have the sugar ready to go before you start cooking the spread. Add the powdered pectin to the pot with the strained buffaloberry mixture; whisk until dissolved. Heat to boiling over high heat, stirring frequently. When mixture comes to a full, rolling boil that can't be stirred down, add the sugar. Cook, stirring constantly, until the mixture again comes to a full, foaming boil. Boil for 1 minute, stirring constantly (if mixture threatens to boil over, move from the heat for a few seconds, then reduce heat slightly and return the pot to the heat). Remove from heat and stir for a minute or two to settle any foam; if there is still foam on top, skim with a clean spoon and discard. Pour into prepared jars, leaving ½ inch headspace; seal with prepared lids and bands. Process in boiling-water bath for 20 minutes at 5,000 feet, or at the recommended time for jam at your elevation (see pg. 183); if you prefer, you can store the spread in the refrigerator where it will keep for a month or longer.

Other recipes in this book featuring buffaloberries:
Six Recipes Using Wild Fruit Juice or Syrup, pgs. 170–174
Wild Berry or Fruit Syrup, pg. 175
Dehydrating Wild Berries and Fruits, pgs. 180–181
Wild Berry or Fruit Leather, pg. 182

CHOKECHERRIES and WILD CHERRIES (*Prunus* spp.)

Chokecherries (*Prunus virginiana* var. *melanocarpa*) are abundant in our area, and have a delicious sweet-tart flavor. In addition, three native wild cherries are found in scattered spots throughout our area: pin cherry (*P. pensylvanica*), bitter cherry (*P. emarginata* var. *emarginata*) and Western sand cherry (*P. pumila* var. *besseyi*). The flesh of pin cherries, chokecherries and bitter cherries is thin in proportion to the pits; sand cherries are meatier, and can be pitted with a regular cherry pitter to make pie or other baked goods. As with many wild fruits, quality varies from tree to tree, but juice from all of them makes an exceptional, sparkling jelly.

Don't crush the pits of any of these fruits during cooking or straining. Cherry pits contain small amounts of a cyanide-forming compound that can cause illness if eaten in large quantities.

Chokecherries are easy to pick because the plants are low-growing and produce plentiful fruit; also, the fruit grows in long clusters so it's easy to pull off a big handful rather than picking one fruit at a time. Sand cherries are also low shrubs that bear heavily, but the fruits grow singly rather than in long clusters. Pin cherry and bitter cherry trees bear a lot of fruit, but it's tough to beat the birds to them; however, the fruit hangs low and a good deal can be gathered from the ground—if you're there at the right time.

Juice and purée prepared from all four species of cherries listed here is interchangeable, so all recipes in this section simply call for chokecherries or chokecherry juice, rather than listing all four species in each recipe. (Note, however, that bitter cherry juice is fairly bitter; it makes good jelly but might be too strong for some of the other recipes that don't have as much sugar.) The only recipe that is not interchangeable is Duck Breast with Cherries (pg. 34), which really does need to be made with large, fleshy sand cherries—unless you have the patience to remove the pits from a gallon of one of the smaller, less-meaty cherries.

To prepare purée or juice, measure the fruit and place in a non-aluminum pot. For purée, add 1 cup water per quart of fruit; for juice, add 2 cups water per quart of fruit. Heat to boiling, then reduce the heat; cover and simmer for about 30 minutes, gently crushing the fruit with a potato masher near the end of cooking. **For purée,** process the cooked fruit through a cone-shaped colander or food mill, then discard the pits. **For juice,** transfer the mixture to a strainer lined with doubled, dampened cheesecloth and let it drip for 30 minutes; if you're making jelly, don't squeeze the fruit or the jelly will be cloudy. After the clear liquid has dripped away, set it aside and squeeze the fruit into a different container; you can use this slightly cloudy juice as a beverage or for cooking. Processed this way, a quart of fruit will yield about 1 cup of purée (slightly more for sand cherries), or about 1½ cups juice.

Purées prepared as above can be sweetened to taste and cooked a bit to thicken if necessary, then dried to make fruit leather (pg. 182); sand cherries make particularly good purée, while bitter cherries are, as you might guess, too bitter to use in this way.

Chokecherry Barbecue Sauce

About 1 cup

This works well with just about any grilled meat, but is particularly good on game such as duck and goose.

1¼ pounds whole chokecherries, stems removed

⅓ cup orange juice

¼ cup chopped shallot

1 tablespoon minced fresh gingerroot

½ teaspoon ground cumin

½ teaspoon freshly ground black pepper

1 small hot red pepper, stem and seeds removed

2 tablespoons tomato paste

2 tablespoons white wine vinegar

¾ teaspoon salt

In heavy-bottomed non-aluminum saucepan, combine chokecherries, orange juice, shallot, gingerroot, cumin, black pepper and hot pepper. Heat to boiling over medium heat, then cook, stirring occasionally, until most of the liquid has cooked away, about 20 minutes. Remove from heat and cool slightly, then process through food mill. Transfer purée to smaller heavy-bottomed non-aluminum saucepan; add tomato paste, vinegar and salt. Simmer over medium-low heat for 20 minutes, stirring occasionally; if sauce is thinner than you like, increase heat slightly and cook until reduced as much as you like.

Chokecherry-Lemonade Sparkler

1 quart; easily increased

This tangy, refreshing beverage goes down well when the mercury heads skyward.

1½ cups chokecherry juice

¾ cup freshly squeezed lemon juice

½ cup sugar, or to taste

1 can (12 ounces) lime-flavored carbonated water

In serving pitcher, combine chokecherry juice, lemon juice and sugar; stir to dissolve sugar. Add carbonated water; pour over ice in tall glasses. Note: If you don't want to serve all of the sparkler at once, mix the chokecherry juice, lemon juice and sugar first, then add to sparkling water as each drink is served.

Chokecherry-Chocolate Marble Bundt Cake
10-inch tube cake (10 servings)

Prepare this for a dinner party or other special event.

For 5,000 feet; see adjustments for other altitudes

1½ cups chokecherry juice

1 teaspoon lemon juice

3¾ cups plus 2 tablespoons all-purpose flour[1, 2, 3]

2 teaspoons baking soda

¾ teaspoon salt

1 cup (2 sticks) butter or margarine, softened

2 cups sugar

3 large eggs

½ teaspoon vanilla extract

1½ cups sour cream

3 (1 ounce) squares semi-sweet chocolate

¾ cup chopped walnuts or pecans

Powdered sugar for dusting

Position oven rack in lower third of oven; heat to 365°F.[1] Grease and flour a 10-inch fluted tube pan; set aside. In small saucepan, combine chokecherry juice and lemon juice; cook over high heat until reduced to 1 cup. Remove from heat and set aside until completely cool. Sift together flour, baking soda and salt into large, microwave-safe mixing bowl; set aside. In another mixing bowl, cream butter and sugar until fluffy. Add eggs one at a time, beating well after each addition. Add 1 cup[1, 3] of the cooled chokecherry juice and vanilla extract; mix well. Add half of the flour mixture; stir with wooden spoon until moistened. Add half of the sour cream; stir until combined. Repeat with remaining flour and sour cream, mixing until just combined.

Place chocolate in the bowl that held the flour. Microwave at 50% power for 60 seconds; remove and check chocolate to see if it's melted. If not, microwave 10 seconds longer, then recheck; repeat until chocolate can be stirred smooth with a *dry* spoon. Add nuts and half of the batter to the melted chocolate; stir well. Spoon half of the plain batter into prepared tube pan. Cover with half of the chocolate batter. Repeat layers. Bake for 50 to 65 minutes,[2, 3] or until a wooden pick inserted in the thickest part comes out cleanly. Cool for 15 minutes; remove from pan and place on a wire rack to cool completely. Dust with powdered sugar before serving.

1. **Below 5,000 feet:** Use 3¾ cups flour. Heat oven to 350°F. Use ⅞ cup reduced juice.

2. **At 7,500 feet:** Add an additional tablespoon of flour. Bake at 365°F for 15 minutes; reduce temperature to 350°F and bake 45–50 minutes longer or until done.

3. **At 10,000 feet:** Add an additional 2 tablespoons of flour. Add 1 tablespoon of water with the reduced chokecherry juice. Bake at 365°F for 15 minutes, then reduce temperature to 350°F and bake for 50–60 minutes longer or until done.

Chokecherry Zabaglione

6 to 8 servings

This light, fluffy dessert is an adaptation of zabaglione (zah-bye-LYOH-neh), a classic Italian dessert which is typically made with Marsala or other sweet wine. Serve it with shortbread cookies, or topped with fresh fruit such as raspberries.

For 5,000 feet; see adjustments for other altitudes

1 cup whipping cream

2 tablespoons plus ⅓ cup sugar, divided

½ teaspoon vanilla extract

5 egg yolks

⅓ cup chokecherry juice

In large mixing bowl, combine cream, 2 tablespoons sugar and the vanilla. Beat with electric mixer until stiff. Refrigerate until needed.

Add 2 inches of water to the bottom of a double boiler[1, 2, 3] that has a large, stovetop-safe top half; heat over medium heat until simmering. In top half of double boiler, combine egg yolks and remaining ⅓ cup sugar. Beat with electric hand mixer until fluffy and light-colored. Add chokecherry juice; beat with mixer until well combined. Place top half of double boiler over the bottom half so the egg mixture in the top half will be heated by the simmering water in the bottom half. Cook, beating constantly with electric mixer, until mixture is thick and holds soft peaks, 8 to 15 minutes.[2, 3] Remove top half of double boiler and place on a heat-proof surface; continue beating for 3 or 4 minutes. Let stand until completely cool, about 10 minutes. Add to mixing bowl with whipped cream, gently folding together with rubber spatula. Refrigerate for 30 minutes, or as long as 2 hours. Serve in parfait glasses.

Tip: If you have leftovers, transfer them to a freezer-safe container and freeze for at least 8 hours. The frozen zabaglione becomes an airy, delicious ice cream.

1. **Below 5,000 feet:** No adjustments necessary.

2. **At 7,500 feet:** A double boiler might not produce enough heat to cook the zabaglione adequately. Start the cooking in the double boiler as directed; if the mixture doesn't get thick enough after 15 minutes, transfer the top half directly to a burner on low heat and continue cooking and beating until it thickens.

3. **At 10,000 feet:** A double boiler will not produce enough heat to cook the zabaglione adequately. Cook it in a heavy-bottomed saucepan placed directly on a burner at the lowest heat setting available, and watch it carefully. If the eggs start to set up (beginning to look like scrambled eggs), remove it from the burner immediately and let it cool a bit, then resume cooking and beating.

Duck Breast with Cherries

2 servings; easily increased

Slow roasting renders much of the duck fat out, leaving moist, tender meat and firm, golden skin. The skin is not super-crispy; depending on individual taste, it may be eaten or cut off.

2 boneless, skin-on Pekin duck breast halves (6½ to 7½ ounces each)

Garlic salt, seasoned salt or plain salt and pepper

1 medium onion

1 cup fresh or previously frozen pitted sand cherry halves,
with any juices collected during pitting or thawing

1 tablespoon balsamic vinegar

1 tablespoon honey

½ teaspoon dried thyme leaves

1 cup chicken broth

2 teaspoons cornstarch

Heat oven to 275°F. Prick duck skin all over with a sharp roasting fork or a very sharp paring knife. Sprinkle duck breast halves on both sides with the seasoning of your choice. Place breast halves together with skin sides out; tie snugly but not too tightly with three pieces of kitchen twine. Place breasts on roasting rack in shallow pan so one half is facing up and the other is facing down. Roast for 3 hours, turning over each hour and pricking skin each time. After 3 hours, spoon out and reserve 1 tablespoon of the rendered fat from the roasting pan; turn and prick skin again and continue roasting for another hour.

While breasts continue to roast, prepare the cherry sauce: Cut onion in half from top to bottom; reserve one half for another use. Cut remaining half crosswise into 2 pieces; cut out and discard root end. Slice the onion pieces vertically into slivers about ¼ inch wide. Heat the 1 tablespoon of duck fat in a medium skillet over medium heat until warm. Add onion; reduce heat to medium-low and cook, stirring occasionally, until caramelized, 15 to 20 minutes (if onions are browning too quickly, reduce heat to low). Add cherries and juice. Cook over medium-low heat, stirring frequently, for 5 minutes; if the mixture is still juicy, cook until fairly dry. Add balsamic vinegar, honey and thyme; cook until liquid has mostly cooked away and mixture is getting sticky, 3 to 5 minutes longer. In small bowl, blend together chicken broth and cornstarch; add to skillet with cherry mixture. Increase heat to medium and cook, stirring frequently, for 5 minutes; mixture should be thickened and bubbly. Transfer mixture to a small casserole; cover and set aside.

After the 4th hour of roasting, cut off the strings from the duck breasts and place breasts, skin side down, in the casserole on top of the cherry mixture. Flip the breast pieces so the skin side is up. Return to oven and roast for 15 minutes longer. Serve duck breasts with the sauce.

 See companion *Wild Berries & Fruits Field Guide of the Rocky Mountain States* – pgs. 184, 188, 270, 272

Homemade Cherry Cordial

About 1 quart

Wild cherries were often used in the past to make a cherry-flavored liqueur. Here's a version of that for you to try.

2 cups whole wild cherries or chokecherries

1½ cups vodka

1½ cups brandy

2 strips orange zest, each about ½ inch wide and 1 inch long (colored rind only, with none of the white pith; see "Zesting Citrus Fruits" below)

4 whole cloves

⅓ cup sugar

⅓ cup water

½ teaspoon glycerin (from the drugstore)

Sterilize a 1-quart canning jar, lid and band as directed on pg. 183. In large bowl, gently crush cherries with a potato masher; pick out and discard pits, squeezing over the bowl to extract any flesh or juice. Transfer cherries and juice to sterilized jar. Add vodka, brandy, orange zest and cloves. Seal jar with sterilized lid and shake well. Set in a cool, dark spot for 4 weeks, shaking occasionally.

At the end of 4 weeks, strain mixture through cheesecloth-lined strainer into a clean bowl; press on the cherries to extract the liquid. Discard the solids. Line a funnel with a paper coffee filter. Strain liquid into a clean, sterilized 1-quart canning jar; set aside.

In small saucepan, combine sugar and water. Heat over medium-low heat, stirring frequently, until sugar dissolves and liquid is clear. Remove from heat; set aside until completely cool. Strain syrup through a clean coffee filter into the jar with the cordial. Add glycerin; seal jar and shake to blend. Let stand, tightly sealed, for 2 or 3 days before serving; store in a cool, dark place for up to 3 months.

Zesting Citrus Fruits

The "zest" is the colored part of the rind only, with none of the bitter white pith. Always wash the fruit well before zesting.

*   **To make zest strips,** *use a very sharp knife to cut off the colored part of the rind, being careful to avoid getting any of the white pith.*

*   **To make grated zest,** *the best tool is a microplane grater; this rasp-like tool looks like it belongs in a woodworker's shop, but it really is superior for grating zest. Hold the grater over a small bowl with the teeth facing up, and draw the fruit over the teeth. When you start to see the lighter part of the rind, rotate the fruit and grate in a fresh spot. If you don't have a microplane grater, use the fine holes on a box grater, or a porcelain ginger grater.*

Pumpkin Tart with Chokecherry Glaze

1 pie (6 to 8 servings)

Chokecherry juice is particularly good with pumpkin pie; the tartness cuts through the richness of the pie filling very well, and the color is lovely.

1 can (15 ounces) pumpkin

8 ounces cream cheese, softened

2 eggs

¾ cup sugar

1 teaspoon rum extract or vanilla extract, optional

1¼ teaspoons cinnamon

½ teaspoon ground ginger

¼ teaspoon allspice

**1 pre-baked pie crust, lightly golden
(see "Blind Baking Pie Crusts," pg. 47)**

3 cups chokecherry juice

2 tablespoons cornstarch mixed with 2 tablespoons cold water

Heat oven to 425°F. Combine pumpkin and cream cheese in mixing bowl. Beat with electric mixer until smooth. Add eggs, sugar, extract, cinnamon, ginger and allspice; beat until smooth. Scrape into pre-baked crust, smoothing top. Bake for 10 minutes, then reduce heat to 375°F and continue baking until set, 30 to 50 minutes longer. Remove from oven; set aside until cool.

While tart is cooling, prepare glaze. Boil chokecherry juice until reduced to 2 cups (see "Reducing Liquid" below). Stir in cornstarch mixture. Cook, stirring constantly, until thickened and bubbly. Remove from heat; set aside to cool slightly. Pour cooled mixture over tart, spreading and smoothing with back of spoon. Serve at room temperature; refrigerate leftovers.

Substitutions: Use elderberry or huckleberry juice in place of the chokecherry juice.

High-altitude note:

Cinnamon and other sweet spices tend to taste less robust in goods baked at high altitude, so you may want to increase the spices slightly at 7,500 feet and above.

 **Reducing Liquid**

When a recipe calls for reducing liquid to a particular volume, it's hard to judge without measuring. Here's a better way. Before you start, measure water in the amount called for after reducing (so if the recipe says to boil 3 cups down to 1 cup, measure 1 cup of water). Place the water in the pan you'll be using, then stand a chopstick in the water. Use a knife to make a small dent in the chopstick at the water level, then discard the water and add the liquid to be reduced. When you think the liquid is getting close to the proper reduction, check it by standing the chopstick in the pan.

Easy Chokecherry Applesauce

About 2½ cups

This fast and easy applesauce is cooked in the microwave. Chokecherry purée provides a lovely color, and a delightfully tangy flavor.

**3 cups sliced apples, wild or purchased
(peeled, cored and sliced before measuring)**

½ cup sugar, or as needed

⅔ cup chokecherry purée

½ teaspoon cinnamon

¼ teaspoon nutmeg

A good pinch of ground cardamom

Combine all ingredients in microwave-safe mixing bowl. Cover with waxed paper. Microwave on high power for 10 minutes or until apples are soft, stirring once halfway through. Cool apple mixture slightly, then mash to desired consistency with potato masher. Taste, and add additional sugar if necessary (stir the sugar into the warm sauce, and heat briefly in the microwave to incorporate the sugar). Serve warm or chilled.

Chokecherry Jelly

4 half-pints

2½ cups chokecherry juice

2 tablespoons lemon juice

Two-thirds of a 1.75-ounce box powdered pectin

½ teaspoon butter, optional (helps reduce foaming)

2¾ cups sugar

Prepare and process as directed in Jelly Instructions (using pectin), pgs. 176–177.

Other recipes in this book featuring chokecherries and wild cherries:
Wild Grape-Chokecherry Wine, pg. 64
Six Recipes Using Wild Fruit Juice or Syrup, pgs. 170–174
Wild Berry or Fruit Syrup, pg. 175
Wild Berry or Fruit Leather, pg. 182
As a variation in Elderberry Meringue Pie, pg. 46
As a variation in Fruit Terrine with Elderberry Gel, pg. 48
As a substitute in Spicy Plum Chutney, pg. 113

CURRANTS (*Ribes* spp.)

Nearly a dozen varieties of currant are found in our area; all can be used in the same way, although their taste varies quite a bit. They can be eaten raw, although most are fairly tart. When properly prepared, however, their tartness accents other flavors; they work well in savory dishes as well as sweet. Flavor varies from plant to plant; before harvesting a large quantity, taste them to be sure they will work for your uses. Golden currant (*Ribes aureum*) are considered the best and tastiest; they're also the largest. Red currants (*R. triste, R. rubrum*) tend to be sweeter than black ones (seven varieties, in addition to golden currant which are black when ripe), but this is not a hard-and-fast rule; juice from red currants is a brighter red color, while that from black currants tends to be darker and somewhat less

Ripe currants retain their quality even if they are left on the plant for a week or more; I usually find, however, that birds and other critters have beaten me to the berries once they're ripe, so don't wait too long to harvest them.

attractive. Also note that some people get digestive upset from eating too many wax currants (*R. cereum*), something to keep in mind when working with these fruits.

Currants grow in racemes, long clusters of multiple flowers that develop into long clusters of fruits. Snip off the entire cluster rather than trying to pick the fruits off individually, unless the fruits have ripened unevenly. At home, wash the clusters and pull individual berries off the stemlets. If you're using them whole for baking or other dishes, also remove the dried flower remnant at the bottom; if you're making juice, don't bother with this step. Currants have small seeds that are noticeable but not objectionable; however, some people prefer to cook the fruit and strain it to remove the seeds.

To prepare currant juice, measure the fruit and place in a non-aluminum pot. Add ½ cup water per quart of fruit. Gently crush the fruit with a potato masher to start the juices flowing. Heat to boiling, then reduce the heat; cover and simmer for about 10 minutes. Transfer the mixture to a strainer lined with doubled, dampened cheesecloth and let it drip for 30 minutes; if you're making jelly, don't squeeze the fruit or the jelly will be cloudy. After the clear liquid has dripped away, set it aside and squeeze the fruit into a different container; you can use this slightly cloudy juice as a beverage or for cooking. Processed this way, a quart of fruit will yield about 2 cups juice.

Currants freeze well. Wash them and remove the blossom remnant, then either spread in a single layer on a baking sheet and freeze overnight, or pack into containers in measured amounts and freeze. If you've frozen them on a baking sheet, pack the frozen berries into containers and store in the freezer; you can measure out what you need and return the rest to the freezer. Currants are also a good choice for dehydrating (see pgs. 180–181); note that the fruit sold in the store as "dried currants" is actually a dried grape, so your home-dried currants will be quite different. They also make good fruit leather (pg. 182).

Currant-Basil Sauce

About ½ cup sauce, enough for 4 servings

Basil adds a sweet, grassy note to the tangy currants in this savory sauce. Serve it over grilled or poached fish such as salmon or trout; it's also delicious with grilled pork tenderloin or chops.

2 tablespoons finely chopped shallots

1 teaspoon olive oil

¼ cup seasoned rice vinegar

2 tablespoons dry, fruity red wine, such as Tempranillo or Beaujolais

2 tablespoons finely chopped fresh basil leaves

1 teaspoon sugar

¾ cup fresh red or black currants (about 4 ounces)

1 tablespoon unsalted butter

Salt and pepper

In small skillet, sauté shallots in oil over medium heat for about 3 minutes. Stir in vinegar, wine, basil and sugar. Cook until liquid reduces by half, 3 to 5 minutes. Add currants; cook, stirring occasionally, until the mixture is saucy, about 5 minutes. Remove from heat; add butter and stir until melted. Season to taste with salt and pepper. Spoon warm sauce over prepared fish or pork.

Salted vs. Unsalted Butter

Many recipes in this book call specifically for unsalted butter. I have long believed that some creameries use fresher cream to make unsalted butter than that which is used for salted butter, because fresher cream is less likely to have "off" flavors, which salt helps cover in less-fresh, salted butter. Even if both types of butter are made from the exact same cream, unsalted butter has a fresher, cleaner taste than salted butter.

If a recipe calls for unsalted butter, you may substitute salted butter, but should reduce any added salt a bit to make up for the extra salt in the butter. If a recipe doesn't specifically call for salted or unsalted butter, feel free to use the type you have on hand; if you tend to like saltier food, then salted butter is a good choice, but if you're watching sodium intake, unsalted butter is a better option.

Red Currant and Blue Cheese Butter
About ½ cup, enough for 8 servings

This is outstanding when melted atop a freshly grilled steak; try it with grilled venison for an extra-special treat.

½ cup (1 stick) unsalted butter, softened
¼ cup red currants (about 1¼ ounces)
1 small clove garlic, pressed
4 ounces blue cheese, crumbled

In mixing bowl, combine butter, currants and garlic. Mash with a fork until well combined. Add blue cheese and mash lightly to combine; some of the blue cheese should retain its texture. Spoon mixture onto a piece of waxed paper, in a line about 8 inches long. Roll up the waxed paper tightly, forming a cylinder; twist the ends closed. Refrigerate for at least 2 hours, or as long as 5 days. To serve, slice off 1-inch-long pieces; place on hot steaks that are fresh from the grill or broiler.

For longer storage, wrap the butter roll in foil and freeze. It will keep for several months in the freezer; you can slice off what you need from the frozen roll and return it to the freezer.

Currant Jelly
4 half-pints

3 cups currant juice
Half of a 1.75-ounce box powdered pectin
½ teaspoon butter, optional (helps reduce foaming)
3¼ cups sugar

Prepare and process as directed in Jelly Instructions (using pectin), pgs. 176–177.

Pears Poached in Spiced Currant Juice

Currant juice combines with pears for a delicious dessert. It would also be perfect on a brunch table. It is prettiest when prepared with red currant juice, but black currant juice will work fine as well.

2 firm but ripe Bosc or Anjou pears

1½ cups currant juice

½ cup ruby Port wine

3 tablespoons honey

1 cinnamon stick

2 whole cloves

**A few strips of orange zest (colored rind only,
    with none of the white pith; see "Zesting Citrus Fruits," pg. 35)**

Ice cream or whipped cream for serving

You'll need a heavy-bottomed 2- to 3-quart non-aluminum saucepan to prepare this; before starting, cut a round of kitchen parchment that will fit snugly inside the saucepan. Peel pears; cut in half lengthwise, and scoop out the seed core with a melon baller or teaspoon.

In saucepan, combine currant juice, Port, honey, cinnamon stick, cloves and orange zest. Heat to boiling over medium-high heat. Reduce heat so mixture simmers. Add pears; cover with kitchen parchment, pressing it directly onto the pears (this wicks the liquid up over the pears, making the color uniform). Simmer, turning occasionally, until pears are just tender, about 25 minutes. Transfer pears to a ceramic or glass mixing bowl.

Increase heat to medium-high and cook until liquid is syrupy; this will take 5 to 15 minutes. Use a wire-mesh strainer to strain reduced liquid over pears, discarding spices; set pears aside until completely cool, about 45 minutes. (The pears can be poached a day in advance; cover and refrigerate, but bring them to room temperature before serving.) Serve pears cut-side down, with syrup poured around; top each pear with a small scoop of vanilla ice cream or some whipped cream.

Overnight Multi-Grain Cereal with Fruit and Nuts

Bulk recipe

This is a wonderful mix to keep on hand. With just a few minutes' prep in the evening, you'll have hearty, cooked breakfast cereal in the morning—and no sticky pan to clean up!

- **³⁄₄ cup dried currants or huckleberries**
- **²⁄₃ cup chopped pecans**
- **½ cup steel-cut (coarse) oatmeal**
- **³⁄₈ cup buckwheat groats**
- **³⁄₈ cup bulgur**
- **¼ cup pepitas (toasted green pumpkin seeds)**
- **¼ cup pearled barley**
- **¼ cup soft wheat berries**
- **2 tablespoons amaranth**

Combine all ingredients in a large bowl; mix well with your hands. Store in a tightly sealed canister.

To prepare: The night before, measure ⅓ cup of the mixture per serving. For each serving, place ⅞ cup water and a pinch of salt in a saucepan or pot. Heat water to boiling. Add the measured mix; stir well. Return to boiling, then cover tightly and remove from the heat. Let stand at room temperature overnight. The next morning, the grains and fruit will be tender; heat on the stovetop or in the microwave, and serve with milk, syrup, butter, sugar or whatever you like. If you cook extra, you can keep it in the refrigerator for several days, heating a portion whenever you like.

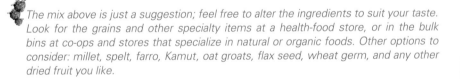

The mix above is just a suggestion; feel free to alter the ingredients to suit your taste. Look for the grains and other specialty items at a health-food store, or in the bulk bins at co-ops and stores that specialize in natural or organic foods. Other options to consider: millet, spelt, farro, Kamut, oat groats, flax seed, wheat germ, and any other dried fruit you like.

Currant Cordial

1 quart

Offer this delightful cordial to guests as a special after-dinner drink. It's also wonderfully warming to sip while sitting around the fireplace on a cold winter's night.

3 cups currant juice

½ cup sugar

1 cup brandy

2 whole cardamom pods

2 strips orange zest (colored rind only, with none of the white pith; see "Zesting Citrus Fruits," pg. 35), each about ½ inch wide and 2 inches long

You'll need a glass bottle that holds at least 40 ounces to hold the cordial; juice is often sold in these types of bottles. Wash it very well, then fill it with boiling water and let stand for at least 5 minutes.

In non-aluminum saucepan, combine currant juice and sugar; heat to boiling over medium-high heat and cook, stirring constantly, until sugar dissolves. Remove from heat and set aside until cool. Drain water from the prepared glass bottle, then use a funnel to pour the juice into it. Add remaining ingredients. Seal tightly and place in a dark, cool cupboard to mellow for a few weeks before drinking.

A cordial is similar to a liqueur, but with a lower alcohol content. If you make this cordial with red currant juice, it's a lovely garnet color; if you use black currant juice, it looks like blackberry brandy.

Other recipes in this book featuring currants:
Six Recipes Using Wild Fruit Juice or Syrup, pgs. 170–174
Wild Berry or Fruit Syrup, pg. 175
Dehydrating Wild Berries and Fruits, pgs. 180–181
Wild Berry or Fruit Leather, pg. 182
As a substitute in Grilled Bananas with Buffaloberry Sauce, pg. 27

Quick ideas for using currants:
If the currants are sweet, serve them raw in a bowl topped with thick cream and lots of sugar.
Add dried currants to hot cereal when cooking. Delicious.

ELDERBERRIES (*Sambucus* spp.)

Two types of elderberries with edible fruits grow in our area: common or black elderberry (*Sambucus nigra* ssp. *canadensis*) and blue elderberry (*S. nigra* ssp. *caerulea*); both can be used interchangeably in recipes. Elderberries have a somewhat musty flavor when sampled raw, but cooking improves the taste, especially when lemon juice is added. Don't taste more than one or two raw, though; many people get an upset stomach from raw elderberries. The seeds also cause digestive problems for some people; if you make an elderberry pie with whole berries, try just a small portion until you are sure you won't have a problem with the seeds.

Elderberry flowers from the two species here can be steeped to make a tea, which is often recommended to relieve headaches. The flower cluster can also be battered and fried to make interesting fritters.

Pick elderberries by snipping the entire fruit cluster off; place them in a bucket until you have as many as you need. The small stemlets that remain attached to the berries taste bad and can also cause digestive problems. The berries should be pulled off the stemlets soon after picking, because once the stemlets start to wilt, they are more difficult to remove. I rinse the clusters as soon as I get home, then just pull the berries off with my fingertips (which are soon stained purple). Some foragers prefer to place the clusters on a rimmed baking sheet that is propped up on one end, then use a fork to rake the berries off the clusters.

To prepare elderberry juice, measure the stemmed fruit and place in a non-aluminum pot. Add 1 cup water per quart of stemmed fruit. Heat to boiling, then reduce the heat; cover and simmer for about 5 minutes. Crush gently with a potato masher, then simmer for about 5 minutes longer. Transfer the mixture to a strainer lined with doubled, dampened cheese-cloth and let it drip for 30 minutes; squeeze once or twice to extract more juice (elderberry juice is so dark that you won't have to worry about the jelly being cloudy if you squeeze the fruit). Processed this way, a quart of fruit will yield about 2 cups juice.

Whole elderberries freeze very well; place measured amounts of stemmed berries in freezer-weight plastic bags or plastic containers, label with the amount, and freeze. Elderberries are also easy to dehydrate (see pgs. 180–181), and can sometimes be found in this form at winemaking supply stores. In addition to being used in winemaking, dried elderberries are used in baked goods, although if you want to try this, keep in mind that the seeds will still be in the dried fruit. To reconstitute dried elderberries, simply cover them generously with warm water and let stand until plumped up. A few reconstituted elderberries added to a batch of muffins, or to an apple pie, will make a delicious and different dessert. The soaking liquid can be added to other fruit juice for an interesting beverage.

Note that there are two elderberries in our area you don't want to confuse with common or blue elderberry: red elderberry (*S racemosa* var. *racemosa*), whose ripe fruits are red, and Rocky Mountain elderberry (*S. racemosa* var. *melanocarpa*), whose ripe fruits are black. Fruits from these two species have a rank flavor and are often regarded as toxic, although there are accounts that consider them edible in moderation when cooked.

Elderberry Liqueur

About 1 quart

This lovely purple liqueur can be served straight in a cordial glass, or on the rocks.

2 cups stemmed fresh elderberries

2 cups water

¾ cup sugar

2 cups vodka

¼ cup freshly squeezed lemon juice

1 teaspoon anise seeds

You'll need a glass bottle that holds at least 40 ounces to hold the liqueur during its steeping period; juice is often sold in these types of bottles. Wash it very well, then fill it with boiling water and let stand for at least 5 minutes.

In blender or food processor, chop elderberries coarsely. In non-aluminum saucepan, combine water and sugar. Heat to boiling over medium-high heat, stirring constantly until sugar dissolves and mixture is clear. Add chopped elderberries; reduce heat to low and cook for 5 minutes, stirring occasionally. Remove from heat and set aside until cool. Drain water from glass bottle, then use a funnel to pour mixture into it. Add vodka, lemon juice and anise seeds. Seal tightly and place in a dark, cool cupboard for 2 to 3 weeks, shaking the bottle every day or two.

After steeping for 2 or 3 weeks, strain the mixture into another clean bottle through a strainer lined with a double layer of cheesecloth; discard mixture in cheesecloth. Refrigerate strained liquid for 8 hours or longer, to allow any sediment to settle. Pour clear liquid into a clean 1-quart bottle through a funnel lined with a paper coffee filter. For best quality, store in refrigerator.

 For an elderberry martini, combine 2 parts elderberry liqueur with 1 part gin in an ice-filled cocktail shaker; shake and strain into a martini glass. Garnish with lemon zest curl.

Elderberry Jelly

4 half-pints

For a delightful variation, also see Elderberry-Sumac Jelly on pg. 49.

2½ cups elderberry juice

3 tablespoons lemon juice

Two-thirds of a 1.75-ounce box powdered pectin

½ teaspoon butter, optional (helps reduce foaming)

2¾ cups sugar

Prepare and process as directed in Jelly Instructions (using pectin), pgs. 176–177.

Elderberry Meringue Pie

1 pie (6 to 8 servings)

This pie looks so pretty, with the dark purple filling and fluffy meringue. It also looks like you spent all day slaving over it, but really, it's quite easy to make.

For 5,000 feet; see adjustments for other altitudes

1 cup plus 1 tablespoon sugar

5 tablespoons cornstarch

⅛ teaspoon salt

1½ cups elderberry juice (or 1 cup elderberry juice plus ½ cup water)

4 egg yolks

2 tablespoons butter

½ cup freshly squeezed lemon juice

1 pre-baked pie crust, lightly golden
(see "Blind Baking Pie Crusts," pg. 47)

Meringue:

6 tablespoons sugar

1 tablespoon cornstarch

Pinch of salt

½ cup water

½ teaspoon vanilla extract

4 egg whites, room temperature*

¼ teaspoon cream of tartar

Position rack in center of oven; heat to 350°F. In medium non-aluminum saucepan, stir sugar, cornstarch and salt together. Whisking constantly, stir in elderberry juice. Cook over medium-high heat, whisking constantly, until mixture boils; reduce heat to low and cook, whisking constantly, about 3 minutes longer. Remove from heat.

In small bowl, beat egg yolks lightly with a fork. Add ½ cup of the warm elderberry mixture to the egg yolks; beat with fork until smooth. Whisk egg yolk mixture into elderberry mixture. Return to medium-high heat and cook, whisking constantly, until thick, 3 to 4 minutes. Remove from heat. Add butter; whisk until dissolved. Add lemon juice; whisk until well blended. Scrape mixture into pre-baked pie crust; set aside while you prepare the meringue.

Prepare the meringue: In medium-sized microwave-safe bowl, whisk together the sugar, cornstarch and salt; add water and whisk until very well blended, with no lumps. Microwave on high until the mixture is thick and clear, about 2 minutes. Set aside to cool for about 15 minutes, then stir in the vanilla.

In very clean mixing bowl, combine egg whites and cream of tartar. Beat with electric mixer on medium speed until foamy. Increase beater speed to high, then gradually add the sugar mixture, beating continuously; continue beating until mixture is glossy and stiff peaks are just beginning to form (do not beat until mixture is completely stiff; the tips should bend slightly when the beater is lifted out). Spoon mixture over filling in crust, spreading all the way to the edges of the filling to seal to the crust; use a spoon to pull some of the meringue up into peaks. Bake for 15 to 20 minutes,[1, 2, 3] or until meringue is golden brown. Cool before serving.

*Use egg whites from pasteurized eggs if concerned about salmonella. You may also be able to purchase cartons of pasteurized egg whites, sold specifically for use in recipes such as meringue, at larger supermarkets.

Variation: Substitute juice from chokecherries or wild cherries for the elderberry juice; increase sugar to 1¼ cups. Or, substitute squashberry or highbush cranberry juice for the elderberry juice; increase sugar to 1⅔ cups.

1. **Below 5,000 feet:** Bake for 20 to 25 minutes.
2. **At 7,500 feet:** Bake for 13 to 17 minutes.
3. **At 10,000 feet:** Meringues are very tricky at 10,000 feet or above, and this recipe is not recommended. For a meringue technique that works at this altitude, see *Pie In the Sky* by Susan G. Purdy.

Blind Baking Pie Crusts

Sometimes, a recipe calls for a pre-baked pie crust. Here's how to make one. Place the rolled-out pastry dough into a pie plate; flute the edges decoratively. Place a large piece of foil inside, pressing it into the corners. Fill the foil with uncooked dry beans; if you do a lot of baking, you can also buy aluminum pie weights for this purpose at specialty cookware stores. Bake at 400°F for 10 minutes. Remove from oven. Carefully lift the foil by the corners, folding it in to contain the beans; place it in a mixing bowl and set it aside. Return the pie crust to the oven. For recipes that will get additional baking, bake until firm and very lightly golden, about 10 minutes more; for recipes that will get little or no additional baking, bake until golden brown, about 15 minutes more. Let crust cool before filling, or as directed in recipe.

The beans can no longer be used for bean recipes, but they can be saved for use when blind baking pies in the future; simply cool them completely, then transfer to a heavyweight plastic bag and store in the cupboard until you need them.

Fruit Terrine with Elderberry Gel

6 to 8 servings

This combines elderberry juice with fresh, purchased fruits for a truly lovely dessert—a clear gel glistening with fruits.

2 tablespoons cold water

2 tablespoons plain gelatin

1 cup elderberry juice

1 cup apple juice

½ cup sugar

1 cup cut-up peaches (fresh or previously frozen), cut into ½-inch pieces before measuring

1 cup fresh raspberries (wild or domestic)

1 cup whole, seedless green grapes (smaller grapes work best here)

A small amount of whipped cream for garnish, optional

Place cold water in a small bowl; sprinkle gelatin over the top. Let stand until gelatin softens, about 5 minutes. While gelatin is softening, in medium saucepan, combine elderberry juice, apple juice and sugar. Cook over medium heat, stirring constantly, until sugar dissolves, about 5 minutes. Remove from heat. Scrape softened gelatin into fruit juices; stir until gelatin is dissolved, 2 to 3 minutes. Cool to lukewarm.

While juice mixture is cooling, arrange peaches, raspberries and grapes in standard-sized glass loaf pan. Pour lukewarm fruit juice mixture over fruits; if any fruit is floating, press it down into the juice. Cover pan with plastic wrap and refrigerate until set, at least 3 hours; terrine can be prepared up to a day in advance.

To serve, run about 2 inches of hot water into the sink, then hold the pan in the sink so the water is level with the top of the gel; let stand in the hot water for about 15 seconds to loosen. (If it isn't loose along the sides, run a table knife between the gel and the pan.) Place a serving plate on top of the loaf pan and invert the two together, holding the plate and pan together tightly. Shake the pan slightly if necessary to release the terrine. Use a very sharp knife to slice crosswise into 6 to 8 pieces; top each serving with a small dollop of whipped cream, if you like.

Variation: Substitute juice from chokecherries or wild cherries for the elderberry juice. Increase sugar to ⅔ cup.

Elderberry-Sumac Jelly

4 half-pints

Elderberry jelly is delicious on its own, but sumac juice raises it to another level. This is one of the finest wild jellies you can make. The idea for this delightful combination comes from the late Euell Gibbons, in his book Stalking the Wild Asparagus.

3 cups stemless fresh elderberries, or 1 cup dried

2½ cups strained sumac juice (pg. 160)

**Two-thirds of a 1.75-ounce box powdered pectin
(see pg. 176 for information on dividing pectin)**

½ teaspoon butter, optional (helps reduce foaming)

2¾ cups sugar

In non-aluminum saucepan, combine elderberries and sumac juice. Heat to a gentle boil. If using fresh elderberries, cook for 5 minutes, then crush gently with potato masher and cook for 5 minutes longer. If using dried elderberries, cook for 10 minutes, then remove from heat and let stand for 20 minutes.

Transfer the mixture to a strainer lined with doubled, dampened cheesecloth and let it drip for 30 minutes; squeeze once or twice to extract more juice. Measure the juice; add water if necessary to bring it up to 2½ cups. Prepare and process as directed in Jelly Instructions (using pectin), pgs. 176–177.

Other recipes in this book featuring elderberries:
Wild Berry Vinegar, pg. 22
Six Recipes Using Wild Fruit Juice or Syrup, pgs. 170–174
Wild Berry or Fruit Syrup, pg. 175
Dehydrating Wild Berries and Fruits, pgs. 180–181
As a substitute in Pumpkin Tart with Chokecherry Glaze, pg. 36

Quick ideas for using elderberries:
Elderberry wine is often considered to be one of the best of the wild fruit wines, but it requires a lot of berries—and the stemlets need to be removed before you start. If you want to try making it, check out *Progressive Winemaking* by Peter Duncan and Bryan Acron.
Use the whole berries to make a pie, following any recipe you've got for blueberry pie; reconstituted dried berries are particularly good for pie. As noted on page 44, eat only a very small portion of this pie until you know you're not going to have a reaction to the seeds.

GOJI BERRIES (*Lycium* spp.)

Goji berry (*Lycium barbarum*; the plant is also called matrimony vine) is grown commercially in Asia, where the fruits are used for both food and medicine. Dried goji berries may sometimes be found at Asian markets in the U.S., where they may also be called medlar or wolfberry. Goji juice is also sold here in health-food stores; it is said to provide numerous health benefits, including boosting the immune system, improving eyesight, regulating the blood pressure, reducing inflammation and numerous other effects. Matrimony vines were brought to the U.S. in the 1880s, and are found in scattered locations throughout our area. Pioneers heading to Utah sometimes planted them around cemeteries, apparently so the plant's thorns could protect the dead; I've seen probable descendants of these plants at old, rural cemeteries in Colorado. The berries are juicy, with a delightful sweet-tart flavor; the seeds are tiny and unnoticeable.

Pale wolfberry fruits were a staple in the diets of Zuñi and other American Indians in the Southwest.

Pale wolfberry (*L. pallidum*) is a related but native plant that favors hot, dry climates; in our area it is found in southern Colorado, southern Utah and throughout most of New Mexico. The berries are edible and likely have the same medicinal value as goji berries, but for eating they are a little less desirable, sometimes having a bitter taste.

Because goji berries appear to have at least some medicinal effects (if one can believe even half of the claims made to this effect), it may be prudent to limit consumption of them and also of the related pale wolfberry, or to discuss it with a physician. Matrimony vines, the plants that produce goji berries, don't seem to be prolific fruit bearers in our area, so it's not likely that a forager would pick enough goji berries to be a problem. Pale wolfberry, however, can produce large quantities of fruits, but the bitterness probably would make it unlikely that a forager would eat a very large quantity at any one time.

I've never made juice or purée from these berries, but the procedure would be the same as for currants (pg. 38). Obviously, they can be dehydrated successfully, since they are sold in this form throughout the world; follow the instructions for dehydrating currants (pg. 180-181). I imagine they would make a tasty fruit leather as well; see instructions on pg. 182.

Refrigerator Cookies with Dried Goji Berries

About 24 cookies

The nutmeg and brandy add a delightfully different taste to these crisp, buttery cookies. Make a batch of the dough in the morning and pop it in the refrigerator. Later in the day, it'll be easy to slice off and have fresh-baked cookies for an after-school snack.

½ cup (1 stick) unsalted butter, softened

¾ cup sugar

1 egg

1 tablespoon brandy or cognac, or ¼ teaspoon brandy flavoring

½ teaspoon nutmeg

1¾ cups all-purpose flour

⅓ to ½ cup dried goji berries

In mixing bowl, cream butter with electric mixer until light and fluffy. Add sugar; beat until fluffy. Add egg and beat well. Add brandy and nutmeg; beat until smooth. In another mixing bowl, combine flour and dried berries; stir to blend. Add flour mixture to butter mixture; stir with a wooden spoon until soft dough forms (do not over-mix, or the cookies will be tough). Transfer dough to a 1-gallon zipper-style food storage bag. Using your hands to press the dough together from the outside, form it into a firmly packed cylinder at the bottom of the bag, rolling it on the counter to smooth the shape; it will be about 2 inches across. Seal the bag and refrigerate for at least 5 hours, or overnight.

When you're ready to bake, heat oven to 350°F. Line 2 baking sheets with kitchen parchment, or spray with nonstick spray. Slit the plastic bag open to expose the roll of dough. Use a very sharp knife to cut the roll into ¼-inch-thick slices; transfer to prepared baking sheets. Bake for 10 minutes, then rotate pans (see "Rotating Cookies while Baking," below). Continue baking until lightly browned around the edges, 9 to 15 minutes longer. Transfer to wire rack to cool.

Substitution: Follow recipe above, substituting any of the following dried wild fruits for the goji berries: barberries, huckleberries, raspberries, serviceberries or strawberries.

Rotating Cookies while Baking

If you're baking more than one sheet of cookies, they tend to bake unevenly because the pan on top blocks heat to the pan (or pans) below it. To help ensure even cooking, rotate the pans about halfway through baking, moving the top pan to the lower shelf and moving the lower pan to the top shelf; as you do this, also rotate the pans so the edge that was at the front of the oven is now in the back of the oven.

Cornmeal Pancakes with Goji

8 or 9 pancakes

These light, crispy cakes make a delicious breakfast or brunch item. For a change of pace, try them with apple butter slathered on top rather than the usual syrup.

¾ cup all-purpose flour, or as needed

½ cup cornmeal (use coarse cornmeal for more texture, if you like)

1 tablespoon sugar

1 teaspoon baking powder

½ teaspoon baking soda

¼ teaspoon salt

1 cup buttermilk, or as needed

1 tablespoon vegetable oil, plus additional as needed for frying

1 large egg

⅔ cup fresh goji berries

Maple syrup and butter for serving, or other toppings of your choice

Heat oven to 200°F. In large mixing bowl, combine ¾ cup flour, the cornmeal, sugar, baking powder, baking soda and salt; stir with a whisk until well blended. In small bowl, whisk together 1 cup buttermilk, 1 tablespoon oil and the egg. Add the buttermilk mixture to the flour mixture and stir gently with a wooden spoon until just mixed. Add the goji berries and stir gently to combine. Depending on your preference, the batter may be too thick or too thin (see tip below); adjust consistency if necessary by adding a little more flour or buttermilk.

Heat a griddle over medium heat until a drop of water sizzles and dances. Film with vegetable oil. Spoon batter onto hot griddle in scant ¼-cup portions. Cook until edges dry out and bubbles form on top. Carefully flip and cook until browned on second side and cooked through. Transfer cooked pancakes to a plate and place in the oven. Cook remaining pancakes, re-oiling griddle as necessary and transferring finished pancakes to oven as you go. Serve hot, with maple syrup and butter.

The consistency of pancake batter affects the pancakes quite a bit, especially with heartier pancakes that contain whole wheat flour and/or cornmeal. Thick batter makes smaller, sturdier pancakes; thin batter makes wider, more delicate pancakes. Feel free to adjust the consistency by adding a little more liquid (for thinner pancakes) or a little more flour (for thicker pancakes) so the pancakes come out just the way you like them. I usually cook a single pancake first, then adjust the consistency if needed for the rest of the batch. If you like thicker pancakes, use a little less heat under the griddle so the pancakes don't burn before they are cooked through.

Chinese Bright Eyes Soup

In China, a similar soup is made to provide both nutrition and medicinal value; it is said to be particularly beneficial to the eyesight. The traditional recipe uses leaves from the goji plant; here, spinach makes a delicious, and easy, substitute.

2 teaspoons toasted (dark) sesame oil

3 cloves garlic, minced

1 tablespoon minced gingerroot

8 cups (about 6 ounces, tightly packed) fresh spinach leaves, washed and spun dry

3 cups chicken broth

1 teaspoon soy sauce, or to taste

1 egg, well beaten

½ to ¾ cup fresh goji berries

In Dutch oven or soup pot, heat oil over medium-high heat until fragrant. Add garlic and ginger-root; stir-fry for about 1 minute. Add spinach; stir-fry until wilted and reduced in volume. Add chicken broth and soy sauce. Heat to boiling, stirring several times; adjust heat so mixture is bubbling gently rather than boiling furiously. Drizzle beaten egg into soup, stirring constantly; the egg should separate into threads or thin ribbons. Cook for about 1 minute. Add goji berries; remove from heat and let stand for about 1 minute.

If you've dehydrated some goji berries, you can substitute them for the fresh ones in this and other recipes in this section. Use a little over half of the amount called for in the recipe, and rehydrate them by soaking in warm water for about 10 minutes before adding to the dish.

Other recipes in this book featuring goji berries:
Six Recipes Using Wild Fruit Juice or Syrup, pgs. 170–174
Wild Berry or Fruit Syrup, pg. 175

GOOSEBERRIES (*Ribes* spp.)

Five types of gooseberries grow in our area: whitestem (*Ribes inerme*), trumpet (*R. leptanthum*), Canadian (*R. oxyacanthoides*), desert (*R. velutinum*) and gooseberry currant (*R. montigenum*). Fruits from these species are similar in taste, so they all work for any gooseberry recipe. Gooseberries are unusual because the fruit can be used in its green stage as well as when fully ripe. They have a tart, refreshing flavor, somewhat reminiscent of rhubarb; ripe gooseberries are sweeter than green ones. Green gooseberries are rich in pectin, so they can be used to make jam without adding commercial pectin; they also make a good pie filling, because the pectin helps thicken the juices naturally.

Most gooseberries are too tart to eat raw, even when ripe, but some, particularly whitestem gooseberries, may be sweet enough to eat out of hand. Try a few when you find a plant with ripe fruit and see what you think.

When picking green gooseberries, choose those that are close to full size, about 3/8 inch across; they will still be firm, but will begin to appear slightly translucent around the edges. Taste one before picking a lot. If the berry is hard and tastes acrid, the gooseberries are underripe; wait a week or so before picking. As summer progresses, you'll see gooseberries in all stages of ripeness on the plant at the same time, and you'll quickly get a feel for judging the correct stage.

Gooseberries grow abundantly on the plants, and you'll often find plants in small colonies, so it's easy to pick a good quantity. The work starts once you get them home, because you'll need to remove the stems and the "pigtail," a withered brown flower remnant at the base of the berry (if you're juicing the fruit, you don't need to remove the stems or tails). To clean green gooseberries, use a very sharp paring knife to slice off the stem and all parts of the pigtail. A knife works best on green gooseberries, which are firm enough to allow slicing. Once gooseberries ripen, the pressure of the knife and your fingertips tends to mangle the berries; sharp scissors work better (or pinch the stems and tails off with your fingernails).

To make gooseberry juice, place washed gooseberries in a medium (4-quart) non-aluminum soup pot (you don't need to remove the stems or tails). Gently crush the fruit with a potato masher to start the flow of juice. Add 1/2 cup water per quart of gooseberries. Heat to boiling, then reduce the heat; cover and simmer for about 10 minutes. Transfer the mixture to a strainer lined with doubled, dampened cheesecloth and let it drip for 30 minutes; if you're making jelly, don't squeeze the fruit or the jelly will be cloudy. After the clear liquid has dripped away, set it aside and squeeze the fruit into a different container; you can use this slightly cloudy juice as a beverage or for cooking. Processed this way, a quart of gooseberries will yield about 2 cups of juice.

Gooseberries freeze well. Simply wash them and remove the stems and tails, then freeze in heavyweight plastic food-storage bags or tightly lidded plastic containers. They can also be dehydrated (see pgs. 180–181); they become chewy, rather like raisins, and are a good addition to trail mixes. Finally, they make excellent fruit leather (pg. 182), although they might need a bit of sweetening first.

Green Gooseberry Pie

1 pie (6 to 8 servings)

This is an old-time recipe from the Midwest, from back in the days when every farmhouse had a gooseberry pie cooling on the windowsill during "goosie season."

3½ cups green gooseberries (about 1¼ pounds)

1½ cups sugar

2 tablespoons minute tapioca

½ teaspoon finely grated orange zest (colored rind only, with none of the white pith; see "Zesting Citrus Fruits," pg. 35)

¼ teaspoon nutmeg

¼ teaspoon salt

Ready-to-use pastry for double-crust pie

1½ tablespoons unsalted butter, cut into small pieces

1 egg yolk, beaten with 1 tablespoon cold water

Position rack in lower third of oven; heat to 375°F. In mixing bowl, combine gooseberries, sugar, tapioca, orange zest, nutmeg and salt. Stir gently until well mixed; set aside for 15 minutes. Meanwhile, fit one pastry into ungreased deep-dish pie plate. Scrape gooseberry mixture into pie plate. Dot with cut-up butter. Moisten edges of pastry in pie plate with a little cold water, then top with second pastry (for the most authentic farmhouse look, make a lattice-top pie; see below). Seal, trim and flute edges. Cut 6 to 8 inch-long slits in the crust. Place pie on baking sheet (to catch drips). Brush top with beaten egg. Bake until crust is golden and filling bubbles through slits, 35 to 40 minutes. Transfer to rack to cool; best served warm, the day it is made.

Making a Lattice-Top Pie

When you're making a pie with a top crust, you can use a lattice top in place of the standard, full top crust; the lattice looks very pretty and homestyle. Here's how.

Fit the bottom crust as usual, and add the filling. Cut the second pastry into ½-inch-wide strips. Position a row of strips, running vertically across the top of the pie and separated by ½ inch. Now begin to weave a row of strips horizontally across the top of the pie, lifting the vertical strips over the horizontal strips in an alternating pattern. Trim all strips even with the edge of the overhanging crust, and pinch all edges very well to seal; flute edge decoratively. Brush with egg wash or any other finish as directed in the recipe; the pie is ready to be baked.

Spicy Gooseberry-Apple Crisp

Gingersnaps make a delightfully different topping on this tasty crisp.

Fruit mixture:

2 large Granny Smith or other tart cooking apples (about 1 pound), peeled, cored and cut into ½-inch chunks

2 cups fresh or previously frozen ripe gooseberries (about 12 ounces)

¾ cup (packed) brown sugar

½ cup dried cranberries (craisins)

1 tablespoon cornstarch

½ teaspoon cinnamon

¼ teaspoon nutmeg

Topping:

3 ounces gingersnap cookies (about 12 medium cookies)

¼ cup (packed) brown sugar

¼ cup white sugar

¼ cup all-purpose flour

6 tablespoons cold butter, cut into ½-inch pieces

Heat oven to 375°F. Spray 8x8-inch baking dish generously with nonstick spray. Add all fruit mixture ingredients, stirring to mix. In food processor, chop gingersnaps very coarsely. Add remaining topping ingredients. Pulse on-and-off a few times until mixture is crumbly, with pieces no larger than the size of a pea. Sprinkle mixture evenly over fruit in baking dish. Bake until the topping is deep golden brown and the fruit is bubbling, 30 to 40 minutes. Cool for at least 45 minutes before serving; best served the day it is made.

Green Gooseberry Jam (no added pectin)

1 cup of cleaned gooseberries yields about ¾ cup jam

Green gooseberries contain enough pectin to make jam; once the berries ripen, commercial pectin (which requires precise amounts of fruit, sugar and pectin) needs to be added to make the mixture set up. Since you don't have to mess with pectin in this recipe, it's easy to make a batch of any size. Measurements are given for 1 cup of cleaned gooseberries; adjust proportionally for the amount of gooseberries you've got.

Note: It takes a bit of time to learn how to cook jam without pectin added. It's better to undercook it; you can always cook it a bit more (even after it's cooled) if it's too thin, but if you overcook it, it will be too stiff to use once it's cooled.

6 ounces fresh or previously frozen green gooseberries (about 1 cup)

3 tablespoons water

6 ounces sugar (1 cup minus 2 tablespoons)

Half a thin pat of butter

Place a small ceramic plate in the freezer; this will be used for testing doneness of the jam. Estimate your final yield based on the information under the title, and prepare half-pint canning jars, bands and new lids as described on pg. 183. Place gooseberries and water in a heavy-bottomed non-aluminum saucepan. Heat over medium heat until simmering, then cover and adjust heat mixture just boils. Cook, covered, for 10 minutes, or until gooseberries are very soft and water has cooked away.

Mash fruit with a potato masher, and place the uncovered saucepan over medium heat. Add a third of the sugar and cook, stirring constantly, for about a minute. Add half of the remaining sugar and cook, stirring constantly, for another minute. Add the remaining sugar and cook for another minute, stirring constantly until all sugar is dissolved.

When sugar has dissolved, add butter; increase heat to high. When the mixture comes to a full boil, cook for 5 minutes, stirring constantly. Remove jam from heat to prevent overcooking while you test for doneness. Place a spoonful on the cold plate and return to the freezer for a minute; finished jam will hold its shape, without weeping around the edges. If the jam is too thin, return to boiling and cook for another minute, then re-test; repeat as needed. Pour into prepared jars, leaving ¼ inch headspace; seal with prepared lids and bands. Process in a boiling-water bath for 20 minutes at 5,000 feet, or at the recommended time at your elevation (see pg. 183); if you prefer, you can store the jam in the refrigerator where it will keep for a month or longer.

Gooseberry Bread with Crumble Topping

8 to 10 servings

Moist with gooseberries, this bread makes a great breakfast or brunch item.

For 5,000 feet; see adjustments for other altitudes

4 tablespoons (half of a stick) unsalted butter, softened

⅓ cup plus 1 tablespoon (packed) brown sugar[1, 3]

1 large egg[3]

2 cups plus 1 tablespoon all-purpose flour[1, 2, 3]

½ cup white sugar[2, 3]

1¼ teaspoons baking powder[1, 2, 3]

¼ teaspoon baking soda[1, 3]

½ teaspoon salt[3]

¾ cup plus 2 tablespoons fresh orange juice[1, 2, 3]

1⅓ cups fresh ripe gooseberries (about 8 ounces)

¾ cup chopped pecans

Crumble topping:

2 tablespoons white sugar

1 tablespoon all-purpose flour

¼ teaspoon cinnamon

1½ tablespoons cold butter, cut into small pieces

Position rack in lower third of oven; heat to 375°F.[1, 2, 3] Spray a standard-sized loaf pan with nonstick spray and dust with flour; set aside. In mixing bowl, beat butter, brown sugar and egg with electric mixer until smooth and creamy. Set a wire-mesh strainer over the mixing bowl. Add flour, white sugar, baking powder, baking soda and salt to strainer. Shake to sift into butter mixture. Stir with wooden spoon until dry ingredients are moistened. Add orange juice; stir until just mixed in. Add gooseberries and pecans; stir to mix. Scrape mixture into prepared loaf pan, smoothing top.

Make the crumble topping: In a small bowl, stir together the sugar, flour and cinnamon. Add butter; use a fork or your fingertips to blend the butter into the sugar mixture, working them together until the mixture is the texture of very coarse sand with some pea-sized particles. Use a spoon to sprinkle the crumble topping over the batter. Bake in the lower third of the oven for 50 to 60 minutes,[3] or until a wooden pick inserted into the center comes out clean; if topping is browning too quickly before cake is done, drape a piece of foil over the top. Place pan on wire rack; remove from pan when cool.

1. Below 5,000 feet: Use ½ cup brown sugar. Use 2 cups flour. Use 1½ teaspoons baking powder. Use ½ teaspoon baking soda. Use ¾ cup orange juice. Position rack in center of oven and heat to 350°F.

2. **At 7,500 feet:** Add an additional tablespoon of flour. Use 3 tablespoons white sugar. Use 1⅛ teaspoons baking powder. Add an additional tablespoon of orange juice. Heat oven to 360°F.

3. **At 10,000 feet:** Use ⅓ cup brown sugar. Use extra-large egg. Use 2¼ cups flour. Use 2½ tablespoons white sugar. Use 1⅛ teaspoons baking powder. Use ⅛ teaspoon baking soda. Increase salt slightly. Add an additional tablespoon of orange juice. Heat oven to 360°F; increase baking time by 5 minutes.

Green Gooseberry Filling   About ½ cup; easily increased

This deliciously tart filling is a nice counterpoint when used in sweet or rich recipes.

6 ounces fresh or previously frozen green gooseberries (about 1 cup)

3 tablespoons sugar, or as needed

2 tablespoons grated apple

1 tablespoon orange juice

Chop gooseberries coarsely by hand or in mini food processor. Combine chopped gooseberries, sugar, apple and orange juice in small, heavy-bottomed saucepan. Heat to boiling over medium-high heat, then cook, stirring frequently, until mixture is no longer runny and looks like chunky applesauce; this will take 9 to 11 minutes. Taste for sweetness, and add a little more sugar if you like. Cool before using.

Use this to prepare Easy Bear Claws (pg. 81), Fruit-Striped Cookie Fingers (pg. 126), or Fruit-Filled Muffins (pg. 155). Refrigerate extra filling, and use to top oatmeal or toast.

Sweet Potato-Gooseberry Casserole 6 servings

Fresh sweet potatoes are a fabulous complement to gooseberries in this easy, savory casserole. Serve it with ham, turkey or pork chops for a perfect meal.

2 garnet yams or other orange-fleshed sweet potatoes, about 1½ pounds total

1 cup fresh or previously frozen gooseberries (green or ripe; about 6 ounces)

¼ cup (packed) golden brown sugar

¼ cup apple juice

3 tablespoons butter, melted, divided

½ teaspoon minced or grated fresh gingerroot

½ cup breadcrumbs

2 tablespoons Parmesan cheese, optional

Position rack in center of oven; heat to 375°F. Heat a large pot of water to boiling. Peel sweet potatoes and dice into ½-inch cubes. As soon as all of the potatoes have been diced, add them to the pot of boiling water; if you wait too long, they will turn brown. Return to boiling; cook until sweet potatoes are just tender (not mushy), 5 to 8 minutes. Drain in colander and allow to drip for a few minutes.

While potatoes are draining, spray 1½-quart casserole dish with nonstick spray; set aside. Chop gooseberries very coarsely in food processor or by hand; transfer to large mixing bowl. Add brown sugar, apple juice, 2 tablespoons of the butter, the gingerroot and drained sweet potatoes to gooseberries in mixing bowl; stir to combine. Transfer to prepared dish. In a small bowl, stir together the breadcrumbs, Parmesan cheese and remaining 1 tablespoon butter; sprinkle evenly over casserole. Bake for 30 minutes.

About sweet potatoes
The best sweet potatoes to use for this dish are dark-orange "yams" such as garnet yams. Actually, these are not yams; they're sweet potatoes. A true yam is a starchy, dry root that is rarely found in American markets. The dark-orange sweet potatoes are more moist and less mealy than pale-colored sweet potatoes. If you can't find garnet yams, look for the darkest sweet potatoes you can find.

Ripe Gooseberry Jelly

3 cups gooseberry juice (prepared from ripe gooseberries)
One-third of a 1.75-ounce box powdered pectin
½ teaspoon butter, optional (helps reduce foaming)
3¼ cups sugar

Prepare and process as directed in Jelly Instructions (using pectin), pgs. 176–177.

Strawberry-Gooseberry Dessert Sauce   About 2 cups

Serve this sauce warm or cold. It's good when used to top pound cake, shortcake, ice cream or waffles and can be used in oatmeal for a sweet flavor booster. You may also enjoy it served simply in a dish; try it warm, perhaps with a dollop of whipped cream.

2 cups fresh or previously frozen gooseberries
(green or ripe; about 12 ounces)
¾ cup sugar
⅓ cup orange juice or water
1 teaspoon minced fresh gingerroot, optional
A pinch of ground cloves
1 cup sliced strawberries, wild or domestic
1 tablespoon cornstarch, blended with 2 tablespoons water

In saucepan, combine gooseberries, sugar, orange juice, gingerroot and cloves. Heat to boiling; reduce heat and simmer for 10 minutes, stirring occasionally. Add strawberries; cook for about 3 minutes longer. Stir in cornstarch mixture; increase heat to medium-high and cook, stirring constantly, until mixture boils and thickens. Cool slightly before serving or refrigerating.

Other recipes in this book featuring gooseberries:
Mahonia-Gooseberry Spritzer, pg. 94
Six Recipes Using Wild Fruit Juice or Syrup, pgs. 170–174
Wild Berry or Fruit Syrup, pg. 175
Dehydrating Wild Berries and Fruits, pgs. 180–181
Wild Berry or Fruit Leather, pg. 182

Quick ideas for using gooseberries:
Substitute gooseberries for cut-up fresh rhubarb in desserts and other recipes.

GRAPES (*Vitis* spp.)

Three types of wild grapes grow in our area; all can be used in the same ways. Riverbank grapes (*Vitis riparia*) are by far the most common, although they are found primarily on the eastern plains. Canyon grape (*V. arizonica*) is extremely similar in appearance, but in our area it grows only in New Mexico and southern Utah. Maple-leaf grapes (*V. acerifolia*) are found in our area only in southeastern Colorado and northeastern Utah. Luckily, all are easy to pick and grow in good quantities when you do find plants, so it's easy to harvest a gallon in a short time. Use scissors to snip off the entire cluster, dropping it into an ice cream pail or large bag. A 1-gallon ice cream pail holds about 3 pounds of grape clusters. When you're ready to process the grapes, rinse them well. I pick the grapes off the stems before processing them; bugs often lurk in the clusters, and by stemming the grapes, I eliminate these pests. (If you've got a large quantity of grapes to process or are using a press, simply remove the largest stems.)

You can store grapes in the refrigerator up to a week; make sure the grapes at the bottom don't get crushed by the grapes above them, or they will start to rot.

Wild grapes contain tartrate, a substance that causes crystallization in jelly. It burns your skin after prolonged contact, and also burns your mouth if you eat very many raw grapes. Tartrate is removed during juicing.

To prepare juice, place washed grapes in a clean container. Mash with a potato masher, mashing gently to avoid breaking up the bitter seeds. Transfer the mixture to a strainer lined with a triple layer of dampened cheesecloth. Gather the cheesecloth up around the grapes, and squeeze to extract as much juice as possible. Return the fruit-filled cheesecloth to the strainer and open it up; pour about ½ cup water into the fruit pulp, then re-gather the cheesecloth and squeeze again. Return the fruit-filled cheesecloth to the strainer and let it drip for 30 minutes. (Wear clean rubber gloves, or rinse your hands immediately after squeezing the grapes to wash off the tartrate.)

After the crushed grapes have dripped as much as they will, pour the liquid into a clean jar; for each quart of stemmed grapes you started with, you'll have about 1½ cups of juice. Refrigerate for 24 hours; a sediment will develop. Carefully pour off the separated liquid into a clean jar; the sediment is fairly solid, but you should pour slowly to avoid stirring it up, and as soon as it nears the stream of liquid you're pouring, stop. Discard the sediment, which contains the tartrate. The amount of sediment varies; it is typically between one-quarter and one-third the total volume of the freshly pressed juice. So each quart of picked grapes yields 1 to 1¼ cups of finished, deep-purple juice.

Grape Jelly (pectin added)

4 half-pints

2 1/2 cups wild grape juice
Half of a 1.75-ounce box powdered pectin
1/2 teaspoon butter, optional (helps reduce foaming)
3 1/2 cups sugar

Prepare and process as directed in Jelly Instructions (using pectin), pgs. 176–177.

Grape Freezer Jelly

3 half-pints

Although the pectin mixture is cooked, the juice is never heated, resulting in sparkling-clear jelly with a clean, bright flavor. Jelly making doesn't get much easier than this.

1 1/2 cups wild grape juice
2 1/2 cups sugar
Half of a 1.75-ounce box powdered pectin
   (see pg. 176 for information on dividing pectin)
1/3 cup plus 1 tablespoon water

Sterilize 3 half-pint jars, bands and new lids as directed on pg. 183. Combine juice and sugar in glass or Pyrex mixing bowl, stirring to dissolve sugar. Let stand for 10 minutes, stirring occasionally.

In small saucepan, combine pectin and water; stir well (mixture may be lumpy). Heat to a full, rolling boil over high heat, stirring constantly. Cook at a rolling boil for 1 minute, stirring constantly. Pour pectin mixture into juice in bowl. Stir constantly with wooden spoon until sugar is completely dissolved and no longer grainy, about 3 minutes; a few grains may remain, but the mixture should no longer look cloudy (or the jelly will be cloudy).

Pour mixture into prepared jars or containers, leaving 1/2 inch headspace; cover with clean lids. Let stand at room temperature for 24 hours; the jelly should be set. If it is not set, refrigerate for several days until set before using or freezing; grape jelly may take as long as a week to set. The jelly will keep for 3 weeks in the refrigerator, or it may be frozen for up to a year.

Wild Grape-Chokecherry Wine

8 to 12 bottles

This is a rich, rounded dry red wine with a full mouthfeel and lots of fruit. It uses almost twice as much fresh fruit as other recipes, but the results are worth it.

Winemaking is actually fairly straightforward, but there are a lot of steps and special instructions to follow. The instructions here assume some familiarity with winemaking; if you are unfamiliar with the procedures, consult *First Steps in Winemaking* by C.J.J. Berry, or my book, *Abundantly Wild,* for more information. You can also get help, advice, and supplies such as fermenters and airlocks, from a good winemaking supply store, as well as from some websites.

5 pounds wild grapes

5 pounds chokecherries, fresh or previously frozen

5 pounds sugar

1½ gallons hot water (not boiling; use hot tap water)

5-gram packet of Montrachet wine yeast

2 Campden tablets, finely crushed

2 teaspoons yeast nutrient

1 teaspoon pectic enzyme

Day 1: Sterilize a 5-gallon container, such as a plastic fermenter or a food-safe 5-gallon plastic bucket, with sulphite solution. Place fruit in sterilized container. Crush fruit with your hands, rinsing hands frequently to wash off tartrate (or wear rubber gloves). Add sugar and hot water; stir well with a sterilized spoon (sterilize by rinsing with sulphite solution or by boiling for 5 minutes). When water cools to 70°F or less, add yeast, Campden tablets, yeast nutrient and pectic enzyme. Cover loosely with muslin. The wine should begin to ferment and bubble in 12 to 24 hours; if it fails to start bubbling, stir with a sterilized spoon to aerate it. When it starts bubbling, the solid ingredients will form a cake on top; this is normal. Let stand for 10 days, stirring occasionally with a sterilized spoon; this stage is called the "primary ferment."

Day 10: Sterilize two clean 1-gallon glass jugs with sulphite solution; also have a half-gallon jug ready in case you need it. Strain liquid through a cheesecloth-lined funnel into the jugs; top off if necessary with white grape juice or water (if you don't have enough for a full second gallon, use the half-gallon jug instead). Cap the jugs with sterilized airlocks and place them in a cool location. The wine will bubble vigorously, and bubbles will come frequently through the airlocks. Ferment for 3 to 4 weeks, until a bubble comes through the airlock only once every minute or two; this stage is called the "secondary ferment."

Day 35 (approximate): The wine will separate into two layers: a top layer of liquid (which may be slightly cloudy) and a bottom layer of sediment. Use a sterilized winemaker's siphon or food-grade plastic hose to siphon the liquid into another sterilized jug, taking care to siphon off only the liquid; avoid disturbing the sediment. This is called "racking." Top off the wine with water as needed to fill the jug to within ½ inch of the top. Re-sterilize the airlock and cap the jug; return it to the cool location. After this, rack the wine as necessary; typically, you'll want to rack it after a month or so because it will have developed another layer of sediment, and again after that as needed. Top off the wine each time with water as needed, and always keep it capped with a sterilized airlock. Fermentation is complete when the water in the airlock is level on both sides; if the water remains pushed up on the release side, fermentation is still occurring, although it may be almost unnoticeable.

Bottling and aging: When you decide that fermentation is complete, use the siphon hose to transfer the wine into clean, sterilized wine bottles. Sterilize new corks, then use a corking device to push the cork into the bottle; if the corker doesn't push the cork all the way in, use the handle of a wooden spoon to complete the job. Many home winemakers run a piece of sterilized string alongside the cork, push the cork halfway in, then pull out the string. This releases pressure from inside the bottle, allowing you to push the cork all the way in.

Rest the bottles on their sides, and let the wine age for at least a month; longer is better, but don't wait too long before checking it. Most homemade wines are best when drunk within a year of being bottled, although some exceptional homemade wines—like this one, if it is properly made—can be bottle-aged for as long as 10 years.

Other recipes in this book featuring wild grapes:
Six Recipes Using Wild Fruit Juice or Syrup, pgs. 170–174
Wild Berry or Fruit Syrup, pg. 175

Quick ideas for using wild grapes:
Blend finished grape juice with apple juice, using one part grape juice to two parts apple juice (or to taste). Sweeten as needed; chill before serving.

GROUND CHERRIES (*Physalis* spp.)

The *Physalis* group is fairly large, and includes not only ground cherries, but tomatillos and the orange-husked ornamental plant commonly called Chinese lantern, which has inedible fruit and does not grow in the wild in our area. All have a ribbed, papery husk enclosing the fruit, which is a pulpy berry with many soft seeds, rather like a small tomato. You probably won't encounter tomatillos in the wild in our area (except perhaps scattered in New Mexico), just one of the numerous varieties of ground cherry. In addition to plants in the *Physalis* group, you may also encounter purple ground cherry (*Quincula lobata*), a very similar plant that was once considered part of the *Physalis* genus (group) but has been moved into its own genus; fruits from this plant are very similar to those from *Physalis* species and can be used in the same way.

Ground cherries were a favorite of early settlers, but today the fruit is little known except to foragers and a few country folk who still remember them.

In our area, ripe ground cherries range from golden yellow, to orange, to purple; it's important to note that ripe ground cherries are never green or black. If you've picked some ground cherries and they are still greenish, let them ripen on the countertop until they soften and are no longer green. If they remain tinged with green, they shouldn't be eaten; unripe ground cherries are somewhat toxic, as are all other parts of the plant, including the papery husk. The husk should be very loose around the fruit as well. If you have fruits with husks that cling tightly, discard these without tasting; they probably aren't ground cherries.

To prepare ground cherries, peel away and discard the papery husk. The berries have a sticky, slightly waxy coating that often holds dust, so they should be rinsed after husking; sometimes, they have dark spots of waxy dirt that can be rubbed off while holding the berry under running water. The seeds in ground cherries are soft and unnoticeable, so they don't need to be removed. A quart of husked ground cherries weighs about 1¼ pounds.

Ground cherries are most commonly cooked into jam or preserves, or used in baked goods such as pies. Most ground cherries can be eaten raw or cooked, although some sources state that smooth or longleaf ground cherry (*P. longifolia*) should be cooked before eating; I can't verify that in any scientific texts, but wanted to pass it along. Ground cherries keep for several weeks in the refrigerator, and can be frozen for longer-term storage; just pack washed berries into plastic bags or containers and freeze with no further preparation. They also dehydrate well (see pgs. 180–181), and can also be used to make fruit leather (pg. 182). Ground cherries may cause diarrhea if eaten in large quantities, and persons who are allergic to tomatoes should not eat ground cherries.

Ground Cherry Pie with Cracker Topping

1 pie (6 to 8 servings)

Here's a twist on a top crust. The cracker topping is crunchy and buttery, and works really well with sunny ground cherries.

For 5,000 feet; see adjustments for other altitudes

Topping:

4 ounces buttery crackers such as Ritz

2 tablespoons butter, melted

1 tablespoon sugar

1 Granny Smith or other cooking apple

1½ cups husked, ripe ground cherries (7½ to 8 ounces)

½ cup sugar

2 tablespoons cornstarch

½ teaspoon cinnamon

¼ teaspoon nutmeg

1 tablespoon lemon juice

**1 pre-baked pie crust, lightly golden
(see "Blind Baking Pie Crusts," pg. 47)**

Place rack in lower third of oven; heat to 400°F.[1, 3] Make the topping: Chop crackers in food processor until medium consistency; you may also place them in a plastic bag and bash them with a rolling pin. Place in medium mixing bowl. Drizzle with melted butter; add sugar and mix well. Set aside.

Peel and core apple, then chop to medium-fine consistency (if you made the cracker crumbs in a food processor, you can chop the apple in it without rinsing it out). In large mixing bowl, stir together chopped apple, ground cherries, sugar, cornstarch, cinnamon and nutmeg. Add lemon juice and stir again. Scrape into pre-baked crust. Spoon cracker topping evenly over filling. Place pie on a baking sheet (to catch drips); cover pie loosely with foil. Bake for 15 minutes,[2, 3] then remove foil and bake until crumb topping is deep golden brown and filling is bubbly, 15 to 25 minutes longer.[3] Cool on wire rack; best served slightly warm, the day it is made.

---

1. **Below 5,000 feet:** Heat oven to 375°F.

2. **At 7,500 feet:** Bake the pie for 20 minutes before removing the foil.

3. **At 10,000 feet:** Heat oven to 425°F. Bake the pie for 20 minutes before removing the foil. After removing the foil, bake for 10 to 15 minutes longer, or until crumb topping is deep golden brown and filling is bubbly.

Ground Cherry Jam (no added pectin) About 3 half-pints

1 quart husked, ripe ground cherries (about 1¼ pounds)

2 cups sugar

¼ cup water

¼ cup freshly squeezed lemon juice

1 cinnamon stick, optional

Please read the notes on no-pectin jam in the Green Gooseberry Jam recipe (pg. 57). Ground cherries have less pectin than green gooseberries, so they require longer cooking, but the basic technique is the same. Before you start, prepare 3 half-pint canning jars, bands and new lids as described on pg. 183.

In a heavy-bottomed non-aluminum 2-quart pot, combine all ingredients. Heat to boiling over high heat, then reduce heat to medium and mash slightly with a potato masher (don't break up the cinnamon stick). Cook fruit at a moderate boil for 30 minutes. Remove jam from the heat to prevent overcooking while you test for doneness. Place a spoonful on a cool plate and place in the freezer for a few minutes; the jam should hold its shape, without weeping around the edges. If the jam is too thin, return to boiling and cook for another few minutes, then re-test; continue as needed until the consistency is correct. Discard cinnamon stick. Pour into prepared jars, leaving ¼ inch headspace; seal with prepared lids and bands. Process in a boiling-water bath for 15 minutes at 5,000 feet, or at the recommended time for your elevation (see pg. 183); if you prefer, you can store the jam in the refrigerator where it will keep for a month or longer.

Ground Cherry Filling About ½ cup; easily increased

¾ teaspoon water

¾ teaspoon cornstarch

5½ ounces husked, ripe ground cherries (about 1 heaping cup)

1 tablespoon sugar

¼ teaspoon vanilla extract

In small bowl, blend together water and cornstarch; set aside. Chop ground cherries coarsely by hand or in mini food processor. In small, heavy-bottomed saucepan, combine ground cherries, sugar and vanilla. Heat to boiling over medium-high heat, then cook, stirring frequently, until mixture is no longer runny; this will take 8 to 10 minutes. Add cornstarch mixture, stirring constantly; cook for 1 to 2 minutes longer, or until thick. Cool before using.

Use this to prepare Easy Bear Claws (pg. 81), Fruit-Striped Cookie Fingers (pg. 126), or Fruit-Filled Muffins (pg. 155). Refrigerate extra filling, and use to top oatmeal or toast.

Ground Cherry Custard Bars

These hold up well in a lunchbox or picnic basket.

½ cup (1 stick) butter, softened
1 cup all-purpose flour
¼ cup powdered sugar
1 cup husked, ripe ground cherries (about 5 ounces)

Custard:
½ cup sugar
3 tablespoons all-purpose flour
¼ teaspoon salt
½ cup whole milk
2 tablespoons freshly squeezed lemon juice
1 teaspoon vanilla extract
3 egg yolks

Spray 8x8-inch baking dish with nonstick spray; set aside. Heat oven to 350°F. In a large bowl, beat butter with electric mixer until light. Add flour and powdered sugar; beat at low speed until well combined (mixture will be crumbly). Press mixture firmly into the bottom and ½ inch up the sides of prepared baking dish. Bake 15 minutes. While crust is baking, prepare the filling; if the 15 minutes is up before the filling is ready, remove the crust from the oven and set it aside.

To start on the filling: With a very sharp knife, cut the ground cherries into quarters and set aside. Make the custard: Stir sugar, flour and salt together in a heavy-bottomed non-aluminum saucepan. In measuring cup, combine milk, lemon juice, vanilla and egg yolks; stir with a fork to break up and beat in the egg yolks. Slowly add milk mixture to sugar mixture in saucepan, whisking constantly; whisk until smooth. Cook over medium heat, stirring almost constantly, until mixture thickens, 5 to 10 minutes. Remove from heat; stir in ground cherries.

Scrape custard mixture into baked crust, spreading evenly. Return to oven and bake until custard is set, 30 to 40 minutes. Cool completely; cut into 16 squares.

Chicken Salad with Ground Cherries and Almonds

4 servings

A lovely luncheon dish. Serve with warm biscuits and chilled iced tea.

1 pound cooked chicken breast, diced

2 green onions, chopped

½ cup finely diced celery

¼ cup mayonnaise (reduced-fat works fine)

1 tablespoon chopped fresh tarragon

1 cup husked, ripe ground cherries (about 5 ounces)*

¼ cup olive oil

1 tablespoon white wine vinegar

2 teaspoons orange juice

½ teaspoon Dijon mustard

Salt and pepper

4 to 5 cups tender salad greens

½ cup sliced almonds

In mixing bowl, stir together chicken, onions, celery, mayonnaise and tarragon; set aside (or refrigerate, if preparing in advance).

When you're ready to serve, cut ground cherries into halves; set aside. Prepare salad dressing: In a small jar, combine oil, vinegar, orange juice and mustard; cover and shake vigorously. Add salt and pepper to taste. In a large bowl, toss dressing with greens. Divide greens between 4 salad plates. Top each with one-quarter of the chicken salad, mounding attractively. Scatter ground cherries over the salad; top with almonds. Serve immediately.

*Some sources say that smooth or longleaf ground cherry (*Physalis longifolia*) should not be eaten raw, so it is best to prepare this with a different species.

 You can prepare the chicken salad mixture in advance and keep in the refrigerator until you're ready to serve; dress the greens and assemble the salad right before serving so the greens stay crisp.

Sweet and Snappy Ground Cherry Salsa   About 1 cup

The fruity, sweet taste of ground cherries makes a wonderful foil to the bite of hot peppers and the tang of fresh cilantro. Enjoy this salsa with chicken fajitas, bean burritos or tostadas, or warm tortilla chips.

1 clove garlic

1 or 2 fresh jalapeño peppers, depending on heat level desired

About ¼ cup fresh cilantro leaves

1 cup husked, ripe ground cherries* (about 5 ounces)

One-quarter of a medium red onion

1 tablespoon seasoned rice vinegar

¼ teaspoon salt, or to taste

Place garlic in food processor and chop until fine. Add pepper(s) and pulse on and off a few times. Add cilantro and process until everything is finely chopped. Transfer mixture to small mixing bowl. Add ground cherries to food processor and chop to medium consistency; the texture doesn't have to be completely even so don't worry if there are a few larger chunks of fruit in the mix. Transfer ground cherries to mixing bowl. Cut onion into ¼-inch dice; add to mixing bowl. Add vinegar and salt. Stir well to mix. Let stand for 15 minutes, then taste for seasoning and adjust salt if necessary. Serve at room temperature; refrigerate leftovers.

*Some sources say that smooth or longleaf ground cherry (*Physalis longifolia*) should not be eaten raw, so it is best to prepare this with a different species.

 This is a very juicy salsa, so you may want to place a fork rather than a spoon into the serving dish. Use any leftover liquid to add spice to a pot of beans or a stir-fry.

Other recipes in this book featuring ground cherries:
Dehydrating Wild Berries and Fruits, pgs. 180–181
Wild Berry or Fruit Leather, pg. 182

Quick ideas for using ground cherries:
Cut in half and add to fruit salads or green salads (note the comment in the intro text on pg. 66 regarding raw ground cherries).
Add dehydrated ground cherries to oatmeal or other hot cereal, either during or after cooking.

HACKBERRIES (*Celtis* spp.)

Two types of hackberry are found in the wild in our area: netleaf (*Celtis reticulata*) and common (*C. occidentalis*) which, in spite of its name, is not at all common in our area, being primarily a Midwestern tree. Hackberries are often planted in urban areas as landscape trees, yet few people notice their fruit; fewer still realize that the small, dark, berry-like drupe is edible and tasty. A few texts refer to the tree as "sugarberry," and mention that the sweet fruit is used primarily as a trail nibble; several note that Native Americans used dried, crushed sugarberry to season venison. Sugarberry is actually a related, similar tree (*C. laevigata*) that is found primarily in the Southeastern U.S. but not in our area.

Ripe netleaf hackberries are reddish; common hackberries are black. The flesh of both species is dry but sweet, with a flavor reminiscent of dates, apples and oranges mixed together. Unfortunately, there is precious little of it; most of the fruit consists of a large pit. Unlike the hard stones in cherries and plums, however, hackberry pits are edible; they are brittle but soft enough to chew. The sensation is unusual, and trail nibblers usually discard the pit.

Pillow Cookies with Hackberry Filling   About 30 cookies

The sweet filling has an unusual texture from the pits. This is a recipe I developed for my book, Abundantly Wild: Collecting and Cooking Wild Edibles in the Upper Midwest.

Filling:
⅔ cup hackberry fruits, stems removed

⅓ cup sugar

½ cup water

½ cup chopped pecans or other nuts

Dough:
½ cup (1 stick) unsalted butter, softened

½ cup (packed) brown sugar

½ cup white sugar

1 egg

1 teaspoon lemon extract, orange extract or vanilla extract

½ teaspoon baking soda

½ teaspoon salt

2 cups all-purpose flour

First, prepare the filling. Pound fruits with mortar and pestle until pits are well pulverized; for the least crunchy filling, pound until fruits are reduced to a smooth paste. (Tip: It's easiest to work in small batches of a tablespoon or two at a time; this way, no large chunks of pit will escape your notice. Scrape pounded fruit into a small saucepan as you go, and continue until all fruit has been pounded.)

Combine pounded fruit with sugar and water in small saucepan. Heat over medium heat, stirring constantly, until boiling gently. Cook for 4 minutes or until thick, stirring constantly. Stir in pecans. Remove from heat and let cool completely before assembling the cookies.

To make dough, cream butter in mixing bowl with electric mixer. Gradually add brown and white sugars, beating until smooth. Add egg, extract, baking soda and salt; beat well. Add flour and beat just until mixed. If you prepare the dough right after cooking the filling, gather the dough into a ball, wrap it tightly and refrigerate until you're ready to bake. Or, simply prepare dough after the filling has cooled, and proceed immediately to baking.

When you're ready to bake, heat oven to 350°F. Lightly spray 2 baking sheets with nonstick spray; set aside. Roll out half of the dough about ⅛ inch thick, or just a bit thicker. Cut into 2-inch circles with a glass or cookie cutter. Place half of the circles on prepared baking sheet, allowing ½ inch between circles. Place 1 teaspoon filling mixture in center of each circle, keeping it away from edges. Place a circle of dough over each mound of filling, forming it into a gentle dome shape over filling and gently pressing the edges together (they will seal together during baking, so don't worry about pressing too hard). Repeat with remaining ingredients to fill the second baking sheet. Bake for 7 minutes, then rotate pans (see "Rotating Cookies while Baking," pg. 51). Continue baking for 6 to 10 minutes longer, or until cookies are golden brown. Cool before serving.

 Hackberry pits are very crunchy even when crushed fairly fine. It is an odd sensation to encounter in a cookie—not unpleasant, just unexpected, rather like finding a piece of eggshell that accidentally got into the dough. But unlike the eggshell, the pieces of pit can be chewed and swallowed. The more time you spend pounding the fruit with the mortar and pestle, the smoother and less crunchy the filling will be.

Quick ideas for using hackberries:
Hackberry fruits can be juiced the same way as chokecherries (pg. 30); the juice can be used to make jelly. Note that it would take a large volume of hackberries to get much juice, since there is so little flesh.
Some foragers pound hackberries very thoroughly as described above, then make fruit leather from the paste; see the instructions for making fruit leather on pg. 182.

HAWTHORNS (*Crataegus* spp.)

Numerous varieties of hawthorn grow in our area, and it's hard to know exactly which species you've found. The fruit, usually called a haw, looks like a crabapple, but the seeds in the fruit are larger. Haws of some varieties, or from individual trees, are small, and there is very little flesh in proportion to the seeds. Nevertheless, what flesh and skin there is has a lot of flavor, so these small haws can be used to make juice. If you're lucky, however, you'll find a tree whose fruits are large, soft and fleshy. These haws have enough flesh to make jam; or, the seeds can be removed and the fruit used in pies and other baked goods. The flavor of a good haw is outstanding—rather like a pear with apple and almond overtones.

All hawthorn fruits are edible. The best for cooking have a large amount of fruit in proportion to the seeds; these can be cut up and used like diced apples.

To prepare large haws for use in pies or other recipes that use pieces of fruit rather than pulp, I use a table knife to cut or break them open. My feeling is that if I have to use a sharp knife, either the haw isn't ripe enough, or it is too hard because it's nothing but seeds. Once the haw is open, scrape out the seeds and any blackish tissue surrounding them; if soft, clean flesh adheres to the seeds, scrape it off with the knife before discarding the seed. Pull or cut away the blossom end and the stem, then feel the flesh carefully with your fingertips to be sure there isn't a tooth-shattering seed hidden in the piece. Place the cleaned, seedless haw chunks, and any flesh you've scraped from the seeds, into a measuring cup. Because haws vary so much in size, it's hard to predict the yield; in general, you'll get about ½ cup of cleaned, ready-to-cook haw chunks from a pound of whole, large haws (roughly a quart, give or take).

To prepare hawthorn juice, place whole haws in non-aluminum pot. Add water to generously cover the fruit. Heat to boiling over high heat, then reduce heat and boil gently for 20 minutes, or until the fruit is very soft. Mash as best you can with a potato masher, making sure that each fruit has been opened. Add a little more water if it looks too dry, and cook for 5 minutes longer; the pulpy, seedy mixture should be well covered with water. Transfer the mixture to a strainer lined with doubled, dampened cheesecloth and let it drip for 30 minutes; if you're making jelly, don't squeeze the fruit or the jelly will be cloudy. After the clear liquid has dripped away, set it aside and squeeze the fruit into a different container; you can use this slightly cloudy juice as a beverage or for cooking. Yield varies quite a bit, because hawthorns vary in size; in general, you'll get 1½ cups of pink juice per pound of hawthorns.

Hawthorn and Sausage Brunch Casserole
6 to 8 servings

Hawthorns work really well with the sausage and cheese in this simple dish. It's a natural for brunch, or even a light supper.

8 ounces breakfast-style pork sausage (casings removed if links)

¼ cup diced onion

1¼ cups whole or 2% milk

3 eggs

½ teaspoon dry mustard powder

4 or 5 slices day-old firm white bread (Italian bread works well)

¾ to 1 cup cleaned, seedless hawthorn chunks

1½ cups shredded mozzarella cheese, divided

Heat oven to 375°F. Spray an 8x8-inch baking dish with nonstick spray; set aside. In medium skillet, cook sausage over medium heat, stirring to break up, until no longer pink. Drain off excess grease. Add onion and cook, stirring frequently, until sausage is lightly browned and onion is tender, about 5 minutes. Set aside to cool slightly.

In large mixing bowl, combine milk, eggs and mustard powder; beat well with a fork and set aside. Now, use a blender to make fresh breadcrumbs. Start by tearing bread into 1-inch chunks. Turn the blender on high. Drop chunks from one slice into the blender, immediately re-covering it; the bread pops up very high and can make quite a mess if you don't keep it covered. Process until bread has been chopped into medium-fine crumbs. Transfer breadcrumbs to a large bowl; repeat with remaining bread. Measure 2½ cups of crumbs; if you have extra crumbs, see tip below.

Add measured crumbs, sausage mixture, hawthorn chunks and 1 cup of the cheese to the milk mixture. Stir well, then scrape into prepared dish. Bake, uncovered, for 25 minutes. Sprinkle remaining cheese over the casserole; bake for 5 to 10 minutes longer, or until eggs are set and cheese has melted. Remove from oven and let stand 10 minutes before serving.

Substitution: Use diced wild pears in place of the hawthorns.

If you have any breadcrumbs remaining, you can spread them out on a baking sheet and let them dry at room temperature for a few days, stirring occasionally; when completely dry, store in a jar and use in any recipe calling for dry breadcrumbs.

Spiced Hawthorn Cider

6 to 8 servings

This flavorful brew is a perfect fall beverage; it's especially good with oatmeal cookies.

2 cups hawthorns

1 quart apple juice

3 cups water

1 cinnamon stick

6 whole cloves

6 whole allspice berries

Zest strips from 1 whole orange (colored rind only, with none of the white pith; see "Zesting Citrus Fruits," pg. 35)

2 tablespoons real maple syrup

Cut the hawthorns in half, then cut away and discard the stems and blossom ends. Combine the hawthorn halves, apple juice and water in a non-aluminum saucepan. Heat to boiling over high heat, then reduce heat and simmer for 15 minutes. Mash gently with a potato masher; simmer for 10 minutes longer. Pour through a wire-mesh strainer lined with doubled cheesecloth; let drip for 15 minutes. Meanwhile, place cloves, allspice berries and orange zest strips on a square of cheesecloth; gather together and tie at the top with kitchen twine. Rinse out the saucepan so you can use it in the next step.

When hawthorns have dripped for 15 minutes, return strained juice to saucepan; discard contents of strainer. Stir in the maple syrup, then add the spice bundle. Heat over medium heat until simmering, then adjust heat as necessary and simmer for 10 minutes. Fish out the spice bundle and discard it. Serve the cider hot, in mugs.

Hawthorn Jelly

3 cups hawthorn juice

Half of a 1.75-ounce box powdered pectin

½ teaspoon butter, optional (helps reduce foaming)

3 cups sugar

Prepare and process as directed in Jelly Instructions (using pectin), pgs. 176–177.

Hawthorn Vinegar

This infused vinegar makes a refreshing and healthful beverage when a tablespoon or so is mixed with chilled sparkling water. It can also be used for salad dressings or marinades.

2 cups (about 8 ounces) whole hawthorns

2½ cups apple cider vinegar, or as needed

Sterilize a 1-quart canning jar as directed on pg. 183. Wash hawthorns well. Cut each hawthorn in half, or into quarters if large; if the seeds are easy to flick out with the tip of your knife, do so, but don't worry about a few seeds that are hard to get at. Remove the blossom ends and stems. Place the hawthorns in the sterilized jar. Add vinegar to cover by 1 inch. Place a piece of plastic wrap over the top of the jar, and seal with the screw band and a lid; shake well. Place the jar in a cool, dark cupboard. Each day for a week, shake the jar again, and top off with more vinegar if needed to keep the hawthorns covered. After that, let the vinegar infuse for five weeks longer, checking it occasionally and giving it a gentle shake. At the end of the six-week period, strain through a wire-mesh strainer lined with several thicknesses of cheesecloth, then strain again through a funnel lined with a paper coffee filter. Store in a glass jar in a cool, dark cupboard for up to three months; refrigerate for longer storage.

Other recipes in this book featuring hawthorns:
Fruits of the Forest Pie, pg. 168
Six Recipes Using Wild Fruit Juice or Syrup, pgs. 170–174
Wild Berry or Fruit Syrup, pg. 175

Quick ideas for using hawthorns:
Use the juice in place of apple juice, for cooking or as a beverage.
Use hawthorn chunks to substitute for chopped apple or pear in recipes for baked
goods. Watch out for the seeds when eating!

HUCKLEBERRIES, BILBERRIES and WILD BLUEBERRIES (*Vaccinium* spp.)

Several related plants with blueberry-like fruits grow in our area. Mountain huckleberries (*Vaccinium membranaceum*) are often considered the best of these, and have a unique sweet-tart flavor. Two bilberry species, dwarf bilberry (*V. caespitosum*) and low bilberry (*V. myrtillus*; sometimes called whortleberry), are also fairly common in our area; their fruits are sweet, similar to blueberries. And although they are uncommon, bog blueberry (*V. uliginosum*) and oval-leaf blueberry (*V. ovalifolium*) may be found occasionally in scattered parts of our area. To avoid cumbersome lists, the text below and the recipes on the following pages simply call for huckleberries. You may use fruits from any of the species above with no adjustments.

Huckleberries are the official state fruit of Idaho. Several Idaho municipalities, including Wallace, Donnelly and Rexburg, have annual huckleberry festivals to celebrate this beloved fruit.

Huckleberries can be used in much the same way as blueberries; they have more flavor than domestic blueberries, probably because they are smaller and have more of the flavorful skin in proportion to the flesh. If you're substituting huckleberries in a recipe that was written for domestic blueberries, use a bit less by volume than called for; the smaller huckleberries pack more closely in the measuring cup, so a cup of huckleberries weighs more (about 6 ounces) than a cup of domestic blueberries (4½ to 5 ounces).

It's easy to gather a decent quantity of huckleberries, once you've found a good patch. Huckleberries are among the first plants to grow in an area that has been swept by wildfire; if you can travel to an area that burned the previous year, you should enjoy phenomenal berry picking.

Huckleberries have soft seeds that are virtually unnoticeable, and the fruits can be eaten raw or cooked (however, it's worth noting that another fruit called huckleberry, the black huckleberry, *Gaylussacia baccata,* has seeds that are best described as crunchy; *Gaylussacia baccata* does not grow in our area, being found only in the eastern half of the U.S.). Huckleberries are rich in anthocyanins, antioxidants believed to reduce the risk of cancer and diabetes, promote heart health, and help prevent age-related memory loss. They store well in the refrigerator, remaining fresh for up to a week; don't wash them until you're ready to use them, though, or they may mold.

Huckleberries freeze well; simply wash and pat dry, then spread in a single layer on a baking sheet and freeze overnight. The next day, transfer the individually frozen berries to freezer containers, and freeze for up to 6 months. Frozen or fresh berries can be successfully dehydrated (see pgs. 180–181) and used in trail mixes and as an out-of-hand snack, or to substitute for raisins or craisins in recipes; they would also make a good fruit leather (pg. 182).

Most people prefer to use these berries whole, but they can be juiced; the juice can be used to make jelly, and is also is an excellent beverage, sweetened as needed. To prepare juice, follow the instructions for making sweetberry juice on pg. 163; to make jelly, follow the proportions for Currant Jelly on pg. 40.

Huckleberry Spirals with Cardamom

8 rolls

Cardamom adds an unusual touch to these rolls. Plan on eating these with a knife and fork, to get every bit of the delicious berry filling.

1 loaf (1 pound) frozen bread dough, thawed according to package directions

All-purpose flour for rolling out dough

2 tablespoons butter, softened

1 cup fresh huckleberries (about 6 ounces)

½ cup chopped pecans

3 tablespoons sugar

½ teaspoon ground cardamom

¼ teaspoon cinnamon

Spray an 8x12-inch baking dish with nonstick spray and line bottom with a piece of waxed paper that has been cut to size; set aside. Roll bread dough on lightly floured worksurface into a rectangle about 8 inches by 12 inches. Spread butter evenly over bread. Sprinkle huckleberries and pecans over bread, keeping an inch away from the long edges. In a small bowl, stir together the sugar, cardamom and cinnamon; sprinkle evenly over bread. Starting with a long edge, roll up bread, jelly-roll fashion; as you roll, tuck the huckleberries in if they pop out. Press the dough together at the long edge once the dough is rolled. Cut into 8 even slices. Place in prepared baking dish with a cut side up; there will be a fair amount of space between the rolls. If some of the berries or nuts fall out, tuck them into the spirals. Cover with plastic wrap and let rise at room temperature for about an hour.

Near the end of the rising time, heat oven to 350°F. Uncover rolls. Bake until cooked through, 25 to 35 minutes; cover dish with foil during the last 10 minutes of baking if rolls are browning too quickly. Remove from oven, and remove foil if used. Let rolls cool for about 5 minutes, then cover with foil, bringing it down the sides of the dish. Place a baking sheet over the dish, and (using potholders) quickly but carefully flip everything over together. Remove the baking dish; peel off the waxed paper if it is stuck to the rolls. Let cool at least 15 minutes before eating; best served warm and fresh.

Huckleberry Streusel Muffins

A tasty streusel topping adds interest to these delicious muffins.

For 5,000 feet; see adjustments for other altitudes

Streusel:

⅓ cup (packed) brown sugar

¼ cup all-purpose flour

½ teaspoon cinnamon

4 tablespoons (half of a stick) cold butter, cut into pieces

½ cup sugar [2, 3]

½ cup (1 stick) butter, softened

2 medium eggs [1, 3]

1 teaspoon vanilla extract

2½ cups all-purpose flour [1, 3]

1 tablespoon baking powder [1, 3]

¼ teaspoon salt

1 cup plus 1 tablespoon buttermilk, divided [1, 3]

1 to 1¼ cups fresh or still-frozen huckleberries (6 to 7½ ounces)

Position rack in lower third of oven; heat to 400°F. [1, 3] Line 12-cup muffin tin with paper liners; set aside. Make the streusel: In a small bowl, stir together the sugar, flour and cinnamon. Add butter; use a fork or your fingertips to blend the butter into the sugar mixture, working them together until mixture is the texture of very coarse sand with some pea-sized particles. Set aside.

In mixing bowl, beat sugar and butter with an electric mixer until smooth. Add egg and vanilla; beat well. Combine flour, baking powder and salt in sifter; sift over the mixing bowl until half of the flour has been added to the butter mixture. Stir with a wooden spoon until just moistened. Add half of the buttermilk; stir to combine. Add remaining flour and buttermilk in the same manner. Add huckleberries; stir gently until incorporated. Spoon batter into prepared muffin cups. Spoon streusel over batter. Bake until golden brown and springy to the touch, 23 to 28 minutes.

Substitution: Use 1¼ cups serviceberries in place of the huckleberries.

---

1. **Below 5,000 feet:** Use 1 large egg. Use 2¼ cups flour. Use 1 tablespoon plus 1 teaspoon baking powder. Use 1 cup whole milk. Heat oven to 375°F.

2. **At 7,500 feet:** Reduce sugar by 1 tablespoon.

3. **At 10,000 feet:** Use ⅓ cup sugar. Use 1 large egg instead of 2 medium eggs. Increase flour by 2 tablespoons. Use 2 teaspoons baking powder. Substitute whole milk for buttermilk. Heat oven to 425°F.

Easy Bear Claws

This quick version of a bakery staple uses refrigerated biscuits to eliminate complicated pastry-making. Quick, easy—and delicious.

For 5,000 feet; see adjustments for other altitudes

1 tube (8 biscuits; 16.3 ounces) refrigerated "grand-sized" flaky biscuits (reduced-fat works fine)

All-purpose flour for rolling dough

½ cup Huckleberry Filling (pg. 91), or other wild fruit filling (see "Filling options" below)

1 egg, beaten with 1 teaspoon water

¼ cup sliced almonds

2 tablespoons coarse sugar, such as turbinado

Heat oven to 400°F.[1, 3] Line 2 rimmed baking sheets with kitchen parchment; set aside.

Separate dough into 8 biscuits. On lightly floured worksurface, gently roll one into an oval that is 4 inches across and about 6 inches long. Spoon one-eighth of the filling mixture onto the center of the dough. Fold the dough over to make a half-moon. Press edges together very well, lifting the edge and pinching all around with your fingertips. Place on a prepared baking sheet. Repeat with remaining dough and filling, keeping at least 1 inch between the rolls.

With a very sharp knife, make 4 cuts through the sealed edge, cutting about halfway into the crescent. Fan the cut strips out slightly to resemble a bear's paw. Brush dough with beaten egg; sprinkle with almonds and sugar. Bake for 9 minutes,[3] then switch the baking sheets so the one underneath moves to the top shelf. Continue baking until golden brown and cooked through, 5 to 8 minutes longer;[1, 3] when the rolls are properly cooked, the dough should not feel mushy when pressed gently with a fingertip. Remove from oven and let stand about a minute, then transfer rolls to wire rack to cool for at least 15 minutes before serving. Best served warm, the day they are made.

Filling options: This recipe works with any of the following fillings: Apple (pg. 10), Apricot or Peach (pg. 12), Blackberry (pg. 23), Green Gooseberry (pg. 59), Ground Cherry (pg. 68), Huckleberry (pg. 91), Mulberry (pg. 102), Pear (pg. 106), Plum (pg. 115), Raspberry (pg. 125), Serviceberry (pg. 138) or Strawberry (pg. 152).

1. **Below 5,000 feet:** Heat oven to 375°F. After switching pan positions, bake for 8 to 12 minutes longer.

2. **At 7,500 feet:** No adjustments needed.

3. **At 10,000 feet:** Heat oven to 410°F. Bake for 7 minutes before switching pan positions. After switching pan positions, reduce heat to 400°F and bake for 5 to 8 minutes longer.

Huckleberry-Cream Cheese Crowns

9 pastries

The puff pastry corners surround a rich, delicious filling, resembling a crown with purple jewels in the center.

1 sheet frozen puff pastry (half of 17.3-ounce package), thawed according to package directions

1½ teaspoons cornstarch

6 tablespoons sugar, divided

⅔ cup fresh or previously frozen huckleberries (about 4 ounces), including any juices

½ teaspoon lemon juice

3 ounces cream cheese, softened

1 egg yolk

½ teaspoon vanilla extract

Position rack at bottom of oven; heat to 375°F. Lightly spray 12-cup muffin tin with nonstick spray. On lightly floured worksurface, roll puff pastry to an 11-inch square. Cut into 9 squares. Place each square into the cup of a standard muffin tin, pressing into the bottom and letting corner points stand straight up. Place pastry-filled muffin tin in refrigerator while you prepare filling.

In small mixing bowl, stir together cornstarch and 3 tablespoons of the sugar. Add huckleberries and lemon juice. Crush the berries lightly against the bowl with a metal spoon to release some juice; stir until moist and well mixed and set aside. In medium mixing bowl, combine cream cheese, egg yolk, vanilla and remaining 3 tablespoons sugar; stir vigorously with a fork until smooth and well blended. Spoon cream-cheese mixture into the pastry cups, dividing equally (about 1 scant tablespoon per cup). Spoon berry mixture on top of the cream cheese mixture, dividing equally (about 1 scant tablespoon per cup). Pour ¼ cup water into each empty cup (to prevent burning during baking). Bake until golden brown, 25 to 35 minutes, rotating pan halfway through. Place pan on wire rack and let cool for 10 minutes, then use a fork to lift out pastries and transfer to wire rack; if pastries are somewhat stuck, loosen edges gently with a table knife. Cool completely before serving; these are best served the day they are baked. They can sit out at room temperature for up to half a day, but should be refrigerated after that (they become firmer, but less crispy, once they've been refrigerated).

Huckleberry Pancakes

When huckleberries are on the breakfast menu, it's worth taking the few extra minutes to whip up a homemade batter.

1 cup whole milk

1½ teaspoons freshly squeezed lemon juice

1 cup plus 2 tablespoons all-purpose flour

1 tablespoon powdered sugar

1¼ teaspoons baking powder

¼ teaspoon salt

2 tablespoons unsalted butter, melted and cooled slightly

1 egg

Nonstick cooking spray (or vegetable oil)

⅔ cup fresh huckleberries (about 4 ounces)

Butter and syrup for serving

In 2-cup measure, stir together milk and lemon juice; set aside while you prepare the other ingredients. Begin heating a griddle over medium heat.

Place a wire-mesh strainer over a mixing bowl. Add flour, powdered sugar, baking powder and salt to strainer; shake to sift into bowl. Add butter and egg to milk; beat with a fork until well blended. Pour all at once into flour mixture; stir with the fork until batter is just combined. Don't over-mix; there should be a number of small lumps in the batter.

Spray hot griddle with nonstick spray (or brush with vegetable oil). Pour batter in ¼-cup batches onto griddle. Immediately scatter about 1 tablespoon of huckleberries over each pancake. Cook until bottom is nicely browned and spotted, and top side has numerous small bubbles beginning to appear. Flip carefully and cook second side until spotted with brown. Transfer to a warm serving plate; cover loosely and keep warm while you cook remaining pancakes. Serve hot, with butter and syrup.

Variation: To use frozen berries, substitute ⅔ cup frozen huckleberries for the fresh berries. While berries are still frozen, place them into a wire-mesh strainer and rinse them briefly under cool water, then spread out in a single layer on a paper towel to dry while you prepare the batter.

Adding the berries to the pancake once it's on the griddle prevents soggy, purple pancakes. This recipe also works beautifully with wild strawberries.

Right-Sized Huckleberry Pie

Servings based on pie size

Huckleberry pie is very juicy, and leftovers don't keep well. With this recipe, you can make a smaller pie, tailored to make just as many servings as you need.

Ready-to-use pastry for single-crust pie

Prepare the crust: Choose an oven-safe skillet that is the size you'd like your pie to be; a 6-inch skillet, for example, will serve four. Fill the skillet with water (or, if using a deep skillet, fill it up to the height you'd like the crust to be). Measure the water, taking note of the amount. Dry the skillet. Heat the oven to 375°F. Roll out the pastry, then cut a circle that is 1 inch wider on all sides than the top of your skillet. Center the pastry in the skillet, allowing the excess to hang evenly over the skillet's edge. Fold the edge of the pastry under, then decoratively crimp the edges; if your skillet is deeper than you want the pie to be, simply make the sides somewhat shallower than the sides of the skillet. (Note, however, that the crust will shrink in height somewhat during baking.) Fit a piece of foil into the pastry, pressing into the corners; blind bake the crust to golden brown as described on pg. 47 (due to the difference between a skillet and a pie plate, it may take longer to bake, or may bake more quickly; simply remove from the oven when it is golden brown). Set aside to cool.

<u>Huckleberry filling:</u>

Fresh huckleberries (do not use previously frozen berries for this recipe); amount based on skillet size

For *each cup* of fresh berries, you'll also need:

3 tablespoons sugar

¼ teaspoon lemon juice

A small pinch of nutmeg

1 tablespoon water

1½ teaspoons cornstarch

Prepare the filling: Three to four hours before you plan to serve the pie, measure out the same amount of huckleberries as the water you measured above. Place *a bit less than half* of the measured huckleberries, along with any accumulated juice, in a heavy-bottomed non-aluminum saucepan; place the rest of the berries in a large mixing bowl and set aside.

Add the sugar, lemon juice and nutmeg to the saucepan; also add a pinch of salt (a single pinch will be enough for up to 4 cups of huckleberries). In a small bowl, blend together the water and cornstarch; set aside. Heat the berry mixture over medium heat, stirring constantly, until the mixture begins bubbling gently. Simmer for 3 minutes, stirring constantly; the berries will pop and the mixture will begin to thicken. Add the cornstarch mixture, stirring constantly; cook until juices are thickened and no longer cloudy, about 1 minute longer. Immediately scrape cooked berry mixture into fresh berries in the bowl; stir to combine. Spoon the mixture into the prepared pie crust. Let stand at room temperature for at least 3 hours before serving.

Putting it into practice: If your skillet holds 3 cups of water, you'll need 3 cups fresh huckleberries, 9 tablespoons sugar (½ cup plus 1 tablespoon), ¾ teaspoon lemon juice, 3 small pinches of nutmeg, 3 tablespoons water, 4½ teaspoons cornstarch (1½ tablespoons) and a pinch of salt. Combine about 1⅓ cups of the berries with the other ingredients in the saucepan; proceed as directed.

Huckleberry Freezer Jam
2 to 3 half-pints

For this easy jam, the fruit is not cooked. It has a fresh, vibrant sweet-tart flavor and a gorgeous reddish-purple color . . . one of the best wild jams ever.

2 cups fresh or previously frozen huckleberries (about 12 ounces), approximate

⅔ cup sugar

2 tablespoons Ball RealFruit Instant Pectin (see below)

Prepare three half-pint canning jars, bands and new lids as described on pg. 183, or have clean plastic freezer containers ready (see tip on pg. 140). Place a single layer of huckleberries in a large mixing bowl; mash with a potato masher until all fruits are crushed but the mixture still has some texture. Transfer to a 2-cup measure; continue mashing until you have 1⅔ cups of mashed berries.

In a clean mixing bowl, stir together sugar and pectin. Add measured, mashed berries. Stir constantly for 3 minutes. Spoon into prepared jars or containers, leaving ½ inch headspace; cover with clean lids. Let stand at room temperature for 30 minutes. Refrigerate or freeze after standing time. Use refrigerated jam within 3 weeks. Frozen jam can be kept for up to a year; thaw frozen jam in refrigerator.

Ball RealFruit Instant Pectin is a fairly new product (as of this writing) and is a real boon to foragers because it simplifies the task of small-batch jam making. It is a different formulation than other powdered pectins, and is not interchangeable with them. Follow the instructions above, or the directions that can be found on the product jar. Look for RealFruit Instant Pectin in plastic jars with the canning supplies.

Salmon with Huckleberry Sauce   2 servings; easily doubled

This luscious, slightly tart pan sauce is the perfect complement to the rich salmon.

¾ pound boneless, skin-on salmon fillet, 1½ inches thick*

1 tablespoon Dijon mustard

2 teaspoons plus 2 tablespoons dry white wine, divided

½ teaspoon dried thyme leaves

Freshly ground black pepper

Small white onion (you won't use all of it), peeled, ends removed

1 tablespoon olive oil or canola oil

1 tablespoon unsalted butter

2 tablespoons minced shallots

½ cup fresh or previously frozen huckleberries (about 3 ounces), including any juices

1 teaspoon honey

Heat oven to 425°F. Cut salmon into two equal pieces; place on plate, skin-side down. In small bowl, stir together mustard, 2 teaspoons wine, and the thyme leaves. Brush generously over the top and sides of the salmon; pour any extra over the top. Grind fresh black pepper to taste over the top. Set salmon aside at room temperature for 15 minutes.

While salmon is marinating, cut the onion in half across the equator (not from top to bottom). Cut one piece in half from top to bottom (so you have two half-moon-shaped pieces), and then slice into vertical wedges about ¼ inch wide at the outside. Add wedges to a measuring cup as you go, slicing until you have about ⅓ cup of wedges. Set measured onion wedges aside; reserve remaining onion for another use.

When you are ready to cook, heat oil in a heavy-bottomed medium skillet over medium-high heat until oil is shimmering. Carefully add salmon to pan, flesh-side down (watch out for splattering oil). Cook for 3 minutes, then flip carefully and cook with the skin-side down for 2 minutes longer. Remove skillet from heat. Transfer salmon to a small baking dish. Place in oven; set a timer for 10 minutes. Discard excess oil from skillet; also scrape out and discard any skin that might be stuck to the skillet.

When the pan has cooled a bit, add the butter and place over medium heat. When butter melts, add onions and shallots; sauté for about 3 minutes. Add huckleberries along with any juice; sauté until juices have mostly cooked away, 3 to 5 minutes. Add honey and remaining 2 tablespoons wine; sauté until mixture has thickened to a sauce-like consistency, 2 to 3 minutes longer. Meanwhile, if the timer rings, remove salmon from oven; if it is done to your liking, cover loosely with foil and set aside, otherwise return to oven and cook for a minute or two longer. The salmon should rest for 5 to 10 minutes before serving; if the sauce is ready before the salmon has rested, simply remove from heat and set aside. To serve, place salmon, flesh-side up, on individual plates; spoon sauce over the middle of the salmon, allowing excess to pool off to the sides.

*If your salmon is 1¼ inches thick, reduce oven cooking time to 9 minutes. If the salmon is 1 inch thick, heat oven to 400°F. Sauté skin side for only 1 minute; oven-cooking time remains 10 minutes. Fillets thinner than 1 inch are not recommended for this recipe.

Huckleberry Mustard
About 1 cup

This pungent purple mustard will enliven sandwiches, grilled sausages or anything you'd top with coarse mustard. Bring a jar of it to a potluck or other get-together for an unusual treat.

⅔ cup fresh or previously frozen huckleberries (about 4 ounces)

⅓ cup dry white wine

3 tablespoons honey

¼ cup yellow mustard seeds

3 tablespoons apple cider vinegar

1 tablespoon dry mustard powder

1 teaspoon salt

In small saucepan, stir together huckleberries, wine and honey. Heat to boiling, then reduce heat and boil very gently for 5 minutes, stirring frequently. Remove from heat; set aside until completely cool. Transfer to blender; pulse on-and-off a few times until berries are coarsely chopped. Add remaining ingredients. Blend on high for 10 seconds; the mustard seeds should be broken and partially chopped but the mixture should not be smooth. Transfer to a clean glass jar and refrigerate for at least 24 hours before using (the taste will be too sharp if you sample it too soon, and the mustard will also thicken slightly during this time). Store in refrigerator for up to several months.

Huckleberry Ice Cream

About 1 quart

Purple and creamy, dotted with huckleberry pieces . . . this is a wild-looking ice cream!

1 cup fresh huckleberries (about 6 ounces)*

2 tablespoons honey

1½ teaspoons lemon juice

A pinch of salt

5 egg yolks

1 egg (white and yolk)

¾ cup sugar

2 cups heavy cream (not ultra-pasteurized)

1 cup whole milk

½ teaspoon vanilla extract

NOTE: It's best to prepare the two parts of the ice cream mixture the day before you plan to churn the ice cream. Also, some ice cream freezers have a container that needs to be frozen for at least 24 hours before churning, so you should take that into account as well.

To prepare the berries: Combine huckleberries, honey, lemon juice and salt in microwave-safe bowl. Microwave on high for 1 minute, then stir with a metal spoon, mashing some of the berries against the side of the bowl; microwave for 1 minute longer. (If you prefer, cook the mixture on the stovetop over medium-high heat until it boils; mash some of the berries and cook for 2 minutes longer.) Cool to room temperature, then refrigerate until completely cold.

To prepare the custard base: In a mixing bowl, whisk together the egg yolks, egg and sugar until smooth; set aside. In heavy-bottomed saucepan, combine cream and milk. Heat over medium-high heat until bubbles appear around the edges. Pour about 1 cup of the hot cream mixture into the egg mixture, whisking constantly; whisk until smooth. Pour the egg mixture into the saucepan with the rest of the cream mixture. Cook over medium-low heat, stirring constantly (a flat-bottomed wooden spatula, or a heat-proof silicone spatula, works very well), until the mixture thickens slightly and reaches 185°F on an instant-read thermometer; this will take about 5 minutes. (Take care not to cook the custard beyond this point, as it will curdle; remove from the heat immediately after it reaches 185°F.) Place a wire-mesh strainer over a clean mixing bowl and strain the mixture through, stirring with a spoon or spatula. Stir vanilla into strained custard. Cool custard slightly, then place a sheet of waxed paper on top of custard, pressing the waxed paper directly against the custard's surface. Cover the bowl with foil and refrigerate until completely cold.

When you're ready to churn, stir huckleberry mixture into custard. Churn according to manufacturer's instructions.

*Frozen huckleberries work fine for this, but be sure to include any juice that is released when they thaw. Total weight of thawed fruit and juice should be about 6 ounces.

Huckleberry Crumb Cake

1 cake (9 servings)

This cake is moist and tender . . . perfect for snacking or dessert.

For 5,000 feet; see adjustments for other altitudes

1½ cups all-purpose flour[2, 3]

½ cup plus 1 tablespoon white sugar, divided

¾ teaspoon baking powder[1, 3]

¼ teaspoon baking soda

¼ teaspoon salt

½ teaspoon cinnamon

⅛ teaspoon freshly grated nutmeg

½ cup (1 stick) cold unsalted butter, divided

½ cup sour cream (reduced fat is fine; do not use fat-free)

1 large egg[3]

½ teaspoon vanilla extract

1 cup fresh huckleberries (about 6 ounces), drained if necessary

2 teaspoons (packed) brown sugar[3]

Position oven rack in center of oven; heat to 375°F.[3] Spray 8x8-inch[2, 3] baking dish with non-stick spray and line bottom with a square of waxed paper that has been cut to size; set aside. Sift together flour, ½ cup white sugar, the baking powder, baking soda, salt, cinnamon and nutmeg into large mixing bowl. Cut off 1½ tablespoons of the butter and set aside; cut remaining butter into ½-inch cubes. Add butter cubes to flour mixture; blend together with a pastry blender or fork until mixture resembles coarse meal with a few pea-sized chunks of butter. Transfer ¾ cup of the flour-butter mixture to a medium mixing bowl; set aside.

In small bowl, beat sour cream, egg and vanilla with a fork until well blended. Add sour cream mixture to the mixing bowl with the main part of the flour-butter mixture; stir until just combined. Gently fold in huckleberries; spread in prepared baking dish. Cut reserved 1½ tablespoons butter into ½-inch cubes; add butter, brown sugar and remaining 1 tablespoon white sugar to reserved flour-butter mixture in medium bowl. Blend with your fingertips until coarse and crumbly. Sprinkle mixture evenly over batter. Bake until golden and a wooden pick inserted into the center comes out clean, 30 to 35 minutes.[2, 3] Cool at least 30 minutes before serving.

1. Below 5,000 feet: Use 1 teaspoon baking powder.

2. At 7,500 feet: Add an additional 1 tablespoon flour. Use 9x9-inch baking dish. Bake for 32 to 37 minutes.

3. At 10,000 feet: Add an additional 2 tablespoons flour. Use ½ teaspoon baking powder. Use 1 extra-large egg. Use 1 teaspoon brown sugar. Heat oven to 390°F. Use 9x9-inch baking dish. Bake for 28 to 35 minutes.

Huckleberry-Maple Breakfast Casserole

6 to 8 servings

A little preparation the night before lets you put a wonderful, warm breakfast together with ease. The maple syrup is a perfect complement to the huckleberries.

1 loaf (1 pound) French bread, cut into ½-inch cubes

**8 ounces cream cheese, cut into ½-inch cubes
(reduced-fat works fine)**

1 to 1½ cups fresh or previously frozen huckleberries (6 to 8½ ounces)

8 eggs

2½ cups whole milk

½ cup real maple syrup

½ teaspoon salt

Spray 9x13-inch baking dish with nonstick spray. Distribute half of the bread cubes in the dish. Top with cream cheese cubes and huckleberries, distributing evenly; top with remaining bread cubes. In large mixing bowl, beat together eggs, milk, syrup and salt until smooth. Pour evenly over bread. Cover and refrigerate overnight.

The next morning, heat oven to 350°F. Uncover dish; bake until top is golden brown and center is set, 35 to 45 minutes. Let stand 10 minutes before serving.

Egg Talk

Many recipes in this book simply call for "eggs" without distinguishing between sizes. For best results, use large eggs, rather than medium or small eggs. If you are watching cholesterol, you may substitute ¼ cup liquid egg substitute for each egg in a recipe; it works great in place of whole eggs in all dishes except custards.

Huckleberry Filling

½ teaspoon water
½ teaspoon cornstarch
6 ounces fresh or previously frozen huckleberries (about 1 cup)
1 heaping tablespoon grated apple
1 tablespoon sugar

In small bowl, blend together water and cornstarch; set aside. In small, heavy-bottomed saucepan, combine huckleberries, apple and sugar. Crush fruit gently with a potato masher to start juices flowing. Heat to boiling over medium-high heat, then cook, stirring frequently and mashing once more, until mixture is no longer runny; this will take 8 to 15 minutes. Add cornstarch mixture, stirring constantly; cook for about 1 minute longer, or until thick. Cool before using.

Use this to prepare Easy Bear Claws (pg. 81), Fruit-Striped Cookie Fingers (pg. 126), or Fruit-Filled Muffins (pg. 155). Refrigerate extra filling, and use to top oatmeal or toast.

Other recipes in this book featuring huckleberries, bilberries and wild blueberries:

Overnight Multi-Grain Cereal with Fruit and Nuts, pg. 42
Two-Berry Freezer Jam, pg. 167
Fruits of the Forest Pie, pg. 168
Dehydrating Wild Berries and Fruits, pgs. 180–181
Wild Berry or Fruit Leather, pg. 182
As a substitute in Blackberry-Apple Crisp, pg. 21
As a substitute in Pumpkin Tart with Chokecherry Glaze, pg. 36
As a substitute in Refrigerator Cookies with Dried Goji Berries, pg. 51
As a substitute in Serviceberry Pudding Cake, pg. 139
As a variation in Strawberry Smoothie, pg. 156

Quick ideas for using huckleberries, bilberries and wild blueberries:

Use fresh huckleberries, bilberries or wild blueberries in any recipe you have that calls for fresh blueberries. You may want to increase the sugar slightly.

JUNIPER BERRIES (*Juniperus* spp.)

Three junipers with edible, berry-like fruits grow in our area: the low-growing common juniper (*Juniperus communis*), and two trees, Rocky Mountain juniper (*J. scopulorum*) and Utah juniper (*J. utahensis*); fruits from all three can be used in the same way. Fruits from these three junipers are used as seasoning. They have a sharp, clean scent and taste; common juniper fruits are one of the main ingredients used in the traditional distillation of gin, and fruits from all three junipers listed here have the same smell. They're usually used in marinades or rubs for meat, and are particularly good with strongly flavored meats such as venison and lamb. Some old-world sausages also use juniper as one of the seasoning ingredients.

Pick juniper fruits in late summer or fall, when they are fully developed and blue, with a dusty bloom. Dry them for a few days at room temperature, then store in a tightly sealed spice bottle in a dark cupboard; they'll keep until the next season.

Red Cabbage with Juniper and Bacon   4 servings

This is a hearty dish that goes well with roasted meats or poultry.

¼ pound thick-cut bacon, cut into ½-inch pieces
Half of a small head of red cabbage, cored and cut into 1-inch chunks
Half of a white onion, cut vertically into ¼-inch-wide wedges
¼ cup chicken broth
3 or 4 juniper fruits, crushed
1 tablespoon white wine vinegar
½ teaspoon dried thyme

In large skillet, sauté bacon over medium heat until crisp. Use slotted spoon to transfer to a plate lined with paper towels; discard all but 1 tablespoon of the drippings. Add cabbage and onion to skillet with drippings. Cook over medium heat, stirring occasionally, for about 5 minutes. Add chicken broth, juniper fruits, vinegar and thyme. Cover and cook for 10 minutes, stirring occasionally. Uncover and cook until juices thicken and cabbage is tender, about 5 minutes longer. Sprinkle bacon over cabbage, stirring to combine; cook for a minute or two, until bacon is hot. Serve immediately.

Other recipes in this book featuring juniper fruits:
Venison Roast with Mountain Ash and Juniper Rub, pg. 99

Quick ideas for using juniper fruits:
Use in any recipe calling for purchased juniper berries.
Simmer crushed juniper fruits in melted butter, then use the mixture to baste poultry
while it is roasting.

MAHONIA: CREEPING GRAPE-HOLLY and
HOLLY-LEAVED BARBERRY (Mahonia spp.)

Two types of Mahonia with edible fruits are found in the wild in our area: the low-growing creeping grape-holly (*Mahonia repens*; also called creeping Oregon grape) and the upright shrub called holly-leaved barberry (*M. aqui-folium*). Both produce similar dusty-looking blue or bluish-purple berries that are somewhat dry and have a single hard seed.

Mahonia's sharp-tipped, holly-like leaves make picking a bit of a chore. Lightweight leather gloves help protect your hands but still allow you to grab onto the berries.

In addition to their distinctive fruits, both plants also share another common trait: stiff, holly-like leaves with sharply pointed teeth. The teeth are a nuisance when you're picking the berries; it's hard to avoid being pricked, and if you pick very many berries, you *will* get pricked—a lot. Some people develop a rash from this, so some care is advised.

Mahonia berries are very sour, but like other sour fruits such as cherries or grapes, they make excellent jelly and other sweetened products. Be sure to gather only fully ripe, bright blue or bluish-purple berries with no tinge of green. Not only are underripe berries even more sour, they may cause digestive upset and should not be picked. Ripe berries remain on the plants for a long time, often until covered by snow; some foragers feel that mahonia berries become sweeter after a frost, and wait to gather them until cold weather sets in. The berries may become somewhat shriveled, but they can still be used to prepare juice.

Ripe mahonia berries are typically juiced because the single seed, although not excessively large, is very hard and inedible. However, winemakers sometimes combine whole mahonia berries with other fruits—particularly apples—to make a delicious, attractive wine; the mahonia doesn't need to be juiced first when making wine because the seeds get strained out during the winemaking process. If you're an amateur vintner, search on the internet for mahonia-apple wine recipes to get some ideas.

To prepare mahonia juice, measure the fruit and place in a non-aluminum pot. Add enough water to just cover the fruit. Heat to boiling, then reduce the heat; cover and simmer for about 15 minutes, gently crushing the fruit with a potato masher about midway through the cooking. Transfer the mixture to a strainer lined with doubled, dampened cheesecloth and let it drip for 30 minutes; if you're making jelly, don't squeeze the fruit or the jelly will be cloudy. After the clear liquid has dripped away, set it aside and squeeze the fruit into a different container; you can use this slightly cloudy juice as a beverage or for cooking. Processed this way, a quart of fruit will yield about 2½ cups of lovely, deep purple juice. Some cooks like to use apple juice, or a mix of apple juice and water, when preparing mahonia juice.

Mahonia-Gooseberry Spritzer

About 2 cups

This is a delightfully refreshing, addictive sipper for hot weather.

2 cups fresh or previously frozen gooseberries* (about 12 ounces)

1 cup mahonia berries, rinsed

1¼ cups water

½ cup sugar

½ cup fresh mint leaves

1 tablespoon freshly squeezed lime juice

1 bottle Prosecco, Cava, Monastrell or other light, sparkling white wine (or sparkling water), chilled

Lime slices for garnish

In saucepan, combine gooseberries, mahonia, water and sugar. Heat to boiling over high heat. Reduce heat to medium-low; cover and simmer for 15 minutes. Remove from heat and add mint leaves; let steep for 5 minutes. Strain through wire-mesh strainer placed over a large bowl; use rubber spatula to press on fruits to extract as much juice as possible. Discard contents of strainer. Cool juice to room temperature, then stir in lime juice. Cover and place in refrigerator until completely chilled; can be prepared in advance and stored in refrigerator for several days. To serve, fill wine glass two-thirds full with chilled sparkling wine; add fruit juice mixture to taste, stirring quickly to blend. Garnish with a half-slice of lime.

*If you don't have gooseberries, substitute ¾ pound of cut-up rhubarb (often available at larger supermarkets in the frozen-fruit section).

Mahonia Jelly

4 half-pints

For a delicious variation, use apple juice rather than water when preparing the mahonia juice.

2½ cups mahonia juice

Half of a 1.75-ounce box powdered pectin

½ teaspoon butter, optional (helps reduce foaming)

3 cups sugar

Prepare and process as directed in Jelly Instructions (using pectin), pgs. 176–177.

Mahonia-Blackberry Turnovers

4 turnovers

The combination of tart mahonia with rich blackberry makes a wonderful filling for these pretty turnovers.

1¼ cups mahonia berries, rinsed

1¼ cups apple juice

½ cup wild or purchased blackberries,
cut in half before measuring if large

¼ cup sugar

1 tablespoon cornstarch

2 teaspoons butter

½ teaspoon vanilla extract

1 sheet frozen puff pastry (half of a 17.3-ounce package),
thawed according to package directions

1 egg yolk, beaten with 1 teaspoon milk

In small, heavy-bottomed non-aluminum saucepan, boil mahonia with apple juice for 10 minutes. Run through food mill; discard seeds. Return purée to saucepan. Add blackberries, sugar, cornstarch, butter and vanilla, stirring until well combined. Heat over medium heat to a gentle boil, then reduce heat to medium-low and cook until very thick, about 10 minutes, stirring frequently (especially near the end of cooking, as it will burn easily). Set aside until cool.

Heat oven to 400°F; line a large baking sheet with kitchen parchment. On lightly floured worksurface, unfold puff pastry sheet; press together the gaps where it was folded and roll to a 10-inch square. Cut into 4 squares, each 5x5 inches. Transfer to prepared baking sheet, keeping slightly apart (you may have to position them at an angle to fit them all on the baking sheet; also remember that each square will be folded into a triangle so some edges won't be close once they are ready to bake). Spoon 1½ tablespoons of the cooled filling in the center of each (refrigerate any leftover filling, and use it to top oatmeal or toast). Moisten edges with a little water and fold into triangle; seal edges with fork. Brush tops with egg yolk mixture, being careful not to let any egg mixture drip down the edges (see tip below). Bake until richly browned and puffed, 13 to 18 minutes. Cool for at least 30 minutes (or completely) before serving, to avoid being burned by the hot filling.

When you're glazing puff pastry turnovers with an egg wash, don't let any of the egg wash drip down the edges onto the baking sheet. If it does, the pastry may not puff properly because the egg acts like glue, holding the edges down and preventing them from separating (puffing).

Open-Faced Peach-Mahonia Tart   1 tart (6 to 8 servings)

For top-notch results, prepare this with local, in-season ripe peaches from one of the many splendid peach orchards in our area.

Ready-to-use pastry for single-crust pie

Mahonia layer:
1½ cups fresh mahonia berries, rinsed
3 tablespoons water
2 tablespoons sugar
1 tablespoon instant tapioca

Almond layer:
¾ cup slivered blanched almonds
3 tablespoons butter, softened slightly
¼ cup sugar
1 egg yolk

5 ripe peaches, peeled and pitted, sliced into ¼-inch-thick wedges
2 tablespoons sugar (coarse sugar is very nice here)
2 tablespoons butter, cut into small bits

Line tart/quiche pan (with removable bottom) with pastry, pressing up the sides so pastry is slightly above rim of pan. Prick crust all over with a fork; chill for at least 30 minutes, or until you are ready to use it. Meanwhile, prepare the mahonia layer: In small saucepan, combine mahonia and water. Place over medium heat and cook until berries begin to soften, then mash gently with a potato masher to get the juices flowing. Cook for 10 minutes, or until very soft, mashing occasionally. Process through food mill; discard seeds. Return purée to saucepan; stir in sugar. Heat to a gentle boil, stirring constantly; cook until sugar dissolves. Add tapioca; stir well, then remove from heat and set aside to cool.

Position oven rack in lower third of oven; heat to 400°F. Prepare the almond layer: Combine all ingredients in food processor, and process until smooth. Place chilled tart crust on baking sheet (lined with parchment to catch drips, if you like). Spread almond filling evenly in crust; spread mahonia mixture evenly over almond layer. Arrange peaches in overlapping rings, packing fairly full to allow for shrinkage. Sprinkle with the 2 tablespoons sugar; scatter butter over the top. Wrap a 1-inch-wide strip of foil around the edge of the pan, folding it over the top of the exposed pastry. Bake for 40 minutes; remove foil strips, and bake tart for 10 to 15 minutes longer, or until crust is nicely golden and peaches are tender. Cool on wire rack for a bit before serving.

Mahonia-Champagne Jam

4 half-pints

Many recipes for mahonia jelly or jam use a combination of apples and mahonia, to mellow the flavor of the mahonia. Here's a jam recipe that is full-on mahonia . . . tart but delicious!

3 cups fresh mahonia berries, rinsed

2 cups champagne

1 tablespoon lemon juice

One-half of a 1.75-ounce package powdered pectin (see pg. 176 for information on dividing pectin)

2½ cups sugar

Prepare 4 half-pint canning jars, bands and new lids as described on pg. 183. In non-aluminum saucepan, combine mahonia berries, champagne and lemon juice. Heat to boiling over medium-high heat, then mash well with a potato masher. Cover and reduce heat; simmer for 15 minutes, stirring several times. Transfer mixture to a food mill, and process into a medium (4-quart) non-aluminum soup pot. Discard seeds and skins from food mill.

Have the sugar ready to go before you start cooking the jam. Add the powdered pectin to the pot with the mahonia purée; stir until dissolved. Heat to boiling over high heat, stirring frequently. When mixture comes to a full, rolling boil that can't be stirred down, add the sugar. Cook, stirring constantly, until the mixture again comes to a full, foaming boil. Boil for 1 minute, stirring constantly (if mixture threatens to boil over, move from the heat for a few seconds, then reduce heat slightly and return the pot to the heat). Remove from heat and stir for a minute or two to settle the foam; if there is still foam on top, skim with a clean spoon and discard. Pour into prepared jars, leaving ½ inch headspace; seal with prepared lids and bands. Process in boiling-water bath for 20 minutes at 5,000 feet, or at the recommended time for your elevation (see pg. 183); if you prefer, you can store the jam in the refrigerator where it will keep for a month or longer.

Other recipes in this book featuring mahonia berries:
Six Recipes Using Wild Fruit Juice or Syrup, pgs. 170–174
Wild Berry or Fruit Syrup, pg. 175

MOUNTAIN ASH (*Sorbus* spp.)

Two varieties of mountain ash inhabit our area: the native Greene's mountain ash (*Sorbus scopulina*; also called Cascade or Western mountain ash), and the introduced European mountain ash (*S. aucuparia*). Most people who see these lovely, highly decorative trees don't know that the fruits are edible. To be sure, they won't convince anyone who eats one raw, right off the tree; they're quite bitter. But they make an interesting seasoning, and also can be juiced to make an unusual jelly.

Mountain ash are easy to gather in quantity; simply snip off the entire cluster. Wait until they are fully ripe before harvesting. Frost softens the berries and makes them a bit less bitter, so many foragers wait until after the first frost to harvest the fruit. Fruits persist through the winter, and it's fun to trek through the woods on snowshoes to pick mountain ash. Harvested mountain ash fruits keep well in the refrigerator; simply place unwashed clusters—still on the stems—in a plastic bag. Twist the top just lightly, to allow some air to enter the bag, and refrigerate as long as 3 weeks. They also dehydrate well; see the instructions on pgs. 180–181.

To prepare juice from fresh mountain ash, pull individual fruits off the stems; discard any that are black, or withered and hard. Measure the picked fruit and place in a non-aluminum pot. Add 2 cups of water per 2 cups of picked fruit. Heat to boiling, then reduce the heat; cover and simmer for about 20 minutes. Gently mash the fruit with a potato masher, and cook for 5 minutes longer. Transfer the mixture to a strainer lined with doubled, dampened cheesecloth and let it drip for 30 minutes, pressing lightly to extract more juice. Processed this way, 2 cups of stemmed, fresh fruit will yield about 1 cup juice.

If you're preparing juice from dried mountain ash, follow the same instructions, increasing the water by half (so for 2 cups of dried mountain ash, you'd use 3 cups of water). Increase cooking time from 20 to 30 minutes.

Sweet Mountain Ash Jelly
2 half-pints

1½ cups mountain ash juice

One-third of a 1.75-ounce box powdered pectin

¼ teaspoon butter, optional (helps reduce foaming)

2 cups sugar

Prepare and process as directed in Jelly Instructions (using pectin), pgs. 176–177.

Venison Roast with Mountain Ash and Juniper Rub

6 to 8 servings

Venison is a natural partner for mountain ash and juniper; both are part of the deer's diet.

Rub:

¼ cup mountain ash berries, crushed

6 juniper berries, crushed

1 teaspoon dried rosemary leaves, crushed

1 teaspoon dried thyme

1 teaspoon paprika

1 teaspoon salt

½ teaspoon freshly ground pepper

2- to 2½-pound venison roast from the hindquarter

2 tablespoons vegetable oil

1 medium onion, diced

1 cup dry red wine

½ cup sour cream

2 tablespoons currant jelly

2 teaspoons all-purpose flour

2 tablespoons cold water

In small bowl, combine all rub ingredients; mix well. Spread rub mixture on all sides of roast, pressing in. Place roast in plastic food-storage bag; seal and refrigerate overnight.

When you're ready to cook, heat oven to 350°F. In Dutch oven, heat oil over medium-high heat. Add roast; brown on all sides. Add onion and wine; cover and bake, basting occasionally, until desired doneness, 20 minutes per pound for rare and up to 30 minutes per pound for medium-well (at higher altitudes, increase roasting time slightly). Transfer roast to a serving plate; cover loosely with foil.

Strain pan juices through wire-mesh strainer into a bowl. Return juices to Dutch oven. Heat to boiling over medium-high heat. Reduce heat and boil gently until liquid is reduced to ¼ cup, 8 to 10 minutes. Stir in sour cream and jelly; cook until jelly melts. In small bowl, stir together flour and water; add to liquid in Dutch oven, stirring constantly. Cook until sauce is smooth and bubbling, 1 to 2 minutes. Serve sauce over sliced roast.

Substitution: Substitute a beef rump roast for the venison. Proceed as directed.

MULBERRIES (*Morus* spp.)

White mulberry (*Morus alba*), originally from China, has been widely planted as an ornamental and has spread into the wild throughout much of North America; its fruits are sweet and juicy. Texas or littleleaf mulberry (*M. microphylla*) is a related native plant that is found in our area only in New Mexico; its fruits are more sour, so may need additional sweetening when used in the recipes here. Fruits of both can be eaten raw or cooked; however, be sure that the fruit you pick is completely ripe and soft, as unripe fruit is not only hard and unpleasant but is also mildly toxic (as are the leaves and all other parts of the plant).

Mulberries are often planted in urban areas, yet few people seem to pick them for eating. It's too bad, because the fruits are sweet and delicious—and if more folks were interested in picking them, there would be fewer mulberries staining the sidewalks!

The hardest part about picking mulberries is reaching the fruit, which is usually high up in the tree. The best way to harvest them is to spread a tarp under the tree, then jostle the branches with a stick; ripe fruit will fall onto the tarp and can be gathered. A short, soft stemlet remains attached to the fruit; this should be removed before eating or cooking the fruit. It's easiest to just pinch it off with your fingernails as you're washing the fruit.

To prepare pulp or juice, measure the fruit and place in a non-aluminum pot. For pulp, add ½ cup water per quart of fruit; for juice, add 1 cup water per quart of fruit. Thoroughly crush the fruit with a potato masher to start the juices flowing. Heat to boiling, then reduce the heat; cover and simmer for about 20 minutes. **For pulp,** the mixture is ready to use; you can also purée it in a food processor to make it smoother if you like. **For juice,** transfer the mixture to a strainer lined with doubled, dampened cheesecloth and let it drip for 30 minutes; if you're making jelly, don't squeeze the fruit or the jelly will be cloudy. After the clear liquid has dripped away, set it aside and squeeze the fruit into a different container; you can use this slightly cloudy juice as a beverage or for cooking, and add the leftover, squeezed fruit to applesauce, pie filling or other cooked fruits. Processed this way, a quart of fruit will yield about 1½ cups of pulp, or about 2 cups juice.

Once you've harvested mulberries, use them within a day or two, as they will spoil quickly. They freeze beautifully; simply pack them into containers or heavyweight plastic bags and freeze. They can be dried successfully (see pgs. 180–181); the texture of a dried mulberry is similar to that of a dried fig. Dried mulberries can be eaten out of hand as a nibble, or rehydrated in warm water and used like fresh berries. They also make a decent fruit leather (pg. 182), particularly if mixed with apples.

Mulberry Thumbprint Cookies

About 28 cookies

Whole mulberries nestle inside a thumbprint pressed into a rich, buttery cookie.

For 5,000 feet; see adjustments for other altitudes

½ cup (1 stick) unsalted butter, softened

¼ cup powdered sugar, plus additional for garnish

1½ teaspoons vanilla extract

1 cup plus 1 tablespoon all-purpose flour[1, 2, 3]

¼ teaspoon salt

¼ cup very finely chopped pecans

¾ cup (approximate) fresh mulberries

In mixing bowl, combine butter, sugar and vanilla. Beat with electric mixer until light and fluffy, about 2 minutes; scrape bowl several times. Place a wire-mesh strainer over the mixing bowl; add flour and salt, then shake strainer to sift flour into the butter mixture. Add nuts. Stir with spatula or wooden spoon until well mixed. Cover and refrigerate for an hour (or longer); this makes the dough easy to handle.

When ready to bake, heat oven to 350°F.[2, 3] Roll chilled dough into balls that are about 1 inch in size. Place on ungreased baking sheet, about 1½ inches apart. Use your thumb to press a large indentation into the center of each ball. Place 3 or 4 mulberries (depending on size) into each indentation. Bake for 10 minutes, then rotate pans (see "Rotating Cookies while Baking," pg. 51). Continue baking for 8 to 15 minutes longer, or until cookies are just set and are lightly golden brown. Remove baking sheet(s) from oven; use the back of a spoon to gently press each group of berries into the dough. Put a little powdered sugar into a wire-mesh strainer and shake it gently over the cookies to dust them lightly. Transfer to wire rack. Cool before serving.

---

1. Below 5,000 feet: Use 1 cup flour.

2. At 7,500 feet: Use 1 cup plus 4 teaspoons flour. Heat oven to 365°F.

3. At 10,000 feet: Use 1 cup plus 1½ tablespoons flour. Heat oven to 365°F.

Mulberry Jelly

4 half-pints

2¾ cups mulberry juice
2 tablespoons lemon juice
Two-thirds of a 1.75-ounce box powdered pectin
½ teaspoon butter, optional (helps reduce foaming)
3½ cups sugar

Prepare and process as directed in Jelly Instructions (using pectin), pgs. 176–177.

Mulberry Filling

About ½ cup; easily increased

½ teaspoon water
½ teaspoon cornstarch
5 ounces mulberries (about 1 cup)
1 tablespoon grated apple
2 teaspoons sugar
1½ teaspoons lemon juice

In small bowl, blend together water and cornstarch; set aside. In small, heavy-bottomed saucepan, combine mulberries, apple, sugar and lemon juice. Crush fruit gently with a potato masher to start juices flowing. Heat to boiling over medium-high heat, then cook, stirring frequently, until mixture is no longer runny; this will take 10 to 12 minutes. Add cornstarch mixture, stirring constantly; cook for about 1 minute longer, or until thick. Cool before using.

Use this to prepare Easy Bear Claws (pg. 81), Fruit-Striped Cookie Fingers (pg. 126), or Fruit-Filled Muffins (pg. 155). Refrigerate extra filling, and use to top oatmeal or toast.

Rice Pudding with Wild Berries

Tender, custardy rice pudding is studded with colorful fruits.

1 tablespoon butter, softened

2¾ cups whole milk

6 egg yolks

¾ cup sugar

½ teaspoon vanilla extract

½ teaspoon lemon extract

1 teaspoon cinnamon

⅛ teaspoon salt

4 cups cooked long-grain rice (from about 1½ cups raw rice)

1 cup mulberries, raspberries or blackberries, cut in half if long

Heat oven to 350°F. Generously butter 9x9-inch baking dish; set aside. In saucepan, heat milk over medium heat until small bubbles appear around the edges; remove from heat. In large mixing bowl, use a whisk to beat egg yolks and sugar until light. Add warm milk, vanilla and lemon extracts, cinnamon and salt; whisk to blend. Add rice and stir with a wooden spoon until well mixed. Add mulberries; stir gently to mix. Scrape mixture into prepared dish. Bake until lightly browned on top, 40 to 50 minutes. Cool for 5 to 10 minutes, and serve while still warm.

Other recipes in this book featuring mulberries:
Six Recipes Using Wild Fruit Juice or Syrup, pgs. 170–174
Wild Berry or Fruit Syrup, pg. 175
Dehydrating Wild Berries and Fruits, pgs. 180–181
Wild Berry or Fruit Leather, pg. 182

Quick ideas for using mulberries:
Mix a few into any baking recipe that uses raspberries. The mulberries have a more solid texture and are generally a bit larger than raspberries, so they should be cut into two shorter halves if longer than ¾ inch to make them more similar to the raspberries.

PEARS (*Pyrus communis*)

Wild pears are found occasionally in our area, as remnants of old orchards or homestead gardens. Some were planted by American Indians as they moved westward; still others have been "planted" by birds, or by humans discarding a pear core into the woods. Regardless of their origins, wild pears are typically much smaller than their domestic cousins, sometimes only an inch across (although often larger, occasionally up to 4 inches in length). Generally, they have only a slight neck, and often, they have no perceptible neck at all, appearing rounded or slightly lumpy. Depending on the original variety, they may develop a reddish blush when ripe, but many are green, yellowish or greenish-yellow when ripe. Pears are ripe when the flesh is no longer hard; like commercial pears, wild pears will soften more if they are allowed to sit at room temperature for a day or two.

Most wild pears are fairly small, sometimes weighing only an ounce or two. Compare that to a domestic pear that tips the scales at 8 to 12 ounces, and you can see that it takes a lot of wild pears to amount to much!

Because wild pears are so much smaller than commercially grown pears, they don't work well for recipes that call for whole, halved or quartered pears. However, chopped wild pears can be used in recipes calling for chopped commercial pears. It may take a lot of wild pears to prepare those recipes, though; the smallest wild pears weigh an ounce or perhaps two. If you've got a mix of ripe and unripe wild pears, refrigerate the ripe ones until the others have ripened, then combine the two batches to prepare your recipe; however, if you're making jam or pear butter, save a few underripe pears to add to the mix, because they have more natural pectin than fully ripe pears.

Wild pears make a delicious fruit leather (pg. 182); this is a great use for fruits that may have insect holes, hail spots or other damage because you can simply cut away the affected portions and use the rest of the fruit. Wild pears are generally not juiced, but if you want to try making pear juice to prepare jelly, follow the directions for apple juice on pg. 8.

Crisp Pear Tart

1 tart (6 to 8 servings)

This gorgeous tart tastes as good as it looks. Serve it for a special occasion.

½ cup ricotta cheese

Ready-to-use pastry for single-crust pie

**3½ cups quartered wild pears (about 1¼ pounds),
peeled, quartered and cored before measuring**

3 tablespoons (packed) brown sugar

A pinch of salt

2 tablespoons unsalted butter

¼ cup ground almonds (1 ounce)

Place ricotta in a wire-mesh strainer set over a bowl; refrigerate while you prepare the pears. Heat oven to 400°F. Fit pastry into a 9-inch quiche pan; fold excess pastry over inside the pan as necessary, then press together to make a thicker edge. Blind-bake pastry to lightly golden (see "Blind Baking Pie Crusts" on pg. 47). Remove pan from oven and set aside to cool; it can sit at room temperature for several hours before final assembly.

Meanwhile, in mixing bowl, combine pears, brown sugar and salt, stirring to coat. Melt butter in large, heavy-bottomed skillet over medium heat. Add pear mixture. Cook, gently stirring occasionally, until juices have been reabsorbed and pears are browning in spots; this will take 20 to 25 minutes. Remove from heat and set aside. The pears can sit at room temperature for up to an hour before final assembly of the tart; for longer storage, refrigerate the pears, then warm to room temperature before using (the ricotta can be allowed to drain for several hours).

When you're ready for final baking, position oven rack 6 inches from broiler element; heat broiler. Spread drained ricotta evenly in bottom of pre-baked tart crust (discard the liquid that has dripped out); sprinkle almonds evenly over ricotta. Cover edges of crust with strips of foil; this prevents over-browning during the final cooking. Spoon pears over almonds, distributing evenly. Place tart under broiler for 3 to 6 minutes, until the pears develop a few brown spots; be careful that the pears don't burn. Remove foil strips; serve immediately.

 The pears are cooked separately from the crust; just before serving, the pears are added to the crust and the whole thing is finished off for a few minutes under the broiler. As a result, the crust remains crisp and flaky, and the filling is flavorful and tender without being mushy.

Pear Filling

About ½ cup; easily increased

1 cup cored, chopped pears

1½ tablespoons lemon juice

2 teaspoons water

1½ tablespoons (packed) brown sugar

A pinch of nutmeg

In small, heavy-bottomed non-aluminum saucepan, combine pears, lemon juice and water. Cook over medium heat, stirring frequently, until pears are tender and mixture has thickened, about 10 minutes. Stir in brown sugar and nutmeg; cook for about a minute longer to dissolve sugar. Cool before using.

Use this to prepare Easy Bear Claws (pg. 81), Fruit-Striped Cookie Fingers (pg. 126), or Fruit-Filled Muffins (pg. 155). Refrigerate extra filling, and use to top oatmeal or toast.

Pear Butter

Variable quantity; make as much as you wish

This rich, dark spread has a wonderful pear flavor. Use it on toast, or spread over pancakes.

Wild pears

Water

Sugar

Optional: Cinnamon, nutmeg, pie spice (any or all, as you prefer)

Cut the pears into quarters, then remove and discard the stems and blossom remnants; add pears to a heavy-bottomed non-aluminum saucepan. (Don't try to make pear butter from less than a quart of wild pears; the amount of the cooking purée will be so small that it will burn.) Add cold water to not quite cover the pear pieces. Heat to boiling over medium-high heat, and boil until the fruit is tender, 10 to 15 minutes. Cool slightly, then strain through a food mill or conical strainer. Discard skins and seeds from food mill.

Proceed as directed for Plum Butter, pg. 110.

Variation: Substitute wild apples for the wild pears, or prepare the butter with a mix of the two fruits.

Smoked Pork Chops with Pears and Mustard

2 servings; easily increased

Mustard and apple cider combine with the pears to make a delicious sauce for smoked pork chops. This dish is perfect for fall, when wild pears are at their full ripeness. Serve with wild rice, or a wild rice blend.

1 tablespoon unsalted butter

2 smoked pork chops (6 to 8 ounces each)

8 ounces quartered, skin-on wild pears (about 1½ cups), quartered and cored before measuring

¼ cup diced onion

1 teaspoon mustard seeds

¾ cup apple cider

1 tablespoon Dijon mustard

In large skillet, melt butter over medium-high heat. Add pork chops and brown on both sides. Transfer chops to a plate; set aside. Add pears, onion and mustard seed to skillet. Cook over medium-high heat, stirring frequently, for 5 minutes, until pears begin to brown in spots. In measuring cup, combine apple cider and Dijon mustard, stirring to blend. Pour into skillet, stirring to loosen browned bits and to combine liquid with pear mixture. Return pork chops to skillet, laying them on top of the pears. Reduce heat to medium and cook for 10 minutes, shaking pan occasionally to prevent sticking and turning chops once. Serve chops with pears and pan sauce.

 The pears can be peeled before using, if you prefer. Personally, I like the texture of the peels in this dish, but it will work just fine either way.

Other recipes in this book using wild pears:
Barberry-Pear Chutney, pg. 19
Wild Berry or Fruit Leather, pg. 182
As a substitute in Hawthorn and Sausage Brunch Casserole, pg. 75

Quick ideas for using wild pears:
Cut a few up and add them to the mix when preparing apple pie.

PLUMS (*Prunus* spp.)

Three plums are found in various parts of our area. American wild plum (*Prunus americana*) is the most common; it is a native plant that is typically a large shrub. Its ripe fruits are reddish to pinkish-purple and look a lot like the ones you buy in the store, only smaller. Cherry plum (*P. cerasifera*) is an introduced tree that is far less common; its fruits look similar to American wild plum. Blackthorn or sole (*P. spinosa*) is another introduced plum species; its ripe fruits are dark purple. American wild plums and cherry plums can be used in any of the recipes in this section that call for wild plums, although eating quality varies from tree to tree; some are too tart to eat raw and are best in cooked dishes. Others are sweet and juicy, begging to be popped into the mouth and savored on the spot. Blackthorn fruits, however, are very astringent; they can be used to make jelly, but would not work well for the other recipes in this section that call for wild plums (see the recipe for Sloe Gin on pg. 114 for a recipe written specifically for blackthorn).

Note that plums don't ripen well off the tree, so it's best to harvest only ripe plums, which will be slightly soft. Unripe plums can cause digestive upset.

Plums can be cut from the pit for use in recipes; they are also used to make purée or, less commonly, juice. Unlike many wild fruits, cut-up plums work well in savory dishes as well as sweet ones. I've never encountered a wild plum whose flesh separated easily and cleanly from the pit; unlike some domestic plums, wild plums cling tightly to the pit. Use a paring knife to cut the flesh away, cutting as close to the pit as you can. Plum skin is a bit sour, but I generally leave the skin on the fruit when I'm pitting. If you wish to remove the skins, drop a few whole plums into a pan of boiling water, then boil until the skin splits slightly; this takes about a minute. Immediately transfer the plums to a bowl filled with ice water. You can now peel the skins off, then cut the flesh away from the pit and proceed with your recipe.

To prepare purée or juice, it's not necessary to remove the pits; cut the plums into rough halves, cutting alongside the pit, and place in a non-aluminum pot. For purée, add enough water to come about one-quarter of the way up the plums; for juice, add enough to come about halfway up. Heat to boiling over high heat, then reduce heat and simmer, stirring occasionally, for 10 minutes, or until the plums are very soft.* **For purée,** transfer the cooked fruit to a food mill and process until the pits are largely scraped clean; remove pits individually, then process the mixture remaining in the food mill until all that's left in the food mill is skins. **For juice,** transfer the cooked fruit to a strainer lined with doubled, dampened cheesecloth and let it drip for 30 minutes; if you're making jelly, don't squeeze the fruit or the jelly will be cloudy. After the clear liquid has dripped away, set it aside and squeeze the fruit into a different container; you can use this slightly cloudy juice as a beverage or for cooking.

Yield varies quite a bit with plums; some are very fleshy and produce a good quantity of cut-up fruit or purée, while others are thin-fleshed, yielding much less. If you've found nicely fleshy wild plums, you'll probably get a cup of cut-up chunks (uncooked) per dozen fruits; a pound of fleshy plums typically produces ½ to ¾ cup of cooked purée, or 1½ cups of juice. Plums can also be dehydrated (pgs. 180–181) or used to prepare fruit leather (pg. 182).

*Don't crush or break the pits during cooking or straining. Plum pits contain small amounts of a cyanide-forming compound that can cause illness if eaten in large quantities.

Plum-Dandy Oatmeal Squares

16 servings

These tasty squares hold up well in a lunchbox.

For 5,000 feet; see adjustments for other altitudes

1½ cups cut-up wild plums, pitted and cut into
½-inch chunks before measuring

¼ cup apple juice, other juice or water[1, 3]

1 tablespoon honey

1½ cups all-purpose flour

½ cup old-fashioned rolled oats (not instant)

1½ cups (packed) golden brown sugar[2, 3]

¼ teaspoon baking soda

A pinch of salt

⅓ cup vegetable oil

3 tablespoons frozen orange juice concentrate

2 tablespoons cold butter, cut into several chunks

In small saucepan, combine plums, apple juice and honey. Heat to boiling over medium-high heat, then reduce heat so mixture is simmering. Cook, stirring frequently, until plums break up and mixture thickens, 10 to 15 minutes.[2, 3] Remove from heat; set aside until cool.

Position rack in lower third of oven; heat to 375°F.[1, 3] Spray 8x8-inch baking dish with nonstick spray and line bottom with a square of waxed paper that has been cut to size; set aside. In mixing bowl, combine flour, rolled oats, brown sugar, baking soda and salt; mix well with a wooden spoon. Remove ½ cup of the flour mixture, transferring to a small bowl; set aside. Add oil and orange juice concentrate to flour remaining in mixing bowl; stir with wooden spoon until well mixed and crumbly. Pat flour mixture into prepared baking dish, pressing firmly. Spoon cooled plum filling over crust, spreading evenly; set aside.

Add cold butter to the ½ cup flour mixture in the small bowl. Rub together with your fingertips until the mixture is crumbly. Sprinkle topping over plum filling. Bake until golden brown, 30 to 40 minutes.[1, 3] Cool on wire rack before cutting into squares.

---

1. **Below 5,000 feet:** Use 3 tablespoons apple juice, other juice or water. Heat oven to 350°F. Bake for 25 to 35 minutes.

2. **At 7,500 feet:** Use 1⅓ cups golden brown sugar. The plum mixture will probably need a longer cooking time to thicken, up to 20 minutes.

3. **At 10,000 feet:** Use ¼ cup plus 1 tablespoon apple juice, other juice or water. Use 1⅓ cups golden brown sugar. The plum mixture will probably need a longer cooking time to thicken, up to 20 minutes. Heat oven to 390°F. Bake for 23 to 33 minutes.

Plum Butter

Variable quantity; make as much as you wish

Plum butter is easy to make in almost any quantity, because it needs no added pectin (and therefore does not require precise measurements). It's fabulous as a spread for toast, or used to top pancakes, waffles or hot cereal.

Wild plums

Water

Sugar

Optional: Cinnamon, cardamom, nutmeg (any or all, as you prefer)

Cut the flesh away from the pits, adding the pitted fruit to a saucepan as you go. (Don't try to make plum butter with fewer than 12 plums; the amount of the cooking purée will be so small that it will burn.) Add cold water to cover the plum pieces. Heat to boiling over medium-high heat, and boil until skins are tender, about 10 minutes. Cool slightly, then strain through a food mill or conical strainer; you could also strain the plums through a wire-mesh strainer, stirring and pushing the fruit through with a wooden spoon.

Measure the strained pulp and transfer to a heavy-bottomed non-aluminum saucepan. Sterilize enough half-pint canning jars, bands and new lids (see pg. 183) to hold the finished plum butter (as a guideline, you'd need 4 half-pint jars for 3 cups of strained pulp). Heat to boiling over medium-high heat, then add ½ to ⅞ cup of sugar per cup of strained plums (the amount depends on the sweetness of the plums and your personal preference), stirring until the sugar dissolves. If using spices, add them now; try ¼ teaspoon of cinnamon or cardamom (or both) per cup of strained pulp, and/or a healthy pinch of nutmeg. Adjust heat so the mixture is boiling, but not so vigorously that the bubbles explode. Cook, stirring frequently, until the mixture is very thick; this will take 15 to 30 minutes, depending on how runny the strained pulp was. Transfer to prepared jars, leaving ½ inch headspace; seal with prepared lids and bands. Process in boiling-water bath for 20 minutes at 5,000 feet, or at the recommended time for jam at your elevation (see pg. 183); if you prefer, you can store the plum butter in the refrigerator where it will keep for a month or longer.

Wild Plum Jelly

4 half-pints

2¾ cups wild plum juice

Half of a 1.75-ounce box powdered pectin

½ teaspoon butter, optional (helps reduce foaming)

3¼ cups sugar

Prepare and process as directed in Jelly Instructions (using pectin), pgs. 176–177.

Asian-Inspired Plum Sauce

About 1¼ cups

This lovely, jewel-like sauce packs a punch from the hot pepper and gingerroot.

2 cloves garlic

1-inch chunk of peeled fresh gingerroot

1 small hot red pepper, seeds and stem removed

Half of a small white onion, cut into 1-inch pieces

Half of a red bell pepper, cored and cut into 1-inch chunks

2 cups cut-up wild plums, pitted and cut into
  ½-inch chunks before measuring

⅓ cup brown sugar

⅓ cup seasoned rice vinegar

¼ cup orange juice

½ teaspoon ground coriander

½ teaspoon salt

In food processor, chop garlic, gingerroot and hot pepper until very fine. Add onion and bell pepper; pulse a few times to chop. Add plums; pulse until everything is chopped to medium texture. Transfer mixture to medium, heavy-bottomed non-aluminum saucepan; add remaining ingredients. Heat to boiling over medium-high heat; reduce heat and simmer, stirring frequently, until thick, 30 to 45 minutes. Transfer to a clean jar; cool completely. Store in refrigerator.

 Serve this with egg rolls or chicken wings, or add it to stir-fries. It's also great when brushed over ribs, pork chops or chicken just before taking them from the grill.

Ham Slice with Piquant Plum Sauce

4 servings

A savory plum sauce adds a sweet-and-tangy note to ham in this easy weeknight supper.

¼ cup minced shallots

1 tablespoon butter

1½ cups cut-up wild plums, pitted and cut into ½- to ¾-inch chunks before measuring

⅓ cup dry sherry

2 tablespoons maple syrup

1 tablespoon coarse (prepared) mustard

¼ teaspoon chili powder blend

1 bone-in ham slice, about 1¼ pounds

Heat oven to 400°F. In saucepan, cook shallots in butter over medium heat, stirring frequently, for 5 minutes. Add plums; cook, stirring frequently, for 5 minutes. Add sherry, maple syrup, mustard and chili powder; stir well. Cook, stirring occasionally, for about 5 minutes, or until plums have softened but still retain their shape. Remove from heat.

Place ham in a baking dish large enough to hold it. Spoon about ⅓ cup of the plum sauce over the ham, spreading evenly. Bake for 10 minutes, or until ham is hot all the way through and sauce is starting to glaze. If you like, turn the broiler on and broil for a minute or so to caramelize the glaze. Cut ham into 4 portions; serve with remaining sauce.

Variation: This recipe would also work with smoked pork chops.

Spicy Plum Chutney

About 1½ cups

This is delicious alongside grilled or broiled meats and fish, and with curry dishes.

4 whole cardamom pods

2 whole allspice berries, or ¼ teaspoon ground allspice

3 cups cut-up wild plums, pitted and cut into ½-inch chunks before measuring

¾ cup diced onion (¼-inch dice)

1 cup diced red bell pepper (¼-inch dice)

¼ cup golden raisins or purchased dried currants

¼ cup (packed) brown sugar

¼ cup balsamic vinegar or red-wine vinegar

1 tablespoon minced crystallized ginger (found in the spice aisle)

½ teaspoon mustard seeds

½ teaspoon salt

¼ teaspoon hot red pepper flakes

Split cardamom pods and transfer seeds to mortar; add allspice berries and crush until mixture is coarse. Combine spice mixture with remaining ingredients in heavy-bottomed non-aluminum saucepan. Heat to boiling over high heat. Reduce heat so mixture simmers steadily and cook until thickened and syrupy, 45 minutes to an hour. Stir frequently, especially near the end of the cooking time, to prevent sticking. Cool and transfer to a clean pint jar; store in refrigerator for up to 3 weeks.

Substitutions: Substitute pin cherries or sand cherries for the plums (you may also substitute chokecherries, if you have the patience to pit 3 cups!).

Sloe Gin

One fifth-sized bottle (approximate)

This home-infused gin is less syrupy than commercially purchased sloe gin, and makes a refreshing drink when mixed with sparkling water.

3 cups sloes (blackthorn fruits)

1½ cups sugar

¼ cup slivered almonds (about 1 ounce)

1 quart gin, approximate

You'll need a glass jar that holds 2 quarts, with a mouth wide enough to insert the sloes; juice is often sold in these types of bottles. Wash it very well, then fill it with boiling water and let stand for at least 5 minutes; place the lid into a small bowl and cover it with boiling water. After 5 minutes, drain the jar and proceed with the recipe while the jar is still hot.

Wash the sloes very well and prick each one several times with the tip of a sharp paring knife, adding to the sterilized jar as you go. Add the sugar and almonds. Pour in gin until the jar is completely full. Seal jar tightly and shake well; the sugar won't all dissolve right away. Place the sealed jar on the countertop and shake several times a day for several days, or until the sugar has dissolved completely. After that, set it in a cool, dark spot to infuse for at least 3 months, shaking twice a week; some people let it infuse for 6 months.

After the infusion period, strain mixture through cheesecloth-lined strainer into a clean bowl; press on the sloes to extract the liquid. Discard the solids. Line a funnel with a paper coffee filter. Strain liquid into a clean, sterilized fifth-sized glass bottle. At this point, the sloe gin is ready to drink, although some people prefer to let it age another few months before drinking.

Plum Filling

About ½ cup; easily increased

This filling is really pretty, and adds wonderful jewel tones to baked goods.

**1 cup cut-up wild plums, pitted and cut into
¼-inch chunks before measuring**

2 tablespoons sugar

1 tablespoon grated apple

1 teaspoon lemon juice

In small, heavy-bottomed saucepan, combine all ingredients. Crush fruit gently with a potato masher to start juices flowing. Heat to boiling over medium-high heat. Reduce heat; cover and simmer, stirring occasionally, until fruit is tender, 5 to 8 minutes. Mash again. Increase heat to medium-high, and boil, stirring frequently, until thick, about 5 minutes. Cool before using.

Use this to prepare Easy Bear Claws (pg. 81), Fruit-Striped Cookie Fingers (pg. 126), or Fruit-Filled Muffins (pg. 155). Refrigerate extra filling, and use to top oatmeal or toast.

Other recipes in this book featuring wild plums:
Six Recipes Using Wild Fruit Juice or Syrup, pgs. 170–174
Wild Berry or Fruit Syrup, pg. 175
Dehydrating Wild Berries and Fruits, pgs. 180–181
Wild Berry or Fruit Leather, pg. 182

Quick ideas for using wild plums:
Use cut-up wild plums in any recipe that calls for domestic plums; you may need to increase the sugar slightly if your plums are tart.
Sweeten plum purée to taste, then use it to make a delicious fruit leather (see pg. 182 for information on making leathers).
Plum juice makes a wonderful breakfast drink when sweetened to taste. If you're making juice to drink rather than to make jelly, don't worry about making clear juice; squeeze the cheesecloth-wrapped fruit to get more juice. The juice will be thicker than that used to make jelly, and the extra body is nice in juice for drinking.

PRICKLY PEAR: FRUITS and PADS (*Opuntia* spp.)

A dozen varieties of this flat-jointed cactus grow in our area; all produce edible fruits (called tunas) and pads (called nopales or nopalitos). Some species have fruits that are very small, slightly bitter or somewhat dry; the best fruits are large and juicy, with sweet flesh. Prickly pears are typically found in dry, sandy or rocky areas. They're easy to recognize; look for flat, spiny cactus pads with deep red egg-shaped or oblong fruits on top. Don't attempt to pick the fruits or pads unless you're wearing thick leather gloves, though; in addition to the stout spines you may see, both pads and fruits are armed with hairlike, virtually invisible spines that break off and lodge in your skin at the slightest touch. Even if a plant has few or no stout spines, you can be assured that the hair-like spines are present. Fruits and pads are prepared differently; see the information below.

Watch out for the fine, invisible spines called glochids; they grow from areoles, rounded buds spaced along the skin of both the fruits and the pads.

To prepare prickly pear fruits: The best way to deal with the invisible spines is to singe them off. Use a tongs to rotate the fruit over a gas flame (stovetop, camping stove, torch or side burner on a gas grill); the fine spines burn off quickly. To peel the singed fruit, cut the ends off, then make a lengthwise slit through the skin and peel the skin off. If the fruit is very small and too difficult to peel, slit it open and scrape the flesh out with a teaspoon.

The seeds are about ⅛ inch across and extremely hard, and most people—including me—prefer to avoid eating them. But if you're confident of your dental work and like a challenge, you can eat the flesh with the seeds intact; they won't make you sick.

For purée, process the peeled fruits, raw or cooked as described below, through a food mill. Eight ounces of uncooked fruit (weighed after peeling) will yield about ½ cup of smooth purée. As an option, place the peeled fruits in a microwave-safe bowl with a little water; cover and microwave at 50% power until the fruit is soft (timing varies depending on quantity, but it's usually just a few minutes). The fruits can be processed in the food mill, or poured into a wire-mesh strainer and stirred vigorously with a spoon to press the softened flesh through the mesh. Yield will be a bit higher with the microwave method, but the purée will be thinner than with the uncooked method. With either method, I scrape the seedy pulp from the food mill afterward and simmer it for 15 minutes with enough water to barely cover it; I strain that through my wire-mesh strainer to get a thin juice, which I add to juice prepared from whole fruits using one of the methods below.

To prepare **uncooked juice**, process peeled fruits in a blender with a small amount of water until the fruit is puréed. Pour everything into a wire-mesh strainer that is set over a large bowl, and let the juice drip into the bowl; stir it vigorously with a wooden spoon to extract as much liquid as possible, then discard the seedy pulp. Eight ounces of fruit (weighed after peeling) will yield about 1 cup of medium-body, slightly cloudy juice. For **cooked juice,** cut the peeled fruits into halves or quarters and place in a saucepan with water to barely cover. Simmer for about 10 minutes, mashing once or twice with a potato masher, then strain through doubled cheesecloth; squeeze the cheesecloth well at the end, then discard the cheesecloth and its contents. This method yields about 1½ cups of clear, thin juice from 8 ounces of peeled fruits.

To collect and prepare prickly pear pads: When you're in the field, look for smaller, thinner pads that are bright green and firm, and are growing off the side or top of a larger pad. Don't cut off a pad that is growing directly from the ground or that has other pads (or fruits) growing from it. To harvest a pad, grab (carefully!) onto the smaller pad you've selected and slice it off the larger pad with a sharp knife, leaving about ½ inch of the base of the smaller pad attached to the larger pad so you don't damage the larger pad. Drop the cut-off pad into a plastic bucket or heavy canvas bag; the spines would poke through plastic bags.

I think it's best to clean the pads outside, so the spines don't end up on the kitchen counter. Cover a picnic table with a thick layer of newspapers. Lay a pad flat on the newspaper with the base (the cut end) towards you. Use a tongs to hold tightly onto the base (I have heard of one forager who uses a clipboard from the office-supply store; the clip holds the base of the pad tightly, and the plastic board is easy to wash afterwards). Hold a very sharp knife, such as a long fish fillet knife, at the base and pointing away from yourself; the knife should be lying flat against the pad. Skim the knife across the surface in a slightly sawing motion to cut off the areoles (the raised buds that the spines grow from); the areoles are raised above the skin like a bump, and are fairly easy to slice off. If the knife misses a few areoles, skim it across the pad again, then use the tip of the knife to cut out any areoles or dark spots you may have missed. Turn the pad so the tip is toward you and slice any areoles off the base.

As you cut off the areoles, the pad will become slimy; wipe your knife on the newspapers occasionally to clean it. When one side of the pad is cleaned, roll up and discard the top layer of newspaper, flip the pad over and clean the other side. Then cut off about ¼ inch of the pad all around the edge and discard that, too; trim off any dry or damaged-looking areas. Finally, rinse the cleaned pad in plenty of cold, running water. I like to run my fingers over both sides as I wash it to be sure I've removed all the spines; I figure it's better to get a spine in my finger than in someone's mouth. (If you do get one of the fine spines in your finger, try to scrape it off; if that doesn't work, put a thick layer of white glue, such as Elmer's, over it and let it dry; it will form a skin that can be peeled off, taking the spine with it.)

Cleaning nopales may feel clumsy at first, but you will get better with practice; for some useful instruction, search online for "cleaning nopales" to find videos that show someone cleaning pads (YouTube is a good place to look).

Whole cleaned pads are excellent when grilled (pg. 122). For most recipes, though, you will want to slice them into strips or cubes and boil them to remove some of the thick, slimy sap-like fluid. Once they are sliced or cut up, they are called "nopalitos" (little nopales).

To boil nopalitos, heat a large pot of salted water to boiling. Add the nopalitos. Return to boiling and cook for 5 to 15 minutes; use the shorter cooking time if you want the nopalitos to retain some of their thick fluid to act as a thickener for stews, and use the longer time if you'll be sautéing the nopalitos or using them in a cold salad. When the nopalitos have cooked as long as you would like, pour everything into a colander set in the sink and let it drain. If you want to retain some of the thick fluid, rinse them with a spray of cold water for about 30 seconds, but for other uses, rinse them for about a minute, stirring them to ensure that all sides get well rinsed. Let the rinsed nopalitos drain completely before using in recipes. Regrettably, the pads change from bright green to dull olive drab after cooking.

Prickly Pear Shrub

About 1½ cups

A shrub is a beverage from Colonial days. Also called "drinking vinegar," shrubs were made with many types of fruit, infused in apple cider vinegar. They offered Colonists the health benefits of vinegar along with the refreshment of a fruity, tangy beverage. Rice vinegar is less harsh than other types and makes a good complement to the prickly pears; the vinegar's acidity is also mellowed by the infusion process. When combined with sparkling water, this makes a lovely, reddish-pink beverage that is unusual and very refreshing.

6 to 8 ounces peeled prickly pear fruits, cut into ¼-inch slices

1½ cups unseasoned rice vinegar

1 cup plus 1 tablespoon sugar

In small, non-aluminum saucepan, combine cut-up prickly pear fruits and vinegar. Heat over medium heat until mixture is just simmering. Let cool slightly, then transfer to a clean 1-pint glass jar; cover and place in the refrigerator to infuse for 24 to 48 hours, shaking the jar occasionally. After the infusion period, strain through a wire-mesh strainer lined with doubled cheesecloth; let it drip for 15 minutes, then discard contents of strainer. Combine strained liquid and sugar in medium non-aluminum saucepan. Heat to boiling over medium-high heat, stirring constantly until sugar dissolves. Boil gently for 5 minutes. Cool and pour into a clean bottle; store in the refrigerator, where it will keep for several weeks. To serve, pour club soda nearly to the top of an ice-filled glass; add a tablespoon of the shrub and stir to mix.

Prickly Margarita

2 servings

Here's a wild twist on a classic cocktail . . . colorful and delicious.

Optional: lime wedge and bar salt for rim of glass

¾ cup prickly pear juice

⅓ cup tequila

¼ cup frozen limeade concentrate, thawed enough to measure

2 tablespoons triple sec liqueur

1 tablespoon sugar, or to taste

¾ cup crushed ice

If you like salty margaritas, run the lime wedge around the edges of two margarita glasses, then dip in salt; set aside. To prepare the margarita, combine prickly pear juice, tequila, limeade concentrate, triple sec and sugar in blender; pulse several times to blend. Taste, and adjust sweetness to taste if necessary. Add crushed ice to blender; pulse several times, then pour into margarita glasses and serve immediately.

Prickly Pear Jelly

2 half-pints

1½ cups prickly pear juice
1 tablespoon lemon juice
One-third of a 1.75-ounce box powdered pectin
¼ teaspoon butter, optional (helps reduce foaming)
1½ cups sugar

Prepare and process as directed in Jelly Instructions (using pectin), pgs. 176–177.

Prickly Pear Vinaigrette

1 cup dressing

This vivid-red dressing is absolutely outstanding on a salad of tender greens that is topped with some crumbled blue cheese and a few chopped walnuts.

½ cup seasoned rice vinegar
½ teaspoon mixed pickling spice
3 ounces peeled prickly pear fruits, cut into ¼-inch slices
⅓ cup extra virgin olive oil
1 teaspoon Dijon mustard
½ teaspoon mixed dried herb blend
1 small garlic clove, pressed or finely minced
Salt and freshly ground pepper to taste

In small, non-aluminum saucepan, combine vinegar and pickling spice. Heat to boiling over high heat; remove from heat and let steep for 10 minutes. Return to stove, and heat just to boiling over medium-high heat. Add prickly pear slices. Adjust heat so mixture is simmering gently, then cook for 10 minutes, mashing after a few minutes. Let cool slightly, then pour into a small wire-mesh strainer set over a 2-cup measure. Let drip for 5 minutes; discard fruit pulp and spices from the strainer. Set liquid aside until completely cool.

In a clean pint jar, combine cooled liquid with olive oil, mustard, herbs and garlic; cover tightly and shake very well to blend. Taste, and add salt and pepper to your preference. Store in the refrigerator in a tightly capped jar; it will keep for several months. Before using, shake well to blend.

Chocolate-Prickly Pear Fudge

32 pieces

Prickly pear and chocolate pair nicely together in this rich, dark fudge.

1½ cups white sugar
½ cup (packed) dark brown sugar
½ cup prickly pear purée
½ cup heavy cream
2 tablespoons light corn syrup
⅛ teaspoon salt
2 ounces unsweetened baking chocolate
3 tablespoons butter, plus additional for greasing pan
½ teaspoon vanilla extract
½ cup chopped walnuts or other nuts, optional

In a heavy-bottomed, deep saucepan or pot, combine white and brown sugars, prickly pear purée, cream, corn syrup, salt and chocolate. Cook over medium heat, stirring constantly with a wooden spoon, until chocolate melts and sugars dissolve; mixture will no longer look cloudy. Continue cooking, stirring almost constantly, until mixture reaches the soft-ball stage (see "Fudge Tips" below for more information); adjust heat as necessary so mixture boils fairly vigorously but does not foam up out of the saucepan. Remove from heat; drop the 3 tablespoons butter, cut into several chunks, into the pot without stirring. Let stand until mixture cools to lukewarm; this will take about 45 minutes. While the mixture cools, butter the inside of a standard-sized loaf pan; set aside until needed.

When mixture has cooled to lukewarm, add vanilla. Stir vigorously with a wooden spoon until mixture loses its glossy sheen and begins to thicken, 7 to 10 minutes. Scrape into the prepared loaf pan; smooth the top with a rubber spatula. Sprinkle with nuts, pressing them gently into the surface with the spatula. Set aside to cool completely, then cut into 32 squares. Store at room temperature in a tightly sealed container for up to a week.

Fudge Tips
- *When heated above boiling, sugar tends to form crystals; the small amount of corn syrup used here helps prevent crystallization.*
- *The soft-ball stage happens at 24°F above the boiling point of water. For a no-thermometer method of testing, drop a small bit of the fudge into a bowl of cold water; when it is at the soft-ball stage, it will form a soft, flexible ball that you can push around with your fingertip. If you prefer to use a candy thermometer, measure the temperature of boiling water in your kitchen before preparing the fudge, then add 24 to the reading and cook the fudge to that number.*
- *Watch the fudge mixture as it's boiling; if it starts to rise rapidly and threatens to boil over, quickly remove the pan from the heat.*

Pork Posole with Nopalitos

4 or 5 servings

In this variation on a classic southwestern dish, nopales help thicken this hearty stew.

2½ pounds bone-in pork shoulder roast

Salt and freshly ground black pepper

2 teaspoons vegetable oil

1 medium yellow onion, cut into 8 chunks

4 cloves garlic, halved

1 tablespoon dried ground ancho chile powder (see tip on pg. 15)

2 teaspoons paprika, preferably smoked Spanish

1 quart chicken broth

1 can (15.5 ounces) white hominy, drained and rinsed

2 small prickly pear pads (about 9 ounces total), cleaned, cut into ½-inch squares, boiled for 5 minutes and rinsed as described on pg. 117

2 teaspoons chopped fresh oregano, or 1 teaspoon dried

Garnishes of your choice (any or all): Diced onions, diced avocados, sliced radishes, lime wedges, crumbled queso fresco cheese, chopped cilantro

Cut pork into 2-inch chunks, working around and freeing the bone; season meat with salt and pepper. Heat oil in Dutch oven over medium-high heat. Add half of the pork chunks, and brown well on all sides. Use tongs to transfer to a bowl; repeat with remaining pork.

When all pork has been browned, pour off all but a medium film of oil. Add onion and garlic; cook over medium heat, stirring occasionally, for about 5 minutes. Add chile and paprika; cook, stirring constantly, for about 30 seconds. Add broth, stirring to loosen any browned bits. Return pork and any juices to Dutch oven; also add the bone from the roast. Heat just to boiling over high heat, then reduce heat and simmer for 2 to 2½ hours, or until pork is tender. Use tongs to transfer pork to a clean dish; set aside until cool enough to handle. Strain cooking liquid from Dutch oven through wire-mesh strainer into a large bowl; discard solids from strainer. Skim fat from cooking liquid (or use a gravy separator); return liquid to Dutch oven.

When pork is cool enough to handle, use your fingers to pull away and discard any fat, gristle or bone; break the pork into bite-sized chunks and return to Dutch oven. Add hominy, drained prickly pear pieces and oregano; add up to a cup of additional water if mixture is too thick, or if you wish a more brothy posole. Heat just to boiling over medium heat; reduce heat and cook at a very gentle boil for about 15 minutes. Serve in wide, shallow soup plates, with garnishes on the side for each diner to add as they choose.

Nopalitos with Bacon and Pine Nuts

4 servings

This is a wonderful combination, and makes a nice side dish to serve with poultry.

2 slices bacon, diced

2 tablespoons pine nuts

¼ cup diced white onion (¼-inch dice)

1 pound prickly pear pads (4 or 5 medium-sized pads), cleaned, cut crosswise into ¼-inch-wide strips, boiled for 10 minutes and rinsed as described on pg. 117

1 tablespoon apple cider vinegar

2 teaspoons sugar

In medium skillet, cook bacon over medium heat until just crisp, stirring frequently. Add pine nuts; cook for about 2 minutes longer, stirring frequently. With slotted spoon, transfer bacon and pine nuts to a small bowl; set aside. Add onion to drippings remaining in skillet; sauté for about 2 minutes. Add nopalito strips; cook for about 2 minutes longer, stirring several times. Return bacon and pine nuts to skillet. Add vinegar and sugar and cook, stirring frequently, for about a minute longer. Serve immediately.

Grilled Nopales

4 appetizer servings per pad

Here's an interesting appetizer that's a good way to introduce people to prickly pear pads. Set out a jar of toothpicks, and bring the whole grilled pad to the table; dice it up and let diners help themselves.

Prickly pear pad(s), cleaned as described on pg. 117 but *not boiled or cut up*

Prepared Caesar dressing or Italian vinaigrette, as needed

Prepare a grill for medium heat. Place a cleaned, rinsed pad on a cutting board, with the base facing away from you. Cut the pad lengthwise (from the tip towards the base), leaving about 1 inch of the base uncut. Now make similar cuts in a fan-shaped pattern, angling the cuts outward from the base so the pad looks somewhat like a hand with spread-out fingers; the cuts (or "fingers") should be about ¾ inch apart at the end of the pad. Place the fan-cut pad in a glass baking dish; repeat with any other pads you wish to prepare. Pour some dressing over the pads, turning them to coat; set aside to marinate for 10 to 15 minutes.

When you're ready to cook, pick up each pad by the uncut base, letting the excess dressing drip back into the dish. Grill until tender and nicely marked on both sides, about 8 minutes total, turning as needed. Serve immediately.

Nopalitos Salad

A traditional Mexican dish, often served at weddings or other festive occasions. As usual with such dishes, there are as many recipe variations as there are cooks. It can be served as a luncheon dish or snack, used as a garnish on tacos or tostadas, or served to accompany grilled meats, fish or poultry.

3 cups diced, cooked, rinsed and drained nopalitos, prepared according to the instructions on pg. 117 (for this dish, cut the pads into ½-inch squares and boil for 15 minutes before rinsing)

½ cup thinly sliced white onion (cut into quarters before slicing)

1 cup diced cherry tomatoes or grape tomatoes (measured after dicing)

½ cup quartered, thinly sliced radishes

¼ cup chopped cilantro

2 tablespoons olive oil

2 tablespoons lime juice

½ teaspoon salt

¼ teaspoon minced garlic

½ cup crumbled queso fresco cheese or feta cheese, optional

In mixing bowl, combine prepared nopalitos, onion, tomatoes, radishes and cilantro. In small jar, combine oil, lime juice, salt and garlic; cover tightly and shake to blend. Pour dressing over vegetables in mixing bowl; toss gently to coat. Cover and refrigerate until well chilled, 30 to 45 minutes; the salad can be prepared up to 3 hours in advance. Transfer mixture to a serving bowl. Sprinkle with cheese, if you like; serve immediately.

 For the salad above, you'll need just under a pound of fresh prickly pear pads (weighed before cleaning or cooking).

Other recipes in this book featuring prickly pear fruits:
Six Recipes Using Wild Fruit Juice or Syrup, pgs. 170–174
Wild Berry or Fruit Syrup, pg. 175

Quick ideas for using prickly pears:
For a delightfully different pink lemonade, use half water, half prickly pear juice when mixing up frozen lemonade concentrate.

RASPBERRIES, DEWBERRIES and THIMBLEBERRIES (*Rubus* spp.)

Red raspberries (*Rubus idaeus*) are common throughout much of our area; they are a favorite of foragers because they are easy to identify, easy to pick and delicious. Whitebark raspberries or black raspberries (*R. leucodermis*) are much less common, but they are well worth seeking out; their fruits look like red raspberries but are black when ripe. Dewberries or dwarf raspberries (*R. pubescens*) are also uncommon; they are low-growing plants rather than upright shrubs like red or whitebark raspberries. All three of these plants have the classic three- or five-part compound leaves familiar to anyone who's see a raspberry plant.

Thimbleberries are very soft and delicate, and get smashed if layered too deeply in the berry bucket. When picking them to bring home, transport them in flat containers, like those used by delis to hold a half pint of coleslaw.

In addition, we have two related shrubs that produce similar fruits but have non-compound leaves. Thimbleberries (*R. parviflorus*) grow as waist-high shrubs with large, maple-like leaves. Their fruits are similar to red raspberries, but wider, flatter and more delicate. Eating quality of thimbleberries varies from plant to plant; sample a few before harvesting in any quantity to be sure they are tasty. Look for fruits that are rich red and soft; pink fruits are underripe and hard, and are usually bitter. Boulder raspberry (*R. deliciosus*) is another large shrub with wide, flat fruits and leaves that somewhat resemble maple leaves. Unfortunately the fruit does not live up to the promise of its scientific name, and is generally seedy and bland; most foragers don't pick it.

All of the fruits listed here are compound drupes, with lots of small seeds. The seeds are noticeable, but not nearly as bothersome as blackberry seeds; however, some cooks prefer to strain them out when making jam or purée. To prepare purée or juice, measure the fruit and place in a non-aluminum pot. For purée, add ½ cup water per quart of fruit; for juice, add 1 cup water per quart of fruit. Gently crush the fruit with a potato masher to start the juices flowing. Heat to boiling, then reduce the heat; cover and simmer for about 10 minutes. **For seedless purée,** process the cooked fruit through a food mill, then discard the seeds; if you don't mind the seeds, the purée is ready after cooking. **For juice,** transfer the mixture to a strainer lined with doubled, dampened cheesecloth and let it drip for 30 minutes; if you're making jelly, don't squeeze the fruit or the jelly will be cloudy. After the clear liquid has dripped away, set it aside and squeeze the fruit into a different container; you can use this slightly cloudy juice as a beverage or for cooking, and add the leftover, squeezed fruit to applesauce, pie filling or other cooked fruits. Processed this way, a quart of red raspberries will yield about 1½ cups of purée, or about 2 cups juice; the yield will be slightly less for black raspberries, dewberries or thimbleberries.

Raspberries and dewberries can be dehydrated successfully (see pgs. 180–181), but thimbleberries are too fragile and would just break apart. All three can also be used to make seedy but tasty fruit leather (pg. 182). To avoid cumbersome ingredients lists, most of the recipes on the following pages simply call for raspberries. You may use red or black raspberries for any of them with no adjustments; if you use thimbleberries, you may wish to increase the sugar slightly, depending on the sweetness of the berries you've picked.

Raspberry Filling

½ teaspoon water

½ teaspoon cornstarch

5 ounces raspberries (about 1 cup)

1 tablespoon grated apple

1 tablespoon sugar

½ teaspoon lemon juice

In small bowl, blend together water and cornstarch; set aside. In small, heavy-bottomed saucepan, combine raspberries, apple, sugar and lemon juice. Crush fruit gently with a potato masher to start juices flowing. Heat to boiling over medium-high heat, then cook, stirring frequently, until mixture is no longer runny; this will take 9 to 11 minutes. Add cornstarch mixture, stirring constantly; cook for 1 to 2 minutes longer, or until thick. Cool before using.

Use this to prepare Easy Bear Claws (pg. 81), Fruit-Striped Cookie Fingers (pg. 126), or Fruit-Filled Muffins (pg. 155). Refrigerate extra filling, and use to top oatmeal or toast.

Raspberry Dip
About 2 cups

This is lovely for a brunch buffet, or as a tea-time snack. Have a pretty jar of toothpicks for the pineapples and pound cake. This recipe also works well with wild strawberries.

16 ounces cream cheese, softened (reduced-fat works fine)

½ cup raspberries (about 2½ ounces)

¼ cup sour cream (reduced-fat works fine)

2 tablespoons honey

1 teaspoon vanilla extract

¼ teaspoon finely grated orange zest (colored rind only, with none of the white pith; see "Zesting Citrus Fruits," pg. 35), optional

Dippers for serving (any or all): Pineapple chunks, pound cake cubes, vanilla wafers, pieces of chocolate bars, or assorted cookies

In food processor, combine all ingredients except dippers; process until smooth. Scrape into serving bowl. Cover and refrigerate for at least 2 hours before serving.

See companion *Wild Berries & Fruits Field Guide of the Rocky Mountain States* – pgs. 134, 138, 140, 254   **125**

Fruit-Striped Cookie Fingers

About 2 dozen cookies

A buttery, rich cookie base is topped with fruit filling in these attractive cookies.

For 5,000 feet; see adjustments for other altitudes

1³⁄₄ cups all-purpose flour,[2, 3] plus additional for rolling dough

¼ cup powdered sugar

⅛ teaspoon salt

½ cup (1 stick) cold butter, cut into small pieces

4 ounces cream cheese, cut into 1-inch chunks

1 egg yolk

1 tablespoon plus 1 teaspoon orange juice[1, 2, 3]

1 teaspoon vanilla extract

½ cup Raspberry Filling (pg. 125), or other wild fruit filling
(see "Filling options" below)

In food processor, combine measured flour, the powdered sugar and salt; pulse a few times. Add butter and cream cheese; pulse until coarse and crumbly. In small bowl, stir together the egg yolk, orange juice and vanilla. Add to flour mixture; pulse a few times, until mixture just begins to come together (do not over-process, or the cookies will be tough). Transfer dough to a gallon-sized plastic food storage bag. Press with your hands (from the outside of the bag) until dough comes together. Flatten dough into a disk; refrigerate at least 1 hour, or up to 1 day.

When ready to bake, heat oven to 390°F.[1, 3] Divide dough into 2 parts; refrigerate one while you roll out the other. On lightly floured worksurface, roll dough about ¼ inch thick, keeping the rolled-out dough as square as possible. Trim one edge in a straight line, then use a small ruler to mark 1-inch divisions. Cut the dough into 1-inch-wide strips, cutting on the marks. Lay a chopstick lengthwise in the center of one strip, and press it down into the dough, rolling it back and forth slightly to make a U-shaped channel about ½ inch wide in the center of the strip. Transfer the strip to an ungreased baking sheet. Repeat with remaining strips, keeping them ½ inch apart on the baking sheet. Spoon filling mixture along the channels, mounding it slightly. Bake until golden brown and firm, 22 to 28 minutes. Remove baking sheets from oven, and immediately use a small knife to cut each strip into 1-inch pieces. Transfer to a wire rack to cool completely. Store at room temperature for up to 5 days; refrigerate or freeze for longer storage.

Filling options: This recipe works with any of the following fillings: Apple (pg. 10), Apricot or Peach (pg. 12), Blackberry (pg. 23), Green Gooseberry (pg. 59), Ground Cherry (pg. 68), Huckleberry (pg. 91), Mulberry (pg. 102), Pear (pg.106), Plum (pg. 115), Raspberry (pg. 125), Serviceberry (pg. 138) or Strawberry (pg. 152).

1. Below 5,000 feet: Use 1 tablespoon orange juice. Heat oven to 375°F.

2. At 7,500 feet: Add an additional tablespoon of flour. Use 1½ tablespoons of orange juice, or as needed.

3. At 10,000 feet: Add an additional 1½ tablespoons of flour. Use 1 tablespoon plus 2 teaspoons of orange juice, or as needed. Heat oven to 400°F.

Raspberry Shortcakes

A classic dessert that really shows off the flavor of fresh-picked raspberries.

Shortcakes:

2 cups all-purpose flour, plus additional for rolling dough

3 tablespoons sugar

1 tablespoon baking powder

½ teaspoon salt

½ cup (1 stick) cold unsalted butter, cut into 8 pieces

⅔ cup whole milk, approximate

Filling:

2 cups fresh raspberries (about 10 ounces)

½ cup sugar, or to taste

1 cup whipping cream

½ teaspoon vanilla extract

Prepare the shortcakes: Heat oven to 425°F, and line a baking sheet with kitchen parchment. In food processor, combine 2 cups flour, the sugar, baking powder and salt; pulse a few times to combine. Add cut-up butter; pulse until mixture resembles coarse meal but still has a few pea-sized pieces of butter. With motor running, add milk in a thin stream through the feed tube; use just enough milk so the mixture comes together (don't add too much milk or over-process the dough, or the shortcakes will be tough).

On lightly floured worksurface, knead dough a few times to form a ball; mixture will be sticky at first, but will become less sticky as it picks up flour from the worksurface. Use a rolling pin to roll about ¾ inch thick. Cut 8 circles, using a 3-inch circular cutter (re-roll scraps once if necessary). Transfer to prepared baking sheet. Bake until dough rises and is golden brown, 10 to 15 minutes. Transfer to wire rack while you prepare the filling.

Prepare the filling: Place raspberries in mixing bowl; sprinkle with sugar, tossing gently to coat. Set aside to marinate for a few minutes. In another mixing bowl, beat whipping cream and vanilla with electric mixer until stiff peaks form.

To assemble the shortcakes, use a knife to split each shortcake horizontally. Place one half on an individual dessert plate. Top with about ¼ cup of the raspberries; place second half of shortcake on top. Dollop whipped cream over the top shortcake half; serve immediately.

Rustic Black Raspberry Tart

5 or 6 servings

This tart is a lovely presentation that is unusual enough to look like a really special treat, but it's super-easy to make. Top with some rich vanilla ice cream for a heavenly dessert.

2½ to 3 cups whitebark raspberries (12 to 15 ounces)

½ cup sugar

3 tablespoons minute tapioca

1 tablespoon lemon juice

Ready-to-use pastry for single-crust pie

2 teaspoons butter, cut into small pieces

Heat oven to 375°F; line a rimmed baking sheet with kitchen parchment. In mixing bowl, combine raspberries, sugar, tapioca and lemon juice; stir gently. Set aside for 15 minutes. After 15 minutes, place pastry on prepared baking sheet. Pile raspberry mixture in the center, staying 1½ inches away from the edges. Working quickly, fold pastry over the edge of the filling, leaving the center exposed; the shape will be irregular, but the filling should be surrounded. Pinch overlapping areas together slightly to seal. Dot exposed filling with butter. Bake until crust is brown and filling is bubbling, 30 to 40 minutes. Let cool slightly before cutting; best served warm, the day it is made.

Ready-to-Use Pie Crust

Many recipes in this book call for "ready-to-use pastry for single- (or double-) crust pie." These days, many cooks choose to purchase ready-made pie crusts from the refrigerator case. These are already rolled out into single-crust form; simply thaw or warm them according to package directions, and use as directed. If you make your own pie crust, roll out the dough (or half the dough at once, if you've made enough for a two-crust pie) on a lightly floured worksurface, and proceed as directed.

Raspberry Jelly

4 half-pints

2¾ cups raspberry juice

Two-thirds of a 1.75-ounce box powdered pectin

½ teaspoon butter, optional (helps reduce foaming)

3⅔ cups sugar

Prepare and process as directed in Jelly Instructions (using pectin), pgs. 176–177.

Raspberry-Balsamic Dressing

About ¾ cup

Serve this with salad made from tender greens; it's especially good if a little feta cheese is added to the salad. You could also drizzle this over cooked, sliced chicken breast that is atop a bed of spinach; garnish with sliced almonds and a few slivers of red onion.

1 cup raspberries (about 5 ounces)

5 tablespoons olive oil

2 tablespoons balsamic vinegar

1 teaspoon Dijon mustard

1 teaspoon honey

½ teaspoon salt

⅛ teaspoon white pepper

1 clove garlic, pressed or very finely minced

Purée raspberries in mini food processor or blender. Scrape into a wire-mesh strainer set over a bowl. Stir with a rubber spatula to press the purée through; discard seeds. Transfer strained purée to a half-pint jar. Add remaining ingredients. Cover tightly and shake well to blend. This will keep in the refrigerator for up to 3 weeks.

Other recipes in this book featuring raspberries, dewberries and thimbleberries:
Wild Berry Vinegar, pg. 22
Fruit Terrine with Elderberry Gel, pg. 48
Rice Pudding with Wild Berries, pg. 103
Fruits of the Forest Pie, pg. 168
Brambleberry Cream Sauce, pg. 169
Six Recipes Using Wild Fruit Juice or Syrup, pgs. 170–174
Wild Berry or Fruit Syrup, pg. 175
Dehydrating Wild Berries and Fruits, pgs. 180–181
Wild Berry or Fruit Leather, pg. 182
As a substitute in Blackberry-Apple Crisp, pg. 21
As a substitute in Grilled Bananas with Buffaloberry Sauce, pg. 27
As a substitute in Refrigerator Cookies with Dried Goji Berries, pg. 51
As a variation in Strawberry Smoothie, pg. 156

Quick ideas for using raspberries, dewberries and thimbleberries:
Scatter a handful on top of a mixed salad, especially one made with tender young greens. Serve with a blue cheese dressing or a mild vinaigrette.
Use in any recipe you've got that calls for raspberries.

ROSE HIPS (*Rosa* spp.)

Roses are found just about everywhere in the wild, and rose hips are easy to gather. Harvest hips when they are deeply colored and slightly soft; some foragers wait until after the first frost. Rose hips, especially the larger varieties, can be nibbled raw, but are more commonly dried to make tea, or stewed to make jam, jelly and other dishes. The fruits are loaded with vitamin C and other nutrients. The tiny seeds inside are rich in vitamin E (Steve Brill, *Identifying and Harvesting Edible and Medicinal Plants*), but they are also very bitter and may irritate the throat and stomach. If you're sampling a fresh hip, avoid eating the seeds or the dried blossom remnants.

Rose hips are so rich in vitamin C that they are used in the manufacture of some vitamin C capsules.

Most people remove the bitter seeds and surrounding hairs from rose hips before drying. To start, cut one hip in half from top to bottom; if you can easily scrape out the seeds, go ahead and process all remaining hips in this fashion, also removing the blossom remnants at the bottom. If the pulp is too sticky to remove the seeds easily, let the whole hips dry at room temperature for a few days, then try again. Don't let them get too dry, or the seeds will be even more difficult to remove. Dry split or whole hips (with the blossom remnants removed) at room temperature on a screen laid over a baking sheet, turning daily; or, dry in food dehydrator or 150°F oven (see pgs. 180–181 for more information on dehydrating). Drying time depends on the size of the hips; split hips dry more quickly than whole hips. Store dried hips in tightly sealed glass jars in a dark location.

To make rose hip purée or juice, remove the stems and blossom ends, then measure the hips and place in a non-aluminum pot. For purée, add 1 cup water per quart of hips; for juice, add 3 cups water per quart of hips. (For a nice variation, use apple juice instead of water.) Heat to boiling, then reduce the heat; cover and simmer until soft, about 15 minutes, gently crushing the hips with a potato masher near the end of cooking.

For purée, process the cooked hips through a cone-shaped colander, or rub through a fine wire-mesh strainer; discard the seeds and skin. (I don't use a food mill with rose hips, because too many of the bitter seeds get into the purée.) **For juice,** transfer the mixture to a strainer lined with doubled, dampened cheesecloth and let it drip for 30 minutes; don't squeeze the fruit because some bitter seeds may get through the cheesecloth. Processed this way, a quart of rose hips will yield about 2 cups of lovely, pinkish-red purée, or about 2½ cups pinkish-red juice.

Rose Hip Tea
Per serving

Combine 1 tablespoon dried rose hips, or 2 tablespoons fresh rose hips, in a saucepan with 1 cup of cold water. Heat to boiling, then remove from heat, cover and let steep for 10 to 15 minutes. Strain and sweeten to taste with sugar, honey or maple syrup; serve with a lemon wedge if you like.

Rose Hip-Apple Jelly (no added pectin)   3 half-pints

Tart apples add both flavor and pectin to this jelly.

½ pound fresh rose hips, blossom ends removed before weighing
½ pound Granny Smith apples, cored and chopped
1 lemon
2 cups sugar, approximate

Please read "Jelly Instructions for Fruits with Natural Pectin" on pgs. 177–178 to learn about testing for doneness. In non-aluminum saucepan, combine rose hips and chopped apples. Add water to cover completely. Cut the lemon into quarters, and remove the rind (including the white pith) and seeds. Add lemon flesh to pan with rose hips. Heat to boiling over high heat. Reduce heat so mixture is simmering, then cover and simmer until all fruit is very soft, about 30 minutes. Mash with a potato masher.

Line a wire-mesh strainer with two thicknesses of damp cheesecloth; place over a non-aluminum pot. Spoon fruit mixture into cheesecloth; let drip for 2 hours without squeezing or stirring. At the end of the 2 hours, prepare 3 half-pint canning jars, bands and new lids as directed on pg. 183.

Discard pulp in cheesecloth. Measure the juice; you should have about 2½ cups. Place measured juice in a non-aluminum pot that holds 3 or 4 quarts. For each cup of juice, measure ⅞ cup of sugar. Heat juice to boiling over medium-high heat. Add sugar and cook, stirring constantly, until sugar dissolves. Increase heat to high and cook, skimming off any foam and stirring frequently, until jelly passes one or more of the doneness tests on pg. 177–178; this typically takes 10 to 15 minutes.

Once the jelly is done, skim any foam off the surface and pour it, while still hot, into the prepared canning jars; seal with prepared lids and bands. Process in a boiling-water bath for 15 minutes at 5,000 feet, or at the recommended time for your elevation (see pg. 183); if you prefer, you can store the jelly in the refrigerator where it will keep for a month or longer.

Substitution: Use 2 cups of chopped wild apples (peeled, cored and chopped before measuring) in place of the purchased Granny Smith apples.

Marlin with Rose Hip Glaze

4 servings

This sweet-tangy glaze would also be good with pork loin chops or tenderloin.

½ cup rose hip purée
3 tablespoons (packed) brown sugar
2 tablespoons Asian fish sauce
1 teaspoon butter
½ teaspoon finely minced fresh gingerroot
1 tablespoon freshly squeezed lime juice
4 pieces marlin, ¾ inch thick (6 to 8 ounces each)
1 tablespoon olive oil

In small non-aluminum saucepan, stir together purée, brown sugar, fish sauce, butter and gingerroot. Cook over medium heat, stirring frequently, until thickened, about 10 minutes. Transfer half of the sauce to a small bowl; stir in lime juice and set aside.

Heat oven to 400°F. Rinse fish; pat dry with paper towels. In heavy, oven-safe skillet, heat olive oil over medium-high heat until shimmering. Add fish in a single layer; cook for 2 minutes, then turn with spatula. Spread the mixture remaining in the saucepan evenly over each fish piece. Transfer skillet to oven; cook until the center is just opaque, 6 to 8 minutes. Transfer to serving plate. Serve with remaining sauce mixture.

Fish sauce is found in the Asian section of large supermarkets, or at specialty markets. I prefer Three Crabs brand from Vietnam; some excellent sauces also come from Thailand. The fish sauce adds a lot of flavor depth, but if you don't have any, substitute Japanese soy sauce such as Kikkoman.

Rose Hip Jelly (pectin added)

4 half-pints

2½ cups rose hip juice
¼ cup lemon juice
Half of a 1.75-ounce box powdered pectin
½ teaspoon butter, optional (helps reduce foaming)
2½ cups sugar

Prepare and process as directed in Jelly Instructions (using pectin), pgs. 176–177.

Rose Hip Soup

This dish is common in the Scandinavian countries, where it is often served to soothe sore throats and colds. It can be served hot or cold; when served cold, it is sometimes diluted with water or apple juice and served as a beverage.

3 cups rose hip juice

2 tablespoons honey, or to taste

2 tablespoons freshly squeezed lemon juice, or to taste

¼ cup ground almonds

1 tablespoon potato starch, or 2 teaspoons cornstarch

1 tablespoon cold water

¼ cup sour cream

Fresh mint sprigs as a garnish

In a non-aluminum saucepan, combine rose hip juice, honey and lemon juice. Heat to boiling, then reduce heat and add ground almonds; simmer for about 5 minutes. In small bowl, blend potato starch and water, then whisk into simmering soup. Cook, whisking constantly, until mixture bubbles and thickens. Taste for seasoning, and adjust with more honey or lemon juice if you like. Divide mixture into 4 bowls. Add a tablespoon of sour cream to each serving; garnish with mint sprig.

Other recipes in this book featuring rose hips:
Six Recipes Using Wild Fruit Juice or Syrup, pgs. 170–174
Wild Berry or Fruit Syrup, pg. 175

Quick ideas for using rose hips:
Stir a few tablespoons of the purée into applesauce.
Mix 1 part rose hip juice with 2 parts apple juice; sweeten to taste, and serve as a breakfast drink.
Add a few tablespoons purée to the mixture when making a smoothie.
Use a mix of one part rose hip juice to three parts water when brewing black or green tea.

RUSSIAN OLIVES (*Elaeagnus angustifolia*)

Fruits from the Russian olive tree are not used very often; it's more of a curiosity than a foraging staple. One advantage is that the trees produce abundant fruit, so it's quite easy to harvest enough to experiment with. Fruits are sweet and can be eaten raw or cooked, although the dry, mealy nature makes them fairly unpalatable when raw.

When harvesting Russian olives, choose those that are yellow or cream-colored; underripe green fruits are very astringent. The fruits have a fairly large pit, which is very hard and inedible; it can be removed by cooking the fruits, then straining and puréeing the flesh.

Russian olive flesh is dry and mealy, but it has a sweet flavor and aroma that is reminiscent of apples.

To make Russian olive purée, place fruits in a saucepan, with enough water to not quite cover. Heat to boiling; reduce heat, cover, and simmer for 10 minutes to soften the fruit. Cool slightly, then process the fruits through a food mill. The pits, which are long and narrow with pointed ends, are thick enough to prevent all of the pulp from going through the mill. Once you've gotten as much flesh through the food mill as possible, scrape out the seedy pulp remaining in the mill and place it in a mixing bowl. Add just enough water to loosen the mixture. Now place this into a colander or some other device that has holes small enough to prevent the seeds from going through; I use the top half of a vegetable steamer saucepan. Stir the mixture with a rubber spatula (or use your hands), pressing the soft flesh through the holes; add a little more water if necessary, and keep at it until you've gotten as much flesh separated as possible. Processed in this fashion, 2 cups of whole fruits (about 8 ounces) will yield about 1 cup of purée. The purée has a fairly solid, almost dry texture, and is pale greenish-gray.

Note: A related shrub, silverberry (*E. commutata*) has very similar fruits. I've never had a chance to work with them, but from what I've heard they could be used in the same way as Russian olive fruits.

Coarse Russian Olive Mustard

About 1¼ cups

Homemade mustard is easy to make, and Russian olive purée makes an interesting base. It provides a good texture, and a hint of sweetness.

½ cup Russian olive purée

⅓ cup white wine vinegar

¼ cup yellow mustard seeds

3 tablespoons brown mustard seeds

1 tablespoon dry sherry

2 teaspoons honey

1 teaspoon salt

¼ teaspoon ground turmeric

¼ teaspoon white pepper, optional (adds heat)

Pinch of ground nutmeg

Combine all ingredients in a glass or ceramic mixing bowl; stir until well blended. Cover tightly and refrigerate overnight.

The next day, transfer the mustard to a blender; add a little water if it is too firm. Process until the mustard is well-blended but still somewhat coarse; add additional water if needed. Taste and adjust seasonings as you like; you may want it sweeter, hotter or more salty. Store in a tightly covered jar in the refrigerator; it will keep for about a month. If it becomes stiff after a while, stir in a little water.

Whole-Grain Pancakes with Russian Olive
10 to 12 pancakes

These good-for-you pancakes are very hearty and filling—and delicious as well!

1 cup white whole wheat flour, or as needed (see note below)

3 tablespoons cornmeal

2 tablespoons ground flaxseed

1 teaspoon baking powder

½ teaspoon baking soda

¼ teaspoon salt

3 tablespoons unsalted roasted sunflower nuts

1 cup buttermilk, or as needed

2 tablespoons (packed) brown sugar

1 tablespoon vegetable oil, plus additional as needed for frying

1 large egg

A few drops almond extract, optional

½ cup Russian olive purée

½ cup room-temperature cooked oatmeal (steel-cut or regular)

Maple syrup and butter for serving, or other toppings of your choice

Heat oven to 200°F. In large mixing bowl, combine 1 cup flour, the cornmeal, ground flaxseed, baking powder, baking soda and salt; stir with a whisk until well blended. Use a wooden spoon to stir in the sunflower nuts. In small bowl, whisk together 1 cup buttermilk, the brown sugar, oil, egg, and almond extract, if using. Add Russian olive purée and oatmeal; stir well. Add the buttermilk mixture to the flour mixture and stir with the wooden spoon gently until just mixed. Depending on the wetness of the Russian olive purée, the batter may be too thick or too thin (see tip on pg. 52); adjust consistency if necessary by adding a little more flour or buttermilk.

Heat a griddle over medium heat until a drop of water sizzles and dances. Film with vegetable oil. Spoon batter onto hot griddle in ¼-cup portions. Cook until edges dry out and bubbles form on top. Carefully flip and cook until browned on second side and cooked through. Transfer cooked pancakes to a plate and place in the oven. Cook remaining pancakes, re-oiling griddle as necessary and transferring finished pancakes to oven as you go. Serve hot, with maple syrup and butter.

 White whole wheat flour is made from wheat that is naturally lighter in color than the type that is used to make regular whole wheat flour. It has all the fiber and nutrition of regular whole wheat flour but produces baked goods (and pancakes!) that are lighter in color and texture than those made with regular whole wheat flour.

Oatmeal Muffins with Russian Olive

6 muffins

This recipe brings out the natural apple-like sweetness of the Russian olive purée.

For 5,000 feet; see adjustments for other altitudes

½ cup Russian olive purée

1 large egg[3]

¼ cup orange juice[2]

¼ cup sugar

2 tablespoons vegetable oil

½ cup quick-cooking rolled oats (not instant)[3]

½ cup plus 1 tablespoon all-purpose flour[1, 2, 3]

1½ teaspoons baking powder[2, 3]

½ teaspoon cinnamon

¼ teaspoon baking soda

½ cup dried cranberries (craisins)

Heat oven to 375°F.[2, 3] Line 6-cup muffin tin with paper liners; set aside. In mixing bowl, combine Russian olive purée and egg; beat together with a fork. Add orange juice, sugar and vegetable oil; beat until well combined. Stir in oatmeal. Place a wire-mesh strainer over the bowl; add flour, baking powder, cinnamon and baking soda. Shake strainer to sift into the bowl; stir with a wooden spoon just until moistened. Add dried cranberries and stir gently. Divide mixture evenly into prepared muffin cups. Bake until a wooden pick inserted into the center of a muffin comes out clean, 20 to 25 minutes.[2, 3] Remove muffin tin from oven and let cool for 15 minutes before removing muffins.

---

1. **Below 5,000 feet:** Use ½ cup flour.

2. **At 7,500 feet:** Use ¼ cup plus 2 teaspoons orange juice. Use ½ cup plus 2 tablespoons flour. Use 1 teaspoon baking powder. Heat oven to 390°F. Bake for 18 to 23 minutes.

3. **At 10,000 feet:** Use 1 extra-large egg. Use ⅓ cup rolled oats. Use ½ cup plus 1 tablespoon flour. Use ¾ teaspoon baking powder. Heat oven to 390°F. Bake for 15 to 20 minutes.

SERVICEBERRIES (*Amelanchier* spp.)

Found throughout our area, serviceberries are surprisingly unfamiliar to many people. But the fruits are not showy, so they're easy to miss unless you're looking for them.

Technically a pome, serviceberries have a small crown on the bottom (like an apple), and small, soft seeds. The seeds can be eaten with no trouble, and I never bother taking them out, but some cooks prefer to strain cooked fruits to remove the seeds. I typically use the fruits whole, in much the same way that I use blueberries. They're also a fantastic trail nibble; the sight of a laden serviceberry tree brings a smile to me when I'm hiking in the summer. They're sweet, with a subtle almond-like flavor, and they provide much-needed refreshment and energy on a hot July day.

Serviceberries were a staple in the diets of American Indians in our area, and were mentioned by explorers Meriwether Lewis and William Clark in the diaries of their western travels.

Even though many of the fruits are up out of reach, it's pretty easy to collect a good quantity of serviceberries if you find an area with several trees. Birds and other wildlife depend on serviceberries for food, so don't try too hard to get at the fruits you can't reach; leave them for the waxwings, robins and grosbeaks. (I have fond memories of picking serviceberries from a small tree that was heavy with them, and dodging the cedar waxwings that were gorging themselves on fruit just a few feet from me.)

Serviceberries can be used whole for baking, or turned into jam; they can also be dehydrated (pgs. 180–181) for use in baked goods or trail mix, or used to make fruit leather (pg. 182). They are easy to freeze; wash the fruits and pat them dry, then spread on a baking sheet in a single layer. Freeze overnight, then transfer to plastic containers and seal tightly.

Serviceberry Filling
About ½ cup; easily increased

1 teaspoon water

½ teaspoon cornstarch

5½ ounces fresh or previously frozen serviceberries (about 1¼ cups)

¼ cup sugar

1 tablespoon grated apple

In small bowl, blend together water and cornstarch; set aside. In small, heavy-bottomed saucepan, combine serviceberries, sugar and apple. Crush fruit gently with a potato masher to start juices flowing. Heat to boiling over medium-high heat, then cook, stirring frequently and mashing once more, until mixture is no longer runny; this will take 7 to 9 minutes. Add cornstarch mixture, stirring constantly; cook for about 1½ minutes longer, or until thick. Cool before using.

Use this to prepare Easy Bear Claws (pg. 81), Fruit-Striped Cookie Fingers (pg. 126), or Fruit-Filled Muffins (pg. 155). Refrigerate extra filling, and use to top oatmeal or toast.

Serviceberry Pudding Cake

6 to 8 servings

This is equally appropriate for breakfast or dessert. It's fabulous when still warm from the oven, but it's also good served at room temperature.

For 5,000 feet; see adjustments for other altitudes

½ cup white sugar

¼ cup cold water[1, 2, 3]

2 tablespoons lemon juice

1½ teaspoons cornstarch

2 cups fresh or still-frozen serviceberries (about 8 ounces; rinse briefly under cold water and pat dry if still frozen)

1 cup plus 2 tablespoons all-purpose flour[1, 2, 3]

⅓ cup (packed) golden brown sugar[1, 3]

1½ teaspoons baking powder[1, 2, 3]

1 teaspoon salt

1 large egg[3]

½ cup whole milk or buttermilk[2, 3]

6 tablespoons unsalted butter, melted and cooled slightly

1 teaspoon vanilla extract

Heat oven to 385°F.[1, 2, 3] Spray an 8x8-inch baking dish with nonstick spray; set aside. In medium non-aluminum saucepan, stir together white sugar, water, lemon juice and cornstarch. Heat over medium heat, stirring constantly, until sugar dissolves, about 3 minutes. Add serviceberries; simmer for about a minute, stirring occasionally. Remove from heat.

In medium bowl, stir together flour, brown sugar, baking powder and salt. In large mixing bowl, combine egg, milk, butter and vanilla; beat with whisk until smooth. Add flour mixture; whisk until smooth. Scrape mixture into prepared baking dish, spreading evenly. Pour serviceberry mixture evenly over the top. Bake until a table knife inserted into the center comes out clean, about 30 minutes. Set pan on rack to cool for 5 or 10 minutes before serving. Cake can be cooled, then covered with foil and kept at room temperature for up to 2 days.

Substitutions: Blueberries or huckleberries can be substituted for the serviceberries.

1. **Below 5,000 feet:** Use 3 tablespoons water. Use 1 cup flour. Use ½ cup brown sugar. Use 2 teaspoons baking powder. Heat oven to 375°F.

2. **At 7,500 feet:** Use ⅓ cup water. Use 1¼ cups flour. Use 1¼ teaspoons baking powder. Use ⅔ cup whole milk or buttermilk. Heat oven to 400°F.

3. **At 10,000 feet:** Use ⅓ cup water. Use 1¼ cups flour. Use ¼ cup brown sugar. Use 1 teaspoon baking powder. Use extra-large egg. Use ⅔ cup whole milk or buttermilk. Heat oven to 400°F.

Serviceberry Freezer Jam

4 half-pints

This jam is easy to make because the fruit is not cooked; commercial pectin is cooked separately, then stirred into the fruit mixture.

1 quart serviceberries

2¾ cups sugar

**Two-thirds of a 1.75-ounce box powdered pectin
(see pg. 176 for information on dividing pectin)**

½ cup water

2 tablespoons lemon juice

Prepare 4 half-pint canning jars, bands and new lids as described on pg. 183, or have clean plastic freezer containers ready (see tip below). Chop fruit to medium consistency in food processor (don't over-process; jam should have small fruit chunks in it). Measure 1¾ cups chopped fruit; use any leftover fruit to top ice cream or cook in other recipes. Place measured fruit and the sugar in a large ceramic or Pyrex mixing bowl. Stir well; set aside for 10 minutes, stirring several times with a wooden spoon.

After fruit has rested for 10 minutes, prepare pectin. In small non-aluminum saucepan, combine pectin, water and lemon juice; stir well (mixture may be lumpy). Heat to a full, rolling boil over high heat, stirring constantly. Cook at a rolling boil for 1 minute, stirring constantly. Pour pectin mixture into fruit in bowl. Stir constantly with a wooden spoon until sugar is completely dissolved and no longer grainy, about 3 minutes; a few grains may remain, but the mixture should no longer look cloudy (or the jam will be cloudy).

Pour into prepared jars or containers, leaving ½ inch headspace; cover with clean lids. Let stand at room temperature for 24 hours; the jam should set (it may be softer than regular jam, especially at first; that's okay). If jam is not set, refrigerate for several days until set before using or freezing. Use within 3 weeks, or freeze until needed; thaw frozen jam in refrigerator.

 Special plastic containers, designed especially for freezing jelly and jam, are available with the canning supplies at the supermarket.

Serviceberry and Ricotta Brunch Ring   12 to 16 servings

This delicious cake gets extra moistness from ricotta cheese. The almonds add a nice texture, and point up the subtly nutty taste of the serviceberries. Leftovers freeze well.

For 5,000 feet; see adjustments for other altitudes

½ cup (1 stick) unsalted butter, softened

1 cup sugar

1 container (15 ounces) ricotta cheese (reduced-fat works fine)

½ cup whole or 2% milk

2 large eggs[2, 3]

1 teaspoon vanilla extract

2½ cups flour[2, 3]

2¼ teaspoons baking powder[1, 2, 3]

½ teaspoon salt

1½ cups fresh or previously frozen serviceberries (about 6½ ounces)

1 cup finely chopped slivered almonds (about 4½ ounces)

Powdered sugar for dusting, optional

Position rack in lower third of oven; heat to 365°F.[1, 3] Grease and flour a 12-cup bundt pan or an angel-food cake pan; set aside. In large mixing bowl, cream butter with electric mixer for about 1 minute. Add sugar; beat for another minute. Add ricotta cheese, milk, eggs and vanilla; beat on medium speed for 2 minutes, scraping bowl several times. Combine flour, baking powder and salt in sifter or wire-mesh strainer; sift or shake mixture into mixing bowl. Add serviceberries and almonds, and stir together with wooden spoon until well mixed.

Spoon mixture into prepared pan, smoothing the top. Bake until a wooden pick inserted into the center comes out clean, 50 to 60 minutes.[1, 3] Cool on a wire rack for 20 minutes, then remove from pan; put the prettiest side up. Dust top with powdered sugar, if you like. Cool until just warm before slicing, or cool completely and serve at room temperature.

---

1. Below 5,000 feet: Use 1 tablespoon baking powder. Position rack in middle of oven; heat to 350°F. Bake for 55 to 65 minutes.

2. At 7,500 feet: Add an additional tablespoon of flour. Use 1¾ teaspoons baking powder. Use 2 extra-large eggs.

3. At 10,000 feet: Add 2 additional tablespoons of flour. Use 1¼ teaspoons baking powder. Use 2 extra-large eggs. Position rack in middle of oven; heat to 375°F. Bake at 375°F for 15 minutes, then reduce temperature to 365°F and bake for 35 to 40 minutes longer or until done.

Serviceberry and Wild Rice Muffins

6 to 8 muffins

Wild rice is a natural with serviceberries in these hearty muffins.

For 5,000 feet; see adjustments for other altitudes

¾ cup plus 1 tablespoon all-purpose flour[1, 2, 3]

¼ cup sugar

1 teaspoon baking powder[2, 3]

¼ teaspoon salt

½ cup fresh or previously frozen serviceberries (about 2 ounces)

¼ cup whole or 2% milk[2]

2 tablespoons butter, melted and cooled slightly

1 large egg[3]

⅓ cup cooked wild rice (see tip below)

Heat oven to 365°F.[1, 2, 3] Line 6-cup muffin tin[2, 3] with paper liners; set aside. Place wire-mesh strainer over large mixing bowl. Add flour, sugar, baking powder and salt; shake into bowl to sift together. Place serviceberries in small bowl; spoon about 2 teaspoons of the flour mixture over them, stirring to coat.

In measuring cup, beat together milk, butter and egg. Pour milk mixture into flour mixture and fold together with rubber spatula. Add floured serviceberries and wild rice; fold together. Spoon into prepared muffin cups. Bake until lightly browned and a wooden pick inserted into the center of a muffin comes out clean, 25 to 30 minutes.[2, 3] Remove muffin tin from oven and let cool for 15 minutes before removing muffins.

---

1. **Below 5,000 feet:** Use ¾ cup flour. Heat oven to 350°F.

2. **At 7,500 feet:** Use ¾ cup plus 2 tablespoons flour. Use ¾ teaspoon baking powder. Use ¼ cup plus 2 teaspoons milk. Heat oven to 390°F. Use 12-cup muffin tin; line 7 cups with paper liners and add ¼ cup water to empty cups. Bake for 23 to 28 minutes.

3. **At 10,000 feet:** Use ¾ cup plus 1 tablespoon flour. Use ½ teaspoon baking powder. Use 1 extra-large egg. Heat oven to 390°F. Use 12-cup muffin tin; line 8 cups with paper liners and add ¼ cup water to empty cups. Bake for 20 to 25 minutes.

Wild-grown, hand-harvested genuine wild rice is very different from commercially bred, paddy-grown "wild" rice. It's nuttier, with a more complex flavor, and it cooks more quickly. Commercial "wild" rice is darker and harder; it takes much longer to cook, and has a flavor that seems muddy by comparison. If you're using hand-finished wild rice in a recipe that was written for the commercial variety, start checking for doneness after 15 minutes; because it doesn't need to cook as long, it usually needs less water, too. (If you're using commercial rice in a recipe that was written for truly wild rice, plan on cooking it as long as an hour, adding additional water as necessary.)

Serviceberry Pie

Chopped almonds add a wonderful texture to this luscious pie.

**3 cups fresh or previously frozen serviceberries, divided
(12 to 13 ounces)**

²/₃ cup sugar

3 tablespoons cornstarch

1 tablespoon lemon juice

1 tablespoon butter, cut into several pieces

½ teaspoon cinnamon

A pinch of salt

A few drops almond extract, optional

Ready-to-use pastry for double-crust pie

⅓ cup finely chopped almonds

1 egg yolk, beaten with 1 tablespoon cold water

In medium non-aluminum saucepan, combine 1 cup of serviceberries with the sugar, cornstarch and lemon juice; stir to mix. Heat to boiling over medium heat, stirring constantly; cook, stirring constantly, until liquid clears and thickens. Remove from heat; stir in butter, cinnamon, salt and extract. Let cool for about 5 minutes, then add remaining 2 cups serviceberries and set aside until completely cool, about 1 hour.

When the serviceberry mixture has cooled, position rack in bottom third of oven; heat to 400°F. Fit one pastry into ungreased pie plate. Scatter almonds evenly in crust. Scrape cooled serviceberry mixture into pie plate. Moisten edges of pastry in pie plate with a little cold water, then top with second pastry. Seal, trim and flute edges. Cut 6 to 8 inch-long slits in the crust. Place pie on baking sheet (to catch drips). Brush top with beaten egg. Bake until crust is golden and filling bubbles through slits, about 30 minutes. Transfer to rack to cool; best served warm.

Old-Fashioned Serviceberry Dumplings   4 servings

This is based on an old recipe for blueberry dumplings; it works just as well with serviceberries. Many recipes like this involve a dumpling mixture that is cooked in hot berry sauce. This one puts the berries inside, where they fill the dumplings with flavor. These make a wonderful, filling breakfast.

1½ cups all-purpose flour, plus additional for rolling out dough

½ cup sugar

1 teaspoon baking powder

½ teaspoon salt

⅜ cup whole or 2% milk

4 tablespoons (half of a stick) unsalted butter, melted and cooled slightly

1 egg

1 cup fresh serviceberries (about 4½ ounces)

For serving: milk, butter, and cinnamon-sugar (½ cup sugar mixed with ½ teaspoon cinnamon)

Start heating a large pot of water to boiling over high heat. Place wire-mesh strainer over mixing bowl. Add 1½ cups flour, the sugar, baking powder and salt; shake to sift into bowl. In measuring cup, combine milk, butter and egg; beat with a fork. Add to flour mixture and stir with wooden spoon until well mixed.

Transfer dough to lightly floured worksurface and knead a few times. Roll out about ¼ inch thick. Cut into 2-inch squares. Divide serviceberries among the squares. Make the dumplings one at a time: Fold corners together over the berries. Work the dough in your hand, squeezing slightly, until you hear or feel the berries popping slightly and the ball of dough is well sealed. Repeat with remaining dough and berries.

Drop dumplings, a few at a time, into boiling water. Cook, stirring gently if they stick to the bottom of the pot, until dumplings float; cook for 3 to 5 minutes longer after they float, or until they are cooked through (use a slotted spoon to transfer one of the first ones to a plate, and cut it open to check). Use slotted spoon to transfer to a bowl; cover and keep warm while you prepare remaining dumplings. Serve warm dumplings in a bowl, with butter, milk and cinnamon-sugar to top.

High-altitude note:

At altitudes above 6,000 feet, you will probably have to boil the dumplings a bit longer to cook them through. Try one at 5 to 6 minutes, then check and adjust timing as necessary.

Microwave Oatmeal with Serviceberries and Nuts

Easy, quick and filling, this is the perfect breakfast.

⅔ cup water

⅓ cup old-fashioned rolled oats (not instant)

2 to 3 tablespoons fresh serviceberries

2 drops of vanilla extract

1 tablespoon chopped pecans

Honey, maple syrup or brown sugar to taste

Cream or whole milk to taste, optional

In microwave-safe bowl that holds 2 to 3 cups, combine water, oats, serviceberries and vanilla. Microwave on high, uncovered, until oatmeal is thick and most of the water has been absorbed, 1½ to 2½ minutes. Remove bowl from microwave; stir well and let stand until all water is absorbed, 30 seconds to 1 minute. Sprinkle with pecans; top with honey and cream to taste.

Other recipes in this book featuring serviceberries:
Fruits of the Forest Pie, pg. 168
Dehydrating Wild Berries and Fruits, pgs. 180–181
Wild Berry or Fruit Leather, pg. 182
As a substitute in Blackberry-Apple Crisp, pg. 21
As a substitute in Refrigerator Cookies with Dried Goji Berries, pg. 51
As a substitute in Huckleberry Streusel Muffins, pg. 80
As a variation in Strawberry Smoothie, pg. 156

Quick ideas for using serviceberries:
Substitute serviceberries for fresh blueberries in recipes. Serviceberries are not quite as juicy as blueberries, so you may need to increase the liquid slightly.
Use 1¼ cups of serviceberries in place of one of the sliced apples when making apple pie.

SQUASHBERRIES and
HIGHBUSH CRANBERRIES (*Viburnum* spp.)

Squashberries (*Viburnum edule*) and highbush cranberries (*V. opulus* var. *americanum*; formerly listed as *V. trilobum*) are related plants with similar fruits that taste a fair amount like cranberries. Fruits of both contain a single flat seed, which is hard and bitter, so they must be processed differently than true cranberries.

Highbush cranberries grow in large clusters on the plants, so it's easy to harvest a good quantity; squashberries grow more sparsely, with much smaller clusters that sometimes contain only a few fruits. Both can be picked when bright red but still hard, or later, when the fruits have softened naturally. If you pick more than you can process, simply pull the fruits off the clusters and freeze them; when thawed, they will be soft and can be processed without cooking. A 1-gallon ice cream pail full of clusters will yield about 2 quarts of cleaned fruits (after the stems have been removed), weighing about 2½ pounds.

*Although unrelated to true cranberries (Vaccinium **spp.**), highbush cranberries taste remarkably like their namesake.*

Because of the large, inedible seeds, squashberries and highbush cranberries must be juiced or puréed before using in recipes. Fruits picked when soft, or softened in the freezer, can be processed without cooking; fruits picked when still hard must be stewed first. To stew squashberries or highbush cranberries, pull off the stems, measure the fruits and place in a non-aluminum pot. For purée, add 1 cup water per quart of stemless fruit; for juice, add 3 cups water per quart of fruit. Heat to boiling, then reduce the heat; cover and simmer for about 5 minutes, gently crushing with a potato masher near the end. If you're working with uncooked fruits that were soft when picked, or have been softened in the freezer, simply combine the fruits with the appropriate amount of water in a clean bucket, and gently crush with a potato masher.

For juice, transfer the prepared fruit to a strainer lined with doubled, dampened cheesecloth and let it drip for 30 minutes; if you're making jelly, don't squeeze the fruit or the jelly will be cloudy. After the clear liquid has dripped away, set it aside and squeeze the fruit into a different container; you can use this slightly cloudy juice as a beverage or for cooking. **For purée,** process the prepared fruit through a food mill, discarding the seeds. A quart of stemmed fruits will yield about 3¼ cups of juice, or about 2 cups of purée.

Squashberries and highbush cranberries are rich in vitamin C; the purée or juice can be added to other fruits when baking, or sweetened and used on its own. The juice is often used to make delicious jelly; the purée can be used to make jam. In his book, *The Forager's Harvest*, wild foods specialist Sam Thayer writes that juice or purée made from highbush cranberries that were picked when soft (or softened in the freezer) and processed without stewing taste better than those made from fruits which have been stewed; I assume that the same holds true for squashberries.

To avoid cumbersome ingredients lists, the recipes that follow all call for squashberries; highbush cranberries can be substituted in equal amounts.

Curried Sweet Potato Soup with
Squashberry Drizzle

4 to 6 servings

This is a splendid autumn soup. The squashberry purée makes a lovely, and flavorful, garnish that looks particularly pretty on the orange soup.

½ cup squashberry purée

2 tablespoons sugar

½ teaspoon finely grated orange zest (colored rind only,
with none of the white pith; see "Zesting Citrus Fruits," pg. 35)

1 medium onion, diced

1 tablespoon olive oil or vegetable oil

1 or 2 cloves garlic, minced or pressed

2 teaspoons freshly grated or finely minced fresh gingerroot

1 tablespoon curry powder

2 pounds orange-fleshed sweet potatoes,
peeled and cut into ½-inch cubes

½ cup diced roasted red bell peppers
(from a jar, or make your own)

1 quart chicken broth

¼ teaspoon salt, or to taste

¼ to ½ cup sour cream (reduced-fat works fine)

Prepare the squashberry drizzle: In a small, heavy-bottomed non-aluminum saucepan, combine purée, sugar and orange zest. Heat to boiling over medium-high heat, then reduce heat and cook at a very gentle boil until slightly thickened, 12 to 18 minutes. Remove from heat and set aside until needed.

In soup pot, sauté onion in oil over medium heat until beginning to soften, about 5 minutes. Add garlic, gingerroot and curry powder; cook, stirring constantly, until very fragrant, 1 to 2 minutes. Add sweet potatoes, roasted peppers, chicken broth and salt. Heat just to boiling, then reduce heat and cook at a very gentle boil until sweet potatoes are soft, about 20 minutes. Use an immersion blender to purée the soup, or purée in batches in a regular blender (be careful to avoid splashing the hot liquid). Check for seasoning and adjust salt if necessary. To serve, ladle puréed soup into individual serving bowls. Spoon some of the squashberry drizzle in several dollops on the surface, then use a chopstick to make a swirl pattern by drawing it through the purée in a circular motion. Gently place a tablespoon or so of sour cream into the center of each bowl. Serve immediately.

Squashberry Spice Cake

9 servings

This cake gets its delightful flavor from the squashberries and the spices. The cream cheese frosting is the perfect finish, but a sprinkling of powdered sugar also works well.

For 5,000 feet; see adjustments for other altitudes

6 tablespoons unsalted butter, softened

⅔ cup white sugar[2, 3]

½ cup (packed) golden brown sugar

1 large egg[2, 3]

1¼ cups plus 1 tablespoon all-purpose flour[1, 2, 3]

¾ teaspoon cinnamon[3]

¾ teaspoon baking powder

½ teaspoon baking soda

¼ teaspoon ground cloves

⅛ teaspoon nutmeg

⅔ cup squashberry purée

½ cup golden raisins

½ cup chopped walnuts

Cream Cheese Frosting (pg. 149) or powdered sugar

Heat oven to 365°F.[1, 2, 3] Grease and flour an 8x8-inch baking dish[2, 3] and line the bottom with a square of waxed paper that has been cut to fit; set aside. In large mixing bowl, beat butter with electric mixer until light. Add white and brown sugars; beat for about 1 minute. Add egg; beat about 1 minute longer.

Place a wire-mesh strainer on a dinner plate. Add flour, cinnamon, baking powder, baking soda, cloves and nutmeg. Shake strainer over the mixing bowl to sift about half of the flour into the butter mixture. Add half of the squashberry purée to the butter mixture; stir well with wooden spoon. Sift remaining flour into mixture; add remaining purée and stir until combined. Stir in raisins and nuts. Scrape into prepared pan, spreading evenly. Bake until a wooden pick inserted in the center comes out clean, 28 to 38 minutes.[1, 2, 3] Transfer pan to wire rack and let stand until cool. Frost with Cream Cheese Frosting (pg. 149), or sprinkle with powdered sugar if you prefer.

---

1. Below 5,000 feet: Use 1¼ cups flour. Heat oven to 350°F. Bake for 35 to 45 minutes.

2. At 7,500 feet: Use ½ cup white sugar. Use 1¼ cups plus 2 tablespoons flour. Use 1 extra-large egg. Heat oven to 375°F. Use 9x9-inch baking dish. Bake for 25 to 35 minutes.

3. At 10,000 feet: Use ⅓ cup white sugar. Use 1 extra-large egg plus 1 additional yolk. Use 1¼ cups plus 3 tablespoons flour. Use 1 teaspoon cinnamon; also add a pinch of salt. Heat oven to 375°F. Use 9x9-inch baking dish. Bake for 25 to 35 minutes.

Cream Cheese Frosting

About 1 cup

4 tablespoons (half of a stick) butter, softened
4 ounces cream cheese, softened (reduced-fat works fine)
1 teaspoon vanilla extract
1 cup powdered sugar

In large mixing bowl, beat butter, cream cheese and vanilla with electric mixer on high until light and fluffy. Hold a wire-mesh strainer over the bowl and add powdered sugar to strainer. Shake strainer to sift into the butter. Beat until smooth. Refrigerate leftover cake for storage if using cream cheese frosting.

Squashberry Jam (no added pectin)

About ¾ cup jam per cup of purée

Make as much of this as you wish; since no pectin is needed, you aren't restricted to specific measurements. For a slightly different flavor, use red wine or Port instead of water when stewing the berries (or when mashing berries that you are processing without cooking).

1 cup squashberry purée
½ cup sugar
1 teaspoon finely grated orange zest (colored rind only,
**   with none of the white pith; see "Zesting Citrus Fruits," pg. 35)**
¼ teaspoon ground allspice
¼ teaspoon cinnamon
Pinch of ground nutmeg

Combine all ingredients in heavy-bottomed small saucepan. Heat to boiling, then reduce heat and cook at a very gentle boil, stirring frequently, until mixture is thickened to jam-like consistency. Cooking time is typically 45 minutes to an hour, depending on how loose the purée is. Transfer to sterilized jar(s). Store in refrigerator, or freeze for longer storage.

Squashberry-Apple Leather About 12 ounces finished leather

This fruit leather has a lovely red color, and sweet-tart taste, from the squashberries. It's a good way to combine two autumn fruits into a useful product that can be kept for a long time.

1½ pounds pie apples such as Granny Smith

1½ cups whole squashberries (about 6 ounces), stems removed before measuring

1¼ cups sugar

1 cup water

Before starting, please read Wild Berry or Fruit Leathers on pg. 182, and prepare your dehydrator or several baking sheets as directed. Cut washed but unpeeled apples into 1-inch chunks, removing stems and blossom ends. Place in medium (4-quart) non-aluminum soup pot. Add squashberries, sugar and water. Heat to boiling over high heat. Reduce heat slightly so mixture boils gently and cook, stirring occasionally, for 15 minutes, or until fruit is very tender. Remove from heat and set aside for about 15 minutes; this cools the mixture and also allows the fruit to absorb some of the liquid.

Transfer mixture to a food mill set over a large mixing bowl. Process to remove seeds and apple skins; you should have about 3 cups of thick purée that is the consistency of applesauce. If the purée is runny, transfer it to heavy-bottomed non-aluminum saucepan; boil gently over medium-high heat until mixture thickens, then cool for 15 minutes before proceeding.

Pour the purée onto prepared baking sheets or dehydrator liners. Tilt the sheets to evenly distribute the purée; it should be about ¼ inch deep. Dry at 130°–150°F for about 3 hours, or until the surface feels fairly solid and leathery. Use a spatula to pry up the edge of a piece of the leather, then peel it off and flip it so the underside is exposed. Continue drying until leathery with no sticky spots; total drying time is generally 7 to 9 hours, but this may vary depending on your equipment, the purée and the weather. If you've used baking sheets lined with plastic wrap, the leather can be peeled off any time; if you've used solid liner sheets with a dehydrator, peel off the leather while it is still warm. Roll up all leathers, and wrap in plastic wrap. They keep well at cool room temperature if properly dried; for long-term storage, wrap the plastic-wrapped rolls in freezer paper and store in the freezer.

Squashberry Jelly
5 half-pints

3 cups squashberry juice
Half of a 1.75-ounce box powdered pectin
½ teaspoon butter, optional (helps reduce foaming)
3½ cups sugar

Prepare and process as directed in Jelly Instructions (using pectin), pgs. 176–177.

Squashberry Sunrise
Per serving

Bright red squashberry syrup stands in for the grenadine in the classic tequila sunrise —a delightful difference!

2 ounces gold tequila
4 to 6 ounces top-quality orange juice
1 tablespoon squashberry syrup (pg. 175)
Orange slice and maraschino cherry, for garnish

Fill a tall glass with ice. Add tequila first, then the orange juice. Now pour the syrup into the glass, as close to the side as possible; it should settle to the bottom and then slowly rise to the top. Garnish with orange slice and cherry. (If your syrup isn't thick enough, the sunrise effect may not work—just stir and enjoy.)

Other recipes in this book featuring squashberries and highbush cranberries:
Wild Berry Vinegar, pg. 22
Six Recipes Using Wild Fruit Juice or Syrup, pgs. 170–174
Wild Berry or Fruit Syrup, pg. 175
As a variation in Elderberry Meringue Pie, pg. 46

Quick ideas for using squashberries and highbush cranberries:
Stir a few tablespoons of the purée into apple, berry or other fruit pie fillings.
Mix 1 part squashberry or highbush cranberry juice with 2 or 3 parts apple juice; sweeten to taste.

STRAWBERRIES (*Fragaria* spp.)

It's fun to watch the reaction of someone who's tasting a wild strawberry for the first time. Wonderment over the tiny size of the fruit changes to awed delight when they taste it. "I never knew strawberries could taste like this!" is a common response—quickly followed by a dive to the ground in search of more strawberries.

Two types of wild strawberries grow in our area: the Virginia strawberry (*Fragaria virginiana*) and the woodland strawberry (*F. vesca*). Both are delicious, although the woodland strawberry may be somewhat tart. Wild strawberries are so tiny that it is hard to gather enough to make, say, a batch of jam—and they're so good that it's tough to stop eating them rather than putting them in the berry pail. I've never made wild strawberry jelly, because I've never wanted to sacrifice enough berries to make juice. However, if you've hit the strawberry jackpot and want to make jelly (or other recipes prepared with juice), follow the instructions for making mulberry juice on pg. 100.

The hardest part about picking enough wild strawberries to make jam is refraining from devouring them on the spot.

When you're using wild strawberries in recipes that were written for domestic berries, don't rely on per-cup measurements. Wild strawberries are so much smaller than their domesticated cousins that they pack more tightly into the cup, so you'd be using more strawberries (by weight) than the recipe intended. Domestic strawberries are also less juicy, so liquid may need to be reduced when substituting wild strawberries.

Wild strawberries can be frozen, but they will be soft when thawed. Spread them in a single layer on a baking sheet lined with waxed paper. Freeze overnight, then pack into tightly sealed plastic containers and store in the coldest part of the freezer. They can also be dehydrated (see pgs. 180–181) or used to make fruit leather (pg. 182).

Strawberry Filling
About ½ cup; easily increased

½ teaspoon water

½ teaspoon cornstarch

6 ounces fresh or previously frozen wild strawberries (about 1 cup)

2 teaspoons sugar

1 teaspoon lemon juice

In small bowl, blend together water and cornstarch; set aside. In small, heavy-bottomed non-aluminum saucepan, combine strawberries, sugar and lemon juice. Crush fruit gently with a potato masher to start juices flowing. Heat to boiling over medium-high heat, then cook, stirring frequently, until mixture is no longer runny; this will take 8 to 10 minutes. Add cornstarch mixture, stirring constantly; cook for about 1 minute longer, or until thick. Cool before using.

Use this to prepare Easy Bear Claws (pg. 81), Fruit-Striped Cookie Fingers (pg. 126), or Fruit-Filled Muffins (pg. 155). Refrigerate extra filling, and use to top oatmeal or toast.

Mixed Greens with Strawberries, Honey Pecans and Blue Cheese

4 first-course servings; easily increased

Here's a salad with a fabulous combination of flavors and textures. It serves four as a first course for a special dinner, or two if presented as the center item for a luncheon. If you like, you can prepare the nuts a day or two in advance.

Honey pecans:

¾ cup pecan halves

1 tablespoon honey

2 teaspoons butter, melted

A pinch of curry powder

Salad:

3 slices thick-cut bacon

6 cups tender mixed salad greens

3 thin slices red onion, quartered after slicing

½ cup blue cheese crumbles

⅔ to ¾ cup fresh wild strawberries (4 to 5 ounces)

⅓ to ½ cup prepared balsamic vinaigrette
   (purchased or homemade; see tip below)

Prepare the nuts: Heat oven to 425°F. Line a small baking sheet with foil; spray with nonstick spray. In a small bowl, stir together the pecans, honey, butter and curry powder. Spread out on foil-lined baking sheet. Bake until nuts are lightly browned, 5 to 7 minutes, stirring twice. Remove from oven before they are as brown as you would like because they will continue to cook for a few minutes after you remove them from the oven. Let nuts cool completely; can be prepared a day or two in advance (store cooled nuts in airtight container at room temperature).

To assemble the salad, shortly before serving, cut the bacon crosswise (across the width) into ⅜-inch pieces. In medium skillet, fry over medium heat until crisp, stirring frequently. Transfer with slotted spoon to a plate lined with paper towels; blot surface with another paper towel.

Divide greens evenly between 4 salad-sized serving plates, or 2 dinner-sized plates. Sprinkle evenly with onions, breaking up the rings a bit. Top with bacon; sprinkle cheese over the bacon. Carefully place the strawberries on top, arranging attractively. Scatter honey pecans over all. Drizzle dressing over salads. Serve immediately.

 For a simple balsamic vinaigrette, combine ¾ cup extra virgin olive oil, ¼ cup balsamic vinegar, 1 teaspoon sugar, 1 teaspoon Dijon mustard and ½ teaspoon salt in a glass jar; cover tightly and shake to blend.

Strawberry Freezer Jam

4 half-pints

Freezer jam is not cooked, so it has a fresher taste and a vibrant color. It is a little softer than cooked jam. Wild strawberries make the best freezer jam in the world, but if you can't bear to part with enough to make a full batch of this, see below for small-batch instructions.

1¼ pounds fresh wild strawberries (about 3½ cups)

4 cups sugar

1 pouch Certo liquid pectin

2 tablespoons freshly squeezed lemon juice

Wash and hull strawberries. Pulse on-and-off in a food processor until fruit is finely chopped (not puréed); if you prefer, mash with a potato masher. Measure finely chopped strawberries; transfer exactly 2 cups to a large ceramic or Pyrex mixing bowl. If you have any leftover chopped strawberries, enjoy them over ice cream; don't use more than 2 cups for this recipe.

Add sugar and stir well; set aside for 10 minutes, stirring several times. Meanwhile, stir pectin and lemon juice together in a small bowl. After strawberries and sugar have stood for 10 minutes, add pectin mixture to strawberries, scraping to get all the pectin into the berries. Stir continuously for 3 minutes; sugar should be completely dissolved. Cover bowl tightly with plastic wrap. Let stand at room temperature for 24 hours; jam should be softly set.

When jam has set for 24 hours, prepare 4 half-pint canning jars, bands and new lids as described on pg. 183, or have clean plastic freezer containers ready (see tip on pg. 140). Divide fruit between prepared containers, leaving ½ inch headspace. Cover and freeze until needed.

Note: Another option for small-batch strawberry freezer jam is to use the recipe found on the package of Ball RealFruit Instant Pectin, which requires about 2½ cups of strawberries and makes 3 half-pints. See the tip on pg. 85 for information on this product.

Small-Batch Strawberry Freezer Jam

2 half-pints

If you don't have enough berries to make a full batch, you can make a half-batch, based on the recipe above using liquid pectin. The only tricky part is measuring half of the pectin. It is extremely thick and clings to the measuring spoon or cup, making accurate measuring difficult. To make it easier, mix up the full batch of pectin and lemon juice in a measuring cup, then use exactly half of that in the strawberry mixture. The lemon juice makes it easier to measure.

Place 1 cup of finely chopped strawberries into a large mixing bowl. Add 2 cups sugar; stir and let stand as directed above. Mix the full pouch of pectin with 2 tablespoons lemon juice in a glass measuring cup (when I tested it, it came out to ½ cup, but the pectin formula may change in the future so you need to check this each time). After strawberries and sugar have stood for 10 minutes, pour *exactly half* of the pectin mixture into the strawberry mixture (I poured pectin into the strawberry mixture until there was ¼ cup left in the measuring cup). Proceed as directed. Discard remaining pectin if you don't have another use for it.

Fruit-Filled Muffins

These make a nice, quick breakfast. Freeze any muffins you won't be eating within a few days, wrapping them tightly in plastic wrap and then in foil.

For 5,000 feet; see adjustments for other altitudes

1³/₄ cups all-purpose flour

¹/₂ to ²/₃ cup sugar, depending on how sweet you want the muffins[3]

2 teaspoons baking powder[2, 3]

¹/₄ teaspoon salt

³/₄ cup whole or 2% milk[1, 3]

¹/₃ cup vegetable oil

1 large egg[3]

1 teaspoon vanilla extract

¹/₂ cup Strawberry Filling (pg. 152), or other wild fruit filling (see "Filling options" below)

Position rack in center of oven; heat to 400°F.[1, 2, 3] Line a 12-cup muffin tin with paper liners; set aside. Place wire-mesh strainer over large mixing bowl. Add flour, sugar, baking powder and salt; shake strainer to sift mixture into bowl. In measuring cup or small bowl, beat together milk, oil, egg and vanilla. Add milk mixture to flour mixture; stir with a wooden spoon until just moistened. Fill prepared muffin cups about half-full with the batter. Drop about 2 teaspoons of the filling onto the center of the batter, keeping away from the edges; spoon remaining batter over filling. Bake until golden brown and springy to the touch, 20 to 25 minutes.

Filling options: This recipe works with any of the following fillings: Apple (pg. 10), Apricot or Peach (pg. 12), Blackberry (pg. 23), Green Gooseberry (pg. 59), Ground Cherry (pg. 68), Huckleberry (pg. 91), Mulberry (pg. 102), Pear (pg. 106), Plum (pg. 115), Raspberry (pg. 125), Serviceberry (pg. 138) or Strawberry (pg. 152).

1. **Below 5,000 feet:** Use ²/₃ cup milk. Heat oven to 375°F.

2. **At 7,500 feet:** Use 1³/₄ teaspoons baking powder. Heat oven to 380°F.

3. **At 10,000 feet:** Use ¹/₃ to ¹/₂ cup sugar. Use 1¹/₂ teaspoons baking powder. Use ²/₃ cup milk. Use 1 medium egg. Position rack in bottom of oven; heat to 415°F.

See companion *Wild Berries & Fruits Field Guide of the Rocky Mountain States* – pg. 84   **155**

Strawberry Smoothie

2 servings

A quick and healthy breakfast with a vibrant flavor.

1 cup soy milk, rice milk or regular milk
½ cup plain yogurt (regular, low-fat or fat-free)
⅓ to ½ cup fresh or previously frozen wild strawberries
2 teaspoons honey or other sweetener of choice
Half of a banana
½ cup ice cubes

In blender, combine milk, yogurt, strawberries, honey and banana. Pulse on-and-off on high a few times, then blend on high for about 15 seconds, or until smooth. Add ice cubes; blend until frothy, about 5 seconds. Serve immediately.

Variation: Substitute ½ cup of any bramble (raspberries, blackberries or dewberries) or soft-seeded berry (blueberries, huckleberries, serviceberries or sweetberries) for the strawberries. Adjust honey as needed, depending on the sweetness of the fruit.

Strawberries and Shortbread

This simple, but interesting, dessert was inspired by a recipe from the well-known French chef, Jacques Pépin.

2 cups fresh wild strawberries (about 12 ounces), divided

2 teaspoons sugar, or to taste

¼ teaspoon vanilla extract

4 ounces shortbread cookies

⅓ cup crème fraîche or sour cream

2 tablespoons (packed) brown sugar

4 sprigs fresh mint for garnish, optional

In mini food processor, process half of the strawberries with the sugar and vanilla; transfer to small bowl. Slice remaining strawberries, then gently stir into the strawberry purée. Place shortbread cookies in plastic bag, and crush coarsely with rolling pin. (If preparing in advance, cover and refrigerate strawberries until serving time; set crushed cookies aside.)

To serve, spoon about 2 tablespoons of the strawberry mixture into each of 4 wine glasses or parfait dishes. Divide shortbread crumbs evenly among glasses. Top evenly with remaining strawberry mixture. Spoon crème fraîche evenly on top; sprinkle with brown sugar and garnish with mint sprig. Let stand 5 to 10 minutes before serving.

Other recipes in this book featuring wild strawberries:
Wild Berry Vinegar, pg. 22
Strawberry-Gooseberry Dessert Sauce, pg. 61
Dehydrating Wild Berries and Fruits, pgs. 180–181
Wild Berry or Fruit Leather, pg. 182
As a substitute in Refrigerator Cookies with Dried Goji Berries, pg. 51
As a substitute in Raspberry Dip, pg. 125
As a variation in Huckleberry Pancakes, pg. 83

Quick ideas for using wild strawberries:
Sprinkle over cold cereal before adding milk and sugar; way better
than sliced bananas!
Add to mixed fruit salads.
Add a few to an apple pie, for a delightful difference.
Enjoy them over ice cream, or in a bowl with a little cream or yogurt.

STRAWBERRY SPINACH (*Chenopodium capitatum*)

Also known as strawberry blite, beet stick, blite goosefoot and Indian ink, this unusual but attractive plant is easy to identify and is often found on waste ground such as roadsides and parking-lot margins. The bright "fruit" is actually a tight cluster of pulpy, tiny red flowers (called a glomerule). These clusters grow in abundance along the stem; although the clusters are very seedy, they are completely edible.

This strange-looking plant may make you think that some kids were playing around and skewered a bunch of strawberries or raspberries on a roadside weed.

They have a taste that is hard to describe; to me, it is mildly sweet, somewhat nutty and vegetal all at the same time, somewhat like a cross between mild wheat bread, strawberries and cauliflower.

The leaves are edible as well, either raw or cooked; they are similar to leaves of the related goosefoot or lamb's-quarters (*C. album*), which grows throughout most of our area but does not have the red flower clusters. Like spinach, leaves of both *Chenopodium* species contain a fair amount of oxalic acid, which prevents absorption of calcium; however, it takes a lot of these leaves to have much effect and the casual forager is unlikely to eat enough to cause any problems. The oxalic acid is broken down during cooking.

Picking strawberry spinach is easy: select stems with soft, bright red clusters and snip them off near the ground, placing them into a plastic bag. At home, place the bag of stems in your vegetable drawer, where they will keep for a day or two. When you're ready to prepare the strawberry spinach, rinse the stems very well with a spray of cold water; pay particular attention to the clusters as grit can be trapped in between the pulpy flowers. Drain the stems well, then pat dry with paper towels. Pull off the clusters with your fingertips (which will soon be stained red) and then pull off the leaves; use both the clusters and the leaves the same day you wash them or they may start to spoil. The stems are generally too tough to eat, but could be added to a stockpot with other vegetables when making broth.

Most foragers who pick strawberry spinach use it to make a salad, with the leaves added to other greens and the bright red flower clusters used as a garnish. The flower clusters are rich with red pigment, and are sometimes used to dye fibers, grasses or other materials. I've never heard of anyone making juice, jam or jelly from the fruits, although I imagine any products like that would have a lovely red color.

If you pick strawberry spinach, you can scatter some of the ripe fruits in an unused corner of your garden. The seeds should sprout the following spring and provide you with a continuous supply of this unusual plant, which makes a nice, edible and attractive garden specimen.

Wild Rice Salad with Strawberry Spinach   8 servings

Both the leaves and the red fruits are used in this attractive salad, which makes an interesting conversation starter at a potluck dinner.

1½ cups uncooked wild rice (see tip on pg. 142), rinsed and drained

2 cups chicken broth

½ cup pine nuts

¼ cup olive oil

2 tablespoons seasoned rice vinegar

1 tablespoon toasted (dark) sesame oil

½ teaspoon Dijon mustard

¾ cup thinly sliced celery

½ cup dried cranberries (craisins)

2 stems of strawberry spinach with soft, red clusters

6 green onions, sliced (white and green parts)

¾ cup frozen green peas, thawed but not cooked

In medium saucepan, combine wild rice and broth. Heat to boiling over medium-high heat, then reduce heat and simmer, loosely covered, until rice is tender, adding hot water if the broth cooks away before the rice is done; timing and the amount of water needed will depend on the type of wild rice you have (see tip on pg. 142). Hand-harvested, truly wild rice generally cooks in 15 to 20 minutes and won't need much if any additional water; commercial paddy-grown rice takes 45 to 60 minutes and may require up to 2 cups of additional water. Remove from heat and set aside until completely cool; drain and discard any excess liquid.

While rice is cooling, lightly toast the pine nuts in a dry, heavy-bottomed skillet over medium heat, stirring constantly, until fragrant and beginning to color, about 2 minutes. Transfer immediately to a small bowl and set aside to cool. Make the dressing: In a small jar, combine olive oil, rice vinegar, sesame oil and mustard; cover tightly and shake well to blend.

To assemble the salad, place drained, cooled rice in a large mixing bowl; add celery, dried cranberries and toasted pine nuts, stirring to combine. Add about half of the dressing to the rice mixture and stir to combine; add additional dressing until the salad is dressed as you prefer. Cover the rice mixture and refrigerate until thoroughly chilled; also refrigerate any remaining dressing and use within a week to dress other salads.

When you are almost ready to serve, rinse the strawberry spinach stems very well, then set aside to drain for a few minutes. Add the green onions and thawed peas to the rice mixture, stirring to combine. Blot the strawberry spinach lightly with paper towels; pull off clusters and leaves (tearing them up if large) and scatter them over the salad. Serve immediately.

Variation: Use a boxed wild-and-white-rice blend instead of just wild rice. Cook according to package instructions, then assemble the salad as directed.

SUMAC (*Rhus* spp.)

Three-leaf sumac (*Rhus trilobata*; sometimes called fragrant sumac or skunkbush) is familiar to almost everyone in our area because it is a widespread shrub that bears small but abundant clusters of fuzzy reddish-orange fruits; in addition to growing extensively in the wild it is also planted as a landscape specimen. Smooth sumac (*R. glabra*) is a taller shrub or small tree that is much less common, but its large pyramid-shaped clusters of tiny red fruits call attention to the plant wherever it grows. Littleleaf sumac (*R. microphylla*) is found in our area only in parts of New Mexico; it is a tall shrub with larger fruits that grow in long, column-like clusters.

Sumac is probably the first unfamiliar wild edible that kids learn about. "Sumac-ade" is a staple at many summer camps; it's easy for kids to identify and pick the bright reddish-orange clusters, and fun to make a tasty beverage out of them.

Ripe fruits of all three are sour but edible and are usually used to make a lemonade-type beverage. The fruits should be harvested when they're fully ripe and a bit sticky; if you wait too long, rain will wash away the flavor. Use a pruning snips to cut off entire clusters; it doesn't hurt the plants, because they reproduce by underground runners.

To prepare juice or other beverages, you can use the whole cluster or pick the berries off the stems; picking is more work, but it eliminates any dirt, spiders or other undesirables that may be hiding inside the cluster. For storage, freeze picked berries in heavy plastic bags; the frozen berries retain all their flavor and can be used later to make sumac juice, tea or whatever you like. Clusters can be frozen as well, but they take up more room; as an option, place them in a loosely sealed paper bag and let them dry, then use them to make tea (they won't make very good juice after they've been dried). Sumac berries have tiny hairs that are somewhat irritating to the throat; they can be removed by straining the liquid through a paper coffee filter.

To make sumac juice, use fresh berry clusters that are still sticky; frozen berries or clusters work as well, as long as they were sticky before freezing. Place clusters or picked berries in a soup pot or plastic bucket, then add cold water just to cover. Squeeze the berries with your hands, and rub them up and down along the sides of the pot as though scrubbing on a washboard. Do this for a few minutes, then let the mixture stand for a few minutes and repeat. I usually let them soak for 10 to 20 minutes after that; I want to extract as much flavor as possible. Strain the mixture through a wire-mesh strainer, then again through a paper coffee filter. Sweeten to taste and serve cold as a lemonade-type beverage; or, use the unsweetened liquid in recipes.

For stronger sumac juice, you can reduce it to approximately half-volume by cooking (however, you are eliminating much of the vitamin C by heating it). Or, add more sumac clusters to already prepared sumac juice and repeat the juice-making process to get a stronger liquid.

Caution: People who are highly allergic to poison ivy, mangoes or cashews should avoid all sumacs, which are in the same family and may cause a severe allergic reaction.

Cedar-Planked Salmon with Sumac-Maple Glaze
4 to 6 servings

Cooking salmon on cedar planks is traditional in the Pacific Northwest. In this version, the salmon is topped with a tangy-sweet glaze made from sumac juice and maple syrup.

Red cedar plank, about ½ inch thick and large enough to hold fish

1 cup strained sumac juice

1-inch chunk peeled fresh gingerroot

1 clove garlic

2 strips orange zest (colored rind only, with none of the white pith; see "Zesting Citrus Fruits," pg. 35), each about 2 inches long by ½ inch wide

¾ cup pure maple syrup (don't use substitutes in this recipe)

1 tablespoon soy sauce

2 teaspoons butter

2-pound fillet of salmon, skin on

Salt and freshly ground pepper

In a clean bucket, soak plank in water to cover for 8 hours or overnight; weight with clean rocks to keep plank submerged. When you're ready to start cooking, prepare the glaze: In small, heavy-bottomed non-aluminum saucepan, boil sumac juice over high heat until reduced to about ⅓ cup (see "Reducing Liquid," pg. 36). While the sumac juice is cooking, chop the gingerroot, garlic and orange zest until fine in a food processor.

When the sumac juice is reduced, add the chopped gingerroot mixture, the maple syrup and soy sauce. Continue boiling until reduced slightly, about 5 minutes. Remove from heat and stir in butter; set aside until cooled to room temperature. While glaze is cooling, prepare grill for high heat. Drain plank and pat dry. Place salmon on plank, skin-side down; season to taste with salt and pepper. Reserve half of the glaze; brush fish with remaining glaze. Place plank on grill grate directly over heat. Cover grill and cook until fish is just opaque, 15 to 25 minutes depending on the thickness of the fish. (The plank may catch fire around the edges near the end of cooking time; don't worry about it unless it gets too strong. If necessary, douse the edges with a spray bottle of water.) When the salmon is almost done, warm reserved sauce over medium heat, then transfer to a small serving bowl. Serve salmon on plank, or transfer fish to a serving platter; pass warmed sauce with the fish. Discard the plank after use.

 Buy untreated cedar from the lumberyard, or look at a specialty shop or upscale grocer for planks that are marketed specifically for cooking.

Sumac Tea

3 servings; easily increased or decreased

Sumac makes a pleasant hot tea that is slightly tart, with floral overtones. It's similar to chamomile tea, or to a mild version of the commercial herbal-tea blend called Red Zinger.

1 quart of sumac clusters, or about 1 cup of picked berries

4 cups water

Honey or sugar to taste, optional

Rinse the sumac clusters briefly, and set aside to drain. Heat water to boiling in saucepan; remove from heat and set aside to cool for about 5 minutes. While water is cooling, cut smaller clusters away from woody stems, discarding stems. Add clusters or picked berries to hot water and let stand for 5 minutes. Use potato masher or large wooden spoon to bruise the sumac; you don't want to crack the seeds doing this, so don't use too much force. Let stand for about 5 minutes longer, then strain through a paper coffee filter. Serve warm or cold, adding sweetening to taste if you like.

Variation: Sumac-Mint Tea
Add a few fresh mint leaves to the hot water with the sumac.

If you want iced tea, chill the brewed tea for an hour before serving. I like hot sumac tea unsweetened, but you can add sugar or honey to taste if you prefer; iced tea tastes better if sweetened lightly. Iced sumac tea is best the day it is made; it begins to turn an unappetizing brown after a day in the refrigerator.

Other recipes in this book featuring sumac:
Elderberry-Sumac Jelly, pg. 49
Six Recipes Using Wild Fruit Juice or Syrup, pgs. 170–174
Wild Berry or Fruit Syrup, pg. 175

SWEETBERRY HONEYSUCKLE (*Lonicera caerulea*)

Several types of sweetberry honeysuckle (sometimes called honeyberries or blue honeysuckle) may be found in parts of our area. Some are native plants, while others are escapees from commercial growing operations in Canada or from test plantings in Idaho and Oregon. Sweetberries are bright or deep blue berries with a dusty bloom; some may have a reddish tint. Shape is variable, depending on the cultivar. Some are nearly an inch long and shaped like a tube with a rounded top; the base may be open or closed in this form. Others are oval or barrel-shaped; some grow as paired, bullet-shaped fruits joined at the base. All are edible and juicy, with a fairly strong tart to sweet-tart flavor; many found in the wild may be somewhat bitter.

The University of Saskatchewan developed a cultivar with berries that are particularly delicious; it is called haskap, a registered name that should be used to refer only to this specific cultivar. Most commercially grown sweetberries are haskaps.

Once you find them, sweetberries are easy to pick because the shrubs are fairly short and often bear heavily. They have soft seeds that are virtually unnoticeable, so they can be used whole in baked goods, jam and other products; they are a bit tart and strong-flavored to eat raw, although there's no harm in doing so. They're rich in anthocyanins, antioxidants with potential health benefits. Sweetberries store well in the refrigerator, remaining fresh for several days; don't wash them until you're ready to use them, though, or they may mold.

Sweetberries are very juicy. They can be frozen but collapse when thawed, so you get flattened berries and a lot of juice. This trait can be used to the cook's advantage; flattened, drained berries work great in baked goods because they won't release juice that would make baked goods soggy. The drained juice can be re-frozen in a jar until enough is accumulated to make jelly (pg. 167) or syrup (pg. 175). Because of their varying sizes and shapes, small amounts of sweetberries are difficult to measure accurately; a cup of fresh berries weighs 3½ to 5 ounces. Previously frozen, thawed berries pack much more closely into the measuring cup than fresh berries; 4 ounces of sweetberries may measure 1 cup when fresh but only ½ cup when previously frozen and then thawed. For this reason, sweetberry recipes in this book give quantities in ounces, followed by approximate cup measures.

To prepare purée or juice in the traditional manner, measure the fruit and place in a non-aluminum pot. For purée, add 2 tablespoons water per quart of fruit; for juice, add ¾ cup water per quart of fruit. Gently crush the fruit with a potato masher to start the juices flowing. Heat to boiling, then reduce the heat; cover and simmer for about 10 minutes. **For purée,** process the cooked fruit through a food mill, then discard the skins. **For juice,** transfer the mixture to a strainer lined with doubled, dampened cheesecloth and let it drip for 30 minutes; if you're making jelly, don't squeeze the fruit or the jelly will be cloudy. After the clear liquid has dripped away, set it aside and squeeze the fruit into a different container; you can use this slightly cloudy juice as a beverage or for cooking. Processed this way, a quart of fruit will yield about 2 cups of purée, or about 2½ cups of juice.

Sweetberries can be dehydrated (see pgs. 180–181) or used for leather (pg. 182). Their bitterness is slightly more noticeable when they have been dehydrated.

Crusty Baked Brie with Sweetberries   6 to 8 servings

This is a knockout appetizer, perfect for a buffet party. The sweet-tart sweetberry filling is a wonderful foil to the rich, runny Brie and buttery pastry.

2 ounces fresh or previously frozen sweetberries (about ½ cup fresh, or ¼ cup thawed berries with juice)

1½ tablespoons sugar

1½ teaspoons instant tapioca

1 tube (8 ounces) refrigerated crescent roll dough

4-inch-wide wheel of Brie (8 ounces; see tip below)

1 egg white, lightly beaten

In small, heavy-bottomed non-aluminum saucepan, stir together sweetberries (including any juices from thawing) and sugar. Heat to boiling over medium heat; mash berries with a potato masher, then adjust heat so mixture boils gently and cook for 5 minutes, stirring frequently. Stir in tapioca and continue to cook, stirring constantly, until mixture is very thick, 1½ to 2 minutes longer; watch carefully so the mixture doesn't burn. Remove from heat and set aside until completely cool; can be prepared in advance and refrigerated until needed.

When you're ready to bake, position rack in lower third of oven; heat to 350°F. Spray a small rimmed baking sheet or 9x9-inch baking dish with nonstick spray; set aside. On lightly floured worksurface, unroll the crescent roll dough. Press the seams together with your fingertips, pinching together firmly to seal; turn dough over and seal the seams on the other side. Cut off a 3-inch-wide strip from one of the short ends and set aside; the dough should now be about 7¾x10 inches. Use a rolling pin to roll the dough to a 10-inch square.

Stand the Brie upright and carefully slice it into two thinner rounds. Place one round, cut side up, in the center of the rolled-out dough. Spread about 2 tablespoons of the cooled sweetberry mixture over the cut surface (don't let it drip down the sides of the Brie); if you have extra sweetberry mixture, refrigerate it and use to top toast or oatmeal. Top with remaining round as though making a sandwich, putting the cut side of the second round down so the Brie rind is on the outside. Bring two opposite corners of the dough up over the Brie and pinch together, then repeat with the other two corners, surrounding the Brie completely with dough. Firmly press all seams together to seal well. Carefully flip the wrapped Brie over and place it, seam-side down, on the prepared baking sheet. Cut out a few leaves or other decorations from the extra dough; brush one side lightly with water and place, damp side down, on the wrapped Brie, pressing gently to adhere. Brush the top and sides of the dough with egg white. Bake until pastry is golden brown, about 30 minutes. Serve immediately with a small knife and small spatula (or a spoon) so guests can serve themselves.

Small wheels of Brie are found in the dairy case at most supermarkets; they typically come in a small round box. For this appetizer, purchase a small wheel of Brie that is still fairly firm to the touch; a soft, fully ripened Brie will be too difficult to cut in half.

Carrot Cake with Sweetberries

9 servings

This moist cake stays fresh for several days, even in dry mountain air.

For 5,000 feet; see adjustments for other altitudes

1⅓ cups all-purpose flour[1, 2, 3]

1 teaspoon baking soda[1, 2, 3]

1 teaspoon cinnamon

¼ teaspoon nutmeg

¼ teaspoon salt

2 large eggs[2, 3]

1 cup white sugar[2, 3]

½ cup vegetable oil

1 teaspoon vanilla extract

1½ cups shredded carrots (spooned into cup, not packed; about 5½ ounces)

½ cup chopped pecans

½ cup previously frozen, drained sweetberries (see note below)

Cream cheese frosting (pg. 149) or powdered sugar, optional

Position rack in lower third of oven; heat to 365°F.[1, 2, 3] Grease and flour an 8x8-inch baking dish;[2, 3] set aside. Sift flour, baking soda, cinnamon, nutmeg and salt into medium bowl; set aside. In large mixing bowl, whisk eggs until well blended. Add sugar, oil and vanilla; whisk until smooth. Add flour mixture; stir with wooden spoon until just mixed. Add carrots, pecans and sweetberries; stir until evenly mixed. Scrape into prepared baking dish. Bake for 45 to 55 minutes,[2, 3] or until a wooden pick inserted into the center comes out clean. Set on rack to cool. Spread prepared frosting over the top or dust with powdered sugar, if you like.

---

1. **Below 5,000 feet:** Reduce flour by 1 tablespoon. Use 1⅛ teaspoons baking soda. Heat oven to 350°F.

2. **At 7,500 feet:** Use 1½ cups flour. Use ¾ teaspoon baking soda. Use 2 extra-large eggs. Use ⅔ cup white sugar and ⅓ cup (packed) light brown sugar. Heat oven to 375°F. Use 9x9-inch baking dish. Bake for 40 to 50 minutes.

3. **At 10,000 feet:** Use 1⅔ cups flour. Use ½ teaspoon baking soda. Use 2 large eggs plus one additional egg white. Use ½ cup white sugar and ⅓ cup (packed) light brown sugar. Heat oven to 375°F. Use 9x9-inch baking dish. Bake for 40 to 50 minutes.

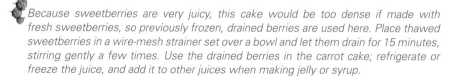

Because sweetberries are very juicy, this cake would be too dense if made with fresh sweetberries, so previously frozen, drained berries are used here. Place thawed sweetberries in a wire-mesh strainer set over a bowl and let them drain for 15 minutes, stirring gently a few times. Use the drained berries in the carrot cake; refrigerate or freeze the juice, and add it to other juices when making jelly or syrup.

Sweetberry-Peach Pandowdy

6 servings

This rustic skillet pie is gorgeous, with caramelized juices peeking out of the browned crust.

½ cup apple cider

¼ cup (packed) golden brown sugar

1 tablespoon freshly squeezed lemon juice

1 tablespoon cornstarch

¼ teaspoon salt

2 tablespoons butter

**4 cups cut-up peaches (sliced into ¼-inch wedges,
then cut into ½-inch chunks)**

1 tablespoon white sugar, plus a bit additional for sprinkling over crust

4 ounces fresh sweetberries (about 1 cup)

½ teaspoon vanilla extract

Ready-to-use pastry for single-crust pie

1 egg white, beaten

Position oven rack in top third of oven; heat to 450°F. In small bowl, stir together cider, brown sugar, lemon juice, cornstarch and salt; set aside. In heavy, oven-safe 10-inch skillet, melt butter over medium heat. Add peaches and 1 tablespoon white sugar, then cook, stirring occasionally, until juices released by peaches have mostly cooked away, about 10 minutes. Add sweetberries and vanilla; cook until juices thicken, about 5 minutes longer, stirring several times. Stir cider mixture again, then pour into skillet; cook, stirring constantly, for about 1 minute, then remove from heat. Level fruit with a spoon; working carefully to avoid burning yourself, place pastry on top of fruit, using a spoon to tuck pastry edges down along the inside edge of the skillet. Brush pastry with egg white; sprinkle with a light dusting of white sugar. Use a sharp knife to make 4 cuts in the pastry in a tic-tac-toe pattern; as you cut, the pastry edges will be partially pushed down into the pan juices. Place skillet on top rack and bake until crust is rich golden brown and juices are bubbling, 20 to 25 minutes. Let cool on wire rack for 15 minutes before serving.

Two-Berry Freezer Jam

3 half-pints

This rich jam is the perfect topper for toast made from whole-grain bread.

6 ounces fresh or previously frozen sweetberries (about 1½ cups fresh, or ¾ cup thawed berries with juice)

2 cups wild or purchased blueberries (about 10 ounces), approximate

¾ cup sugar

2 tablespoons Ball RealFruit Instant Pectin (see tip on pg. 85)

Prepare three half-pint canning jars, bands and new lids as described on pg. 183, or have clean plastic freezer containers ready (see tip on pg. 140). Place a single layer of sweetberries in a large mixing bowl; mash with a potato masher until all fruits are crushed but the mixture still has some texture. Transfer to a 2-cup measure; continue mashing until all of the sweetberries have been mashed. Repeat with blueberries, adding to the measuring cup with the sweetberries as each layer is crushed; continue until you have 1⅔ cups of mashed berries.

In a clean mixing bowl, stir together sugar and pectin. Add measured, mashed berries. Stir constantly for 3 minutes. Spoon into prepared jars or containers, leaving ½ inch headspace; cover with clean lids. Let stand at room temperature for 30 minutes. Refrigerate or freeze after standing time. Use refrigerated jam within 3 weeks. Frozen jam can be kept for up to a year; thaw frozen jam in refrigerator.

Sweetberry Jelly

2 half-pints

1½ cups sweetberry juice

1 tablespoon lemon juice

One-third of a 1.75-ounce box powdered pectin

¼ teaspoon butter, optional (helps reduce foaming)

1½ cups sugar

Prepare and process as directed in Jelly Instructions (using pectin), pgs. 176–177.

Other recipes in this book featuring sweetberries:
Six Recipes Using Wild Fruit Juice or Syrup, pgs. 170–174
Wild Berry or Fruit Syrup, pg. 175
Dehydrating Wild Berries and Fruits, pgs. 180–181
Wild Berry or Fruit Leather, pg. 182
As a variation in Strawberry Smoothie, pg. 156

MIXED BERRY DISHES

Following are two very special recipes that use a mixed bag of wild berries or other wild fruits. Substitutions are given for some of the fruits, in case you are missing one of the species listed.

Fruits of the Forest Pie   1 pie (6 to 8 servings)

This uses a mixture of brambles and berries—heaven in a pie crust. Use what you have on hand (or in the freezer) to fill the amounts noted.

Ready-to-use pastry for two-crust pie

1½ cups huckleberries, serviceberries, bilberries or blueberries— all one type, or a mix

1½ cups brambles such as raspberries (red or whitebark), thimbleberries, blackberries or dewberries—all one type, or a mix

½ cup grated apple, hawthorn or sweet crabapples*

¾ to 1 cup sugar, depending on the sweetness of the berries

1 tablespoon cornstarch

1 tablespoon butter, cut into small pieces

Optional wash: 1 egg lightly beaten with 1 tablespoon milk

Position rack in lower third of oven; heat to 425°F. Line pie plate with one crust; set aside. In mixing bowl, combine berries, brambles, apple, sugar and cornstarch; stir gently to combine. Spoon into bottom crust. Scatter cut-up butter over the fruit. Brush crust edges lightly with water; top with second crust, crimping edges to seal (or, make a lattice crust; see "Making a Lattice-Top Pie," pg. 55). Brush crust with egg mixture; cut several slits in crust. Place pie on a baking sheet (to catch drips). Bake for 10 minutes, then reduce heat to 350°F and cook until crust is rich golden brown and filling bubbles through slits, 35 to 45 minutes longer; if top crust is browning too quickly near the end of baking time, place a piece of foil loosely over the top. Cool on wire rack; best served slightly warm, the day it is made.

*The native wild crabapples (*Peraphyllum ramosissimum*, which grow on a tall shrub rather than a tree) may be too tart or bitter for this recipe. Crabapples from planted trees (*Malus* spp.) work fine. If you're not sure about crabapples you've found, taste a few; if they have a pleasant flavor they will work fine, but if not, use purchased apples instead.

Brambleberry Cream Sauce

About 2 cups (enough for 6 to 8 servings)

Serve this sauce warm with crêpes, over angel food cake or biscuits, on cereal or pancakes, or however you like.

4 tablespoons (half of a stick) cold unsalted butter, divided

2 tablespoons all-purpose flour

1 cup heavy cream

⅔ cup sugar

¼ teaspoon salt

¾ cup red raspberries, thimbleberries or red dewberries—all one type, or a mix

¾ cup whitebark raspberries, blackberries or black dewberries—all one type, or a mix

In heavy-bottomed saucepan, melt 2 tablespoons of the butter over medium heat. Whisk in flour. Cook, whisking constantly, until mixture thickens and turns golden; don't let it burn. Whisk in cream, sugar and salt. Cook over medium heat, whisking frequently, until mixture bubbles and thickens to sauce-like consistency; this will take 3 or 4 minutes. Stir in berries. Cook, stirring gently a few times, for about a minute. Remove from heat. Quickly cut remaining butter into 4 pieces. Add a piece to the warm sauce and stir until it melts. Repeat with remaining butter, adding just one piece at a time and stirring until it melts. Serve immediately, or keep warm until ready to serve.

SIX RECIPES USING
WILD FRUIT JUICE or SYRUP

Here are a half-dozen recipes that work well with juice or syrup you've made from just about any type of wild fruit. One or two suggested juices are listed with most recipes, but feel free to experiment, substituting a different type of juice for the one listed. You may need to increase the amount of sweetening if your juice is particularly tart.

Wild Fruit Sorbet
About 3 cups

This basic recipe works with any wild fruit juice in this book, except mountain ash; you need an ice-cream maker to prepare this. Depending on the type of fruit juice you use, your sorbet may be pink, purple, rich purple, greenish or red. For an attractive presentation, place a small scoop of the sorbet in a dish with a small scoop of lemon sherbet and another of vanilla ice cream; garnish with a shortbread or ginger cookie.

1 cup sugar

⅝ cup water

1¾ cups blackberry juice or other wild fruit juice

A pinch of salt

1 egg white (from commercially pasteurized egg if concerned about salmonella)

If using ice-cream maker that requires pre-freezing, place it in freezer as directed by manufacturer, generally 12 to 24 hours. Combine sugar and water in small saucepan. Heat to boiling, stirring just until sugar dissolves. Remove from heat; cool to room temperature, then place in freezer for 30 minutes, or in refrigerator for at least 2 hours, until completely chilled. Combine sugar mixture, wild fruit juice and salt in a 1-quart jar; chill overnight.

Transfer mixture to prepared ice-cream maker and churn until slushy and beginning to hold a soft shape, 7 to 10 minutes. In small bowl, beat egg white with a fork for 45 seconds, then add to ice-cream maker with slush. Continue to churn until mixture freezes to a soft ice-cream consistency, 12 to 15 minutes longer. The sorbet will be very soft at this point. Scoop sorbet into plastic container and freeze for at least 3 hours; mixture can be frozen for up to a week. It will remain scoopable for several days; if it becomes too hard to scoop, place container in the refrigerator for about 30 minutes to soften the sorbet slightly before serving.

Wild Fruit Gels (Gumdrops)

This works great with the juice from any wild fruit in this book, except mountain ash. Juice from dark fruits like chokecherries, raspberries or blackberries makes attractive, deeply colored gels; for example, juice from squashberries makes stunning, bright-red gels. Note: This is based on a recipe that appeared in Family Circle *magazine in the early 1970s. I've cut the recipe in half; if you want to make a full batch, simply double the ingredients and use an 8x8-inch baking dish.*

**Half of a 1.75-ounce box powdered pectin
(see pg. 176 for information on dividing pectin)**

³⁄₈ cup wild fruit juice

¼ teaspoon baking soda

½ cup sugar, plus additional for rolling the gels

½ cup white corn syrup

You'll need two medium saucepans (large, if you're doubling the recipe), two long-handled spoons and a standard-sized loaf pan (glass or nonstick metal work best). Wet the inside of the loaf pan, then line it with plastic wrap, smoothing it out (the water helps hold the wrap in place).

Combine the pectin, fruit juice and baking soda in one pan; combine the ½ cup sugar and the corn syrup in the other. Place a spoon in each pan, and keep those spoons separate from one another throughout the procedure.

Stir both mixtures well, and place both pans over medium-high heat. The pectin mixture will foam up at the beginning; stirring will prevent it from boiling over. Cook both mixtures, stirring alternately, until the foam subsides from the pectin mixture and the sugar mixture is boiling vigorously, about 5 minutes. Pour the pectin mixture in a thin, steady stream into the sugar mixture, stirring constantly. Boil the mixture, stirring constantly, for 1 minute longer. Pour the mixture immediately into the loaf pan. Let stand at room temperature, covered very loosely with a piece of cheesecloth to discourage flies, until completely cool; this will take about 2 hours. (Alternately, you can pour the mixture into tiny molds, if you have them.) Place another piece of plastic wrap on top, pressing it against the surface of the mixture; refrigerate for at least 3 hours and as long as overnight.

Unmold gelled mixture onto a cutting board; remove plastic wrap. Cut into 1-inch squares with a sharp knife (dip it in very hot water, then dry off, to make cutting easier). Roll gels in sugar, and arrange in a single layer on a serving plate. Refrigerate or freeze for longer storage, keeping a little space between gels and using waxed paper between layers.

Panna Cotta with Fruit Gel Topping

6 servings

Panna cotta means "cooked cream"; it's an elegant but simple Italian dessert. You'll need 6 small ramekins to prepare this version that is crowned with glistening fruit gel.

1 cup sliced strawberries (store-bought berries work fine)
1 cup dark-colored wild fruit juice such as chokecherry
½ to ¾ cup sugar
2 tablespoons cold water
1½ teaspoons unflavored gelatin

Panna cotta:
2 tablespoons cold water
2 teaspoons unflavored gelatin
1 cup half-and-half
½ cup (packed) golden brown sugar
2 cups buttermilk
1 teaspoon vanilla extract

Lightly spray 6 ramekins (1 cup each) with nonstick spray. Arrange in a baking dish that holds them comfortably. Divide strawberries evenly between ramekins; set aside. In small, non-aluminum saucepan, combine juice and ½ cup sugar. Heat the mixture over medium heat, stirring constantly, until sugar dissolves. Cool slightly and taste for sweetness; add additional sugar as needed until the sweetness is the way you like it.

Pour cold water into small bowl. Sprinkle gelatin evenly over water; set aside for 5 minutes. Near the end of the 5 minutes, heat fruit juice mixture over medium-high heat until it is boiling gently. Scrape the gelatin mixture into the fruit juice, stirring vigorously to combine. Boil gently for about a minute, then remove from heat and pour into individual ramekins, dividing equally. Freeze until just set, about 30 minutes; or refrigerate until set, 2 to 3 hours.

When the gel is set, prepare the panna cotta: Pour cold water into small bowl. Sprinkle gelatin evenly over water; set aside for 5 minutes. In medium, non-aluminum saucepan, stir together half-and-half and brown sugar; heat over medium-high heat, stirring constantly, until sugar dissolves. Scrape the gelatin mixture into the half-and-half, stirring vigorously to combine. Remove from heat and cool to lukewarm, stirring frequently. Stir in buttermilk and vanilla. Pour over set gel; cover each dish with plastic wrap and refrigerate until firm, about 4 hours. These can be prepared up to 2 days in advance.

To serve, run a thin knife around the edge of each ramekin, then hold one ramekin in a shallow pan of very hot water for a few seconds to loosen bottom. Place an individual dessert plate over the ramekin and flip the two over as one, holding together tightly. Gently remove ramekin; repeat with remaining desserts. Serve immediately.

Wild Silk Pie with Cream Cheese Topping

1 pie (8 servings)

This pie is very sweet and rich, so a little goes a long way.

1 purchased shortbread crust or deep graham-cracker crust

1 can (14 ounces) sweetened condensed milk (reduced-fat works fine)

4 egg yolks

1 whole egg

¾ cup wild fruit syrup, or ⅔ cup wild fruit juice mixed with ⅔ cup sugar

2 packages (3 ounces each) cream cheese, softened

½ cup powdered sugar

½ cup sour cream (reduced-fat works fine)

1 teaspoon vanilla extract

Heat oven to 350°F. Bake the crust for 5 minutes. Remove from oven and set aside to cool while you prepare the filling. Reduce oven to 325°F.

In large mixing bowl, combine sweetened condensed milk, egg yolks, whole egg and syrup (or juice/sugar mixture). Beat with electric mixer or sturdy whisk until smooth and completely combined. Place prepared crust onto a baking sheet, and pour in the condensed-milk mixture. Bake in center of oven for about 45 minutes, or until knife inserted in center of pie comes out clean.

While pie is baking, prepare cream cheese topping: In medium mixing bowl, combine cream cheese, powdered sugar, sour cream and vanilla. Beat with electric mixer or wooden spoon until smooth and uniform. When pie filling tests done, remove pie from oven and spread cream cheese mixture evenly over the top, spreading gently with rubber spatula. Return to oven and bake for 10 to 15 minutes longer, or until cream cheese mixture can be touched lightly without sticking. Remove pie from oven and cool completely before covering and placing in refrigerator to chill for several hours. Serve cold.

Cappuccino with Flavor Shot Per serving

Just like at the expensive coffee house! You need an espresso machine to make these, but that piece of equipment is becoming quite common in the well-stocked kitchen.

1 tablespoon chokecherry syrup or other wild fruit syrup per serving, or to taste

Cold, fresh milk (skim, lowfat or whole)

Finely ground espresso coffee beans

Prepare the espresso maker, getting it up to temperature and ready to steam. Pour the syrup into a large mug; set it aside while you prepare the milk and coffee. Fill the metal pitcher about half full; clip a milk thermometer inside the pitcher so its tip is just below the surface of the milk. Froth the milk with the steam wand, holding the pitcher so the wand is at an angle with the tip just under the surface of the milk. Steam to a temperature of 150°F. Set aside; the temperature will rise another 5°F while it sits.

Pack a full measure of finely ground espresso into the filter basket and tamp it firmly. Pull a shot into a shot glass or other measure, then pour into the mug; for a double, pull a second shot and add it to the mug. Immediately pour the steamed milk into the cup, holding back the froth with a spoon; fill the mug half to two-thirds full of steamed milk. Spoon the froth over the coffee, filling the mug to the brim.

Some baristas chill the metal milk pitcher for a few minutes in the freezer to produce better froth. Also, some steam the milk first, then "pull the shot" of espresso; others make the espresso before steaming the milk.

Italian Cremosa Soda Per serving

A cooling beverage that is welcome in hot weather.

3 tablespoons raspberry syrup or other wild fruit syrup

½ cup cold whole milk, or a mix of milk and half-and-half

Crushed ice

Carbonated water

In a tall glass, stir together the syrup and milk. Fill glass half full with crushed ice; add carbonated water to the brim. Serve with a straw, and a tall spoon for mixing.

GENERAL INSTRUCTIONS and INFORMATION

The information that follows applies to a number of fruits in this book. Here you'll find information on making syrup, jelly and jam; dehydrating fruits and making fruit leathers; sterilizing canning jars; and processing in a water-bath canner.

Wild Berry or Fruit Syrup   About 1½ cups syrup per cup of juice

This works great with juice from a variety of wild berries and other wild fruits. Use it as you would use maple syrup: on pancakes, over ice cream, on hot cereal, etc. For a refreshing beverage, pour a few tablespoons of syrup into a glass of sparkling water with ice cubes, or add a bit of syrup to a glass of chilled white wine.

1 cup juice from wild berries or other wild fruit

Sugar as directed in Group lists below

3 tablespoons corn syrup

Group A (use 1 cup sugar per cup of juice): Apples, blackberries, buffaloberries, chokecherries, crabapples, currants, dewberries, goji berries, grapes, hawthorns, mulberries, raspberries, sweetberries, wild cherries.

Group B (use 1¼ cups sugar per cup of juice): Barberries, elderberries (also add 1 teaspoon lemon juice), gooseberries, plums, prickly pear fruits, rose hips, thimbleberries.

Group C (use 1½ cups sugar per cup of juice): Highbush cranberries, mahonia berries, squashberries, sumac.

Prepare jars, bands and new lids as directed on pg. 183 (even if you won't be canning the syrup, it's a good idea to sterilize the jars and lids as directed). In medium non-aluminum saucepan, combine juice and sugar. Heat over medium-high heat, stirring constantly, until sugar dissolves and mixture just begins to boil. Adjust heat so mixture boils gently. Add corn syrup and cook, stirring almost constantly, for 5 minutes; watch for boilover and adjust the heat to prevent a too-vigorous boil. After 5 minutes, pour into hot, sterilized jars; seal with new lids and clean bands. Cool and store in the refrigerator; if you prefer, process in a boiling-water bath for 15 minutes at 5,000 feet, or at the recommended time for jelly at your elevation (see pg. 183).

 The instructions are for 1 cup of prepared juice; however, you can proportionally increase the ingredients for any amount of juice.

Jelly Instructions (using pectin)

Pectin is a substance that helps fruit juices set, or jell, when making jelly or jam. Most fruits—wild or domestic—don't have enough natural pectin to set properly, so pectin needs to be added. Packaged pectin comes in two forms: a powder, typically sold in a 1.75-ounce box, and a liquid, typically sold in a box containing two 3-ounce pouches. The packages contain helpful inserts with recipes for common domestic fruits; some of these, such as raspberries, apples and currants, also grow in the wild, so you can use the recipes in the box for those fruits—if you have enough juice. Other wild fruits are not included on the insert, but those that make good jelly have been included in this book. Recipes for jelly are found throughout this book, with individual fruit accounts; the instructions below are general, and apply to all jelly recipes that use packaged pectin.

Recipes that come with packaged pectin are very specific, calling for precise amounts of fruit juice, sugar and pectin, and exact cooking procedures. However, these recipes require a lot of juice—as much as 7 cups, depending on the type of fruit. A box of powdered pectin makes more jelly—and requires more juice—than a pouch of liquid pectin. For example, a batch of currant jelly made with Sure-Jell powdered pectin, prepared according to the recipe in the box, requires 6½ cups of juice and yields 9 cups of jelly; a batch made with Certo liquid pectin requires 5 cups of juice and yields 8 cups of jelly.

Wild fruit juice is not always easy to come by, and you may want to use some of it for other recipes rather than making, say, 10 jars of one type of jelly. Liquid pectin allows you to make a smaller amount, but it still might use more juice than you want. Another option is to divide the pectin to make small-batch jelly; this requires a bit of tinkering.

Dividing the pectin: The most challenging task is dividing the packaged pectin into smaller amounts, and it's important to measure accurately. The best method is to weigh the contents of a full box of pectin on a gram scale (ounce scales are not precise enough), then weigh out the portion you need. For example, the powder in a 1.75-ounce box of Sure-Jell pectin I checked weighs 51 grams, so if a recipe calls for ⅔ of a box, use 34 grams (51 divided by 3 is 17; multiply by 2 to get 34). If you don't have a gram scale, measure the powder very carefully with measuring spoons (scoop or spoon the powder into the measuring spoon until it is completely full, then level off the top with the back of a knife), then divide accordingly. The same box of powdered pectin that weighs 51 grams measures 16½ teaspoons (5 tablespoons plus 1½ teaspoons) with my measuring spoons, so ⅔ of a box would be 11 teaspoons (16.5 divided by 3 is 5.5; multiply by 2 to get 11).

Small-batch jelly also cooks slightly differently than large-batch jelly, such as those on the insert in the pectin box; the smaller batch loses proportionally more liquid due to evaporation than a larger batch. If you're experimenting with your own small-batch recipes, you'll need to add just a bit more liquid than what would be indicated by simply dividing a full-batch recipe. Standard recipes also account for varying amounts of natural pectin that is in specific fruits, and so use varying amounts of juice in proportion to the added pectin depending on the type of fruit. Wild fruits vary quite a bit in natural pectin content, especially if they're not fully ripe. And some jellies take a week or even longer to set up—wild cherry is one I've had this experience with.

In summary, when working with wild fruits, you may occasionally end up with jelly that doesn't set, or jelly that is too firm. If the jelly is still liquid-like 10 days after processing, use it like syrup; it will be delicious. If the jelly is too solid, you can melt it and stir in a little water before using. Another option for too-firm jelly (or jam) is to serve it as "cheese." Set the jar in a pan of very hot water for a few minutes, then slide the jelly out onto a plate. Slice it, and serve it on its own, or use the slices to top toast that's been smeared with cream cheese. Gooseberries are often prepared as "cheese" in England and served in this fashion. It's a delicious solution for jelly or jam that is too thick to spread.

How to cook jelly with added pectin: Prepare half-pint canning jars, bands and new lids as described on pg. 183. Measure the sugar you'll need, and set it aside so it is ready to use. Combine juice, and lemon juice if listed, in a non-aluminum saucepan or pot that holds at least four times the amount of juice you're using. Whisk in pectin until dissolved; add butter if using (it helps reduce foaming). Heat to boiling over high heat, stirring frequently. When mixture comes to a full, rolling boil that can't be stirred down, add the sugar. Cook, stirring constantly, until the mixture again comes to a full, foaming boil. Boil for 1 minute, stirring constantly (if mixture threatens to boil over, move pan from heat for a few seconds, then reduce heat slightly and return pan to heat). Remove from heat, and stir for a minute or two to settle the foam; if there is still foam on top, skim with a clean spoon and discard. Pour into prepared jars, leaving ¼ inch headspace; seal with prepared lids and bands. Process in a boiling-water bath for 15 minutes at 5,000 feet, or at the recommended time for your elevation (see pg. 183); if you prefer, you can store the jelly in the refrigerator where it will keep for a month or longer.

Jelly Instructions for Fruits with Natural Pectin

Some fruit juices, such as apple juice, have enough natural pectin that they will set without the addition of commercial pectin. However, natural pectin content varies depending on the ripeness of the fruit, time of year and other conditions, so exact cooking times can't be given; the times listed in individual recipes are a general guideline. There are three ways to test for doneness; here are directions for all three. Use whichever you prefer; you may even want to use two tests on a batch of jelly until you gain experience in jelly-making.

The temperature method is the most scientific test to judge doneness. At 8°F above the boiling point of water, the sugar concentration is high enough that the liquid should jell when it cools; once your mixture reaches that point, it's done. Because the boiling temperature of water changes with altitude and other factors, it's necessary to measure the boiling temperature of water in your kitchen on the day you'll be making jelly (it can change slightly from day to day, depending on atmospheric conditions and other factors). Plus, thermometers may read slightly differently so it's important to test the temperature of boiling water with the same thermometer you'll be using to check the jelly. Add 8 to the boiling temperature shown on your thermometer that day, then cook your jelly to that temperature (so if your thermometer reads 202°F for a pan of boiling water, cook your jelly to 210°F).

The temperature method works well, but it can be difficult to get a reading when the jelly is cooking. Candy thermometers can be clipped to the side of the pan and monitored throughout cooking, but most need to be immersed into an inch (or more) of boiling liquid to read properly, and that's difficult with a small batch of jelly. Instant-read thermometers require less immersion, but they can't be left in place for more than a few minutes. You can hold them with a tongs and put the tip into the mixture, but it's steamy work because, in spite of the name, these thermometers don't really read "instantly"; it can take up to two minutes.

The spoon test is also called the sheeting test. To use this method, dip a clean, cool metal spoon into the jelly kettle to spoon up a bit of the mixture. Quickly raise it a foot above the jelly kettle, out of the steam, and turn it sideways so the mixture drips back into the kettle off the side of the spoon. If the mixture forms two large drips that flow together and fall off the spoon in a sheet, it is done; get it off the heat immediately. Sometimes, your range hood gets in the way of this test; and, you need a supply of clean, cool spoons in case you need to test the jelly several times.

The cold-plate test is foolproof and easy to use, but sometimes, it's hard to know when to start testing. Many cooks use the spoon test as a preliminary, and follow up with the cold-plate test to confirm doneness. To use the cold-plate test, place a ceramic plate in the freezer to chill when you start boiling the jelly mixture. When you think the jelly is approaching doneness, drop a teaspoon of the mixture onto the cold plate and return it to the freezer for about a minute. Remove the plate from the freezer, and push at the jelly with your fingertip. If the surface wrinkles and the jelly seems firm, with no weeping around the edge, the jelly is done; get it off the heat immediately. If it is not done, return the plate to the freezer and continue cooking the jelly, testing again in a few minutes.

Here are recipes for specific wild-fruit jellies (also see "Freezer jams and jellies" on pg. 179):

Jam Instructions (using pectin)

Making jam with added pectin is similar to making pectin-added jelly, but you start with puréed or crushed fruit rather than juice. For most small-batch jam recipes in this book, you'll need to divide the pectin as instructed in the jelly instructions on pg. 176. Another option is to use Ball RealFruit Instant Pectin, which is a fairly new product (as of this writing); look for it in a plastic jar with the canning supplies. It is formulated especially for small-batch jam making and includes several recipes on the label. Several recipes in this book use this product; see below. (Note that instant pectin is a different formulation than other pectin products and it is not interchangeable with them.)

Prepare half-pint canning jars, bands and new lids as described on pg. 183. Measure the sugar you'll need, and set it aside so it is ready to use. Combine puréed or crushed fruit, and lemon juice if listed, in a non-aluminum saucepan or pot that holds at least four times the amount of purée or crushed fruit you're using. Whisk in powdered pectin until dissolved; add butter if using (it helps reduce foaming). Heat to boiling over high heat, stirring frequently. When mixture comes to a full, rolling boil that can't be stirred down, add the sugar. Cook, stirring constantly, until the mixture again comes to a full, foaming boil. Boil for 1 minute, stirring constantly; if mixture threatens to boil over, move from heat for a few seconds, then reduce heat slightly and return pan to heat before it stops boiling. Remove from heat, and stir for a minute or two to settle the foam; if there is still foam on top, skim with a clean spoon and discard. Pour into prepared jars, leaving ¼ inch headspace; seal with prepared lids and bands. Process in a boiling-water bath for 20 minutes at 5,000 feet, or at the recommended time at your elevation (see pg. 183); if you prefer, you can store the jam in the refrigerator where it will keep for a month or longer.

Here are recipes for specific wild-fruit jams using pectin:
Smoother Blackberry Jam, pg. 25
Spiced Buffaloberry Spread, pg. 29
Mahonia-Champagne Jam, pg. 97

Freezer jams and jellies are made with added pectin, but the fruit is not cooked. Jams and jellies made in this way have a brighter, fresher flavor than those made with cooked fruit. Freezer jams and jellies are so named because jars aren't processed in a boiling-water bath; rather, they are stored in the freezer for up to a year (or in the refrigerator, where they will keep for several weeks). Instructions are included with each recipe.

Here are recipes for specific freezer jams and jellies made with wild fruits:
Blackberry jam, pg. 24
Grape jelly, pg. 63
Huckleberry, bilberry or blueberry jam, pg. 85 (using instant pectin)
Serviceberry jam, pg. 140
Strawberry jam, pg. 154 (using regular or instant pectin)
Sweetberry-blueberry jam, pg. 167 (using instant pectin)

Dehydrating Wild Berries and Fruits

Home drying, or dehydrating, is an excellent preservation method for many wild fruits. It works on a simple principle: Warm air is circulated over prepared foods to remove the moisture. Food is held on a tray that allows maximum air flow. Several home dehydrators are available; your oven can also be used. Dehydrators come with their own trays. For oven dehydrating, stretch a piece of bridal-veil netting over a cake-cooling rack, then secure it with twist-ties. Fruit leathers need to be dried on a solid liner sheet (dehydrator) or plastic-lined baking sheet (oven); see pg. 182 for information on fruit leathers.

Fruits can generally be dried with no preparation other than washing and perhaps slicing. (In comparison, vegetables generally need to be blanched, or parboiled, before dehydrating.) As a general rule, if a fruit can be frozen with no special preparation, it can also be dried with no special preparation. Some fruits dehydrate better if they are first syrup-blanched; the dried fruit will be softer and stickier than untreated fruit, and will have more vibrant color. To prepare the syrup, combine 1 cup sugar and 1 cup white corn syrup with 2 cups water. Heat to boiling, stirring until sugar dissolves. Add fruit; reduce heat and simmer for 5 minutes. Drain and rinse fruit in cold water before drying.

Arrange foods on the trays in even layers, ideally with air space between each piece. However, keep in mind that the food will shrink as it dries, so the spaces between the foods will grow. Stir, turn over or rearrange the food periodically during drying, to separate pieces that may be stuck together and to promote even drying.

Quality home dehydrators have thermostats; 145°F works well for fruits. If you're drying in the oven, set it to the lowest setting, and prop the door slightly ajar with a ball of foil or an empty can; this allows moisture to escape, and also keeps the temperature down.

To check foods for dryness, remove a piece or two from the dehydrator or oven, and cool to room temperature before judging doneness. (If you're making fruit leather, remove the entire tray and let it cool slightly before checking.) Some individual pieces may be dry sooner than others; simply remove them from the trays and continue drying the rest until everything is finished. Let the food stand at room temperature for an hour or so, then pack into clean glass jars, seal tightly and store in a cool, dark location. Check it several times over the next few days to be sure that moisture isn't developing inside the jars; if you see any moisture, take the food out and dry it some more in the dehydrator or oven. Properly dehydrated foods retain their quality and freshness for a year or longer. If you notice any mold, however, discard the entire contents of the jar *without tasting*; moisture has gotten in somehow and compromised the food, and it is no longer safe.

Note: The information here comes largely from my books, *Abundantly Wild: Collecting and Cooking Wild Edibles in the Upper Midwest*, and *The Back-Country Kitchen: Camp Cooking for Canoeists, Hikers and Anglers.*

Barberries: Frozen or fresh barberries both dry well, and require no pretreatment. Doneness test: Leathery, deep red, wrinkled, slightly flattened when dry. Drying time: 6 to 10 hours.

Buffaloberries: Frozen or fresh berries both dry well, and require no pretreatment. Doneness test: Leathery, not sticky, wrinkled, slightly flattened when dry. Drying time: 6 to 10 hours.

Currants or gooseberries: Frozen or fresh berries both dry well, and require no pretreatment; fresh berries can be dipped briefly into boiling water to "check" (break) the skin, which reduces drying time. Doneness test: Hard, dark, wrinkled; frozen and "checked" berries will be slightly flattened when dry. Drying time: 8 to 10 hours.

Elderberries: Spread washed elderberries (stemlets removed) on mesh liners over drying trays (elderberries get quite small when dried, and will fall through normal dryer trays). Doneness test: Shrunken and hard. Drying time: 4 to 5 hours.

Ground cherries: Frozen or fresh ground cherries both dry well. Wash and cut into halves; arrange, cut-side up, on dryer trays. Doneness test: They will shrink and flatten quite a bit, becoming leathery; color will deepen. Drying time: About 5 hours.

Huckleberries, bilberries or blueberries: Frozen or fresh huckleberries, bilberries and blueberries all dry well, and require no pretreatment; fresh berries can be dipped briefly into boiling water to "check" (break) the skin, which reduces drying time. Doneness test: Hard, dark, wrinkled; frozen and "checked" berries will be slightly flattened when dry. Drying time: 6 to 12 hours.

Mountain ash berries: These mealy berries dry well at room temperature; simply spread them on baking sheets and let stand at room temperature until dry, stirring several times a day. To hasten drying, spread individual berries, or even small berry clusters, on the tray of a food dehydrator or baking sheet for oven drying. Doneness test: Leathery and hard, deep brick color. Drying time (dehydrator or oven): 3 to 4 hours.

Plums: Halve plums and remove pits. Plums can be dried with no further pretreatment, or syrup-blanched first. Arrange plum halves, blanched or not, cut-side up, on dryer trays. Doneness test: Shrunken, firm and leathery; blanched plums will be softer and stickier when dry, while untreated fruit will be harder and more chewy. Drying time: 8 to 24 hours, depending on size of fruit.

Raspberries, dewberries or mulberries: Spread in single layer on solid liner sheets or baking sheets (for oven drying) to catch drips; no pretreatment is needed. If you like, transfer fruits to regular (ventilated) dryer trays after an hour or 2, after any juices have been released, to hasten drying. Doneness test: Leathery and shrunken. Drying time: 4 to 10 hours; raspberries dry more quickly than dewberries or mulberries.

Serviceberries: Remove stem and blossom ends. Cut fruits in half for quicker drying, or dry whole. Arrange in single layer on trays. Doneness test: Shrunken and leathery. Drying time: 6 to 10 hours.

Strawberries: Wash; remove cap. Arrange on trays no more than 2 deep. Doneness test: Leathery and somewhat spongy. Drying time: 4 to 8 hours, depending on size.

Sweetberries: Spread in single layer on solid liner sheets or baking sheets (for oven drying) to catch drips; no pretreatment is needed. If you like, transfer fruits to regular (ventilated) dryer trays after an hour or 2, after any juices have been released, to hasten drying. Doneness test: Leathery and shrunken. Drying time: 4 to 10 hours.

Wild Berry or Fruit Leather

Most fruits can be dried into a leather; generally, all you need to do is simply purée the fruit in a blender or food processor, sweeten to taste as needed, and dry in a food dehydrator or low oven. (Please read the general information on dehydrating foods on pg. 180.) Hard fruits, such as apples and pears, should be cooked in a little water with a few drops of lemon juice before puréeing; soft berries can be puréed and dried with no cooking.

The purée to be dried into a leather should be fairly thick—a consistency like applesauce works well. If you try to dry a purée that is too thin or watery, the leather will take forever to dry, and may be brittle once dry. If the fruit you're working with is watery, or the purée too runny, cook it down for a bit to thicken it before spreading on the drying sheets.

You can add spices to your purées to vary the flavor; try cinnamon or nutmeg with apple or plum purée, or a bit of orange extract with berry purée. For additional interest, sprinkle the purée before drying with finely chopped nuts, shredded coconut or granola.

Commercial dryers come with solid liner sheets that work well, but I've found that some of them need to be sprayed with nonstick spray, especially if the fruit is extremely sticky. Experiment with a small batch of purée to see how your liner sheets perform. If you're drying in the oven or in a homemade dryer, line rimmed baking sheets with plastic wrap, then tape the wrap to the rims of the baking sheets to keep it in place during filling and drying. One standard-sized sheet will hold about 2 cups of purée.

Pour the purée onto prepared baking sheets or dehydrator liners. Tilt the sheets to evenly distribute the purée; it should be about ¼ inch deep. Dry at 130°–150°F until leathery with no sticky spots; peel from the sheets and flip once during drying if the bottom is not drying properly. Total drying time is generally 4 to 10 hours, but this may vary depending on your equipment, the purée and the weather. If you've used baking sheets lined with plastic wrap, the leather can be peeled off any time; if you've used solid liner sheets with a dehydrator, peel off the leather while it is still warm. Roll up all leathers, and wrap in plastic wrap. They keep well at cool room temperature if properly dried; for long-term storage, wrap the plastic-wrapped rolls in freezer wrap and store in the freezer.

Sterilizing Jars and Canning

Jars and lids used for canning need to be sterilized before filling. It's also a good idea to sterilize jars for jams and jellies even if you plan to store the finished product in the refrigerator or freezer. Modern canning jars have two-piece tops: a flat lid, and a screw-on band. When you're canning, always start with a brand-new lid; the rubber seal won't work if the lid has been used before. Bands can be re-used a number of times, but if they start to get corroded, get rid of them and buy new bands.

Always use jars specially made for canning. These jars can be re-used many times, unless they develop a nick or crack. Inspect each jar by holding it up to the light, looking for cracks or fractures. Then, when you are washing the jar prior to sterilizing it, run your wet finger over the top rim of the jar, checking for nicks. Even a small nick will cause canning failure; if you find jars like this in your collection, pack them up for recycling.

All of the jelly and jam recipes in this book call for half-pint jars. These are small enough to fit in a large pot such as a Dutch oven, so you don't have to use a full-sized water bath canner. The jars shouldn't sit directly on the bottom of the pot because they might crack from the heat. If you have a rack or a pasta-cooking insert for your pot, use that to raise the jars above the bottom; otherwise, line the bottom of the pot with a clean, thick towel.

Jelly and jam should be poured into the jars the minute they are done cooking, so the jars must be sterilized and ready to go before you start cooking. Wash jars, bands and lids in hot, soapy water, inspecting the rim; rinse well. Place jars on the rack in the pot, then add water to cover them by an inch. Heat to boiling over high heat. Boil the jars for 10 minutes, then turn off the heat and let the jars sit in the hot water until you're ready to fill them. Meanwhile, place washed lids and bands in a saucepan; cover with water. Heat to a vigorous simmer. Cover and remove from heat.

When the jelly or jam is ready, use canning tongs to remove one jar from the pot, pouring its water back into the pot. Fill the jar with food, leaving the amount of head space indicated in the recipe ("head space" is the empty area at the top of the jar). Wipe the jar rim and threads with a clean paper towel. Place a hot lid and band on top, and screw the band on so it is just finger-tight. If you will be canning the food, return the jar to the pot and repeat with remaining food; otherwise, place the filled jar on a rack to cool.

How to process food in a boiling-water bath
Once the jars are filled and returned to the pot, add additional hot water if necessary to cover the jars by 1 inch. Heat to boiling over high heat, then begin timing and boil for the amount of time indicated in the recipe or in the altitude section below. Use canning tongs to remove the jars from the pot, grasping them below the bands (if you grasp the band itself, you could break the seal). Place jars on a thick towel, away from drafts, to cool. When cool, check each jar for a proper seal. The center of the lid should be depressed, and it should not move up and down when pressed with a finger. If any jars are improperly sealed, refrigerate and enjoy as you would any opened jelly or jam. Sealed jars can be stored in a cool, dark place for up to a year.

Adjusting boiling-water-bath processing time for various altitudes
Because water boils at different temperatures at different altitudes, processing times must be adjusted based on your altitude to ensure that the canned food is safe. The instructions in this book all include time for processing at 5,000 feet (highlighted below); see the chart for a complete range of altitudes based on the food you're canning. (This information is taken from the insert in a package of Sure-Jell pectin; it is the standard used by all authorities.)

ALTITUDE	Sea level–1,000 ft.	1,001–3,000 ft.	3,001–6,000 ft.	6,001–8,000 ft.	8,001–10,000 ft.
Jelly	5 minutes	10 minutes	15 minutes	20 minutes	25 minutes
Jam	10 minutes	15 minutes	20 minutes	25 minutes	30 minutes

BIBLIOGRAPHY

Bittman, Mark. *How to Cook Everything*. New York, NY: Macmillan, a Simon & Schuster Macmillan Company, 1998.

Corriher, Shirley O. *CookWise: The Hows & Whys of Successful Cooking*. New York, NY: William Morrow and Company, Inc., 1997.

Derig, Betty B. and Fuller, Margaret C. *Wild Berries of the West*. Missoula, MT: Mountain Press Publishing Company, 2001.

Freitus, Joe and Haberman, Salli. *Wild Jams & Jellies*. Mechanicsburg, PA: Stackpole Books, 1977.

Gibbons, Euell. *Stalking the Wild Asparagus*. New York, NY: David McKay Company, Inc., 1962.

Harrington, H.D. *Edible Native Plants of the Rocky Mountains*. Albuquerque: The University of New Mexico Press, 1967.

Hibler, Janie. *The Berry Bible*. New York, NY: William Morrow, an imprint of HarperCollins Publishers Inc., 2004.

Krumm, Bob. *The Rocky Mountain Berry Book*. Guilford, CT: The Globe Pequot Press, 1991.

Liddell, Caroline and Weir, Robin. *Frozen Desserts*. New York, NY: St. Martin's Griffin, 1996.

Lyle, Katie Letcher. *The Wild Berry Book: Romance, Recipes and Remedies*. Minnetonka, MN: NorthWord Press, 1994.

Marrone, Teresa. *Abundantly Wild: Collecting and Cooking Wild Edibles in the Upper Midwest* and *The Seasonal Cabin Cookbook*. Cambridge, MN: Adventure Publications, Inc., 2004 and 2001.

Marrone, Teresa. *The Back-Country Kitchen: Camp Cooking for Canoeists, Hikers and Anglers*. Minneapolis, MN: Northern Trails Press, 1996.

Purdy, Susan G. *Pie in the Sky: Successful Baking at High Altitudes*. New York: William Morrow, an imprint of HarperCollins Publishers, 2005.

Seebeck, Cattail Bob. *Best-Tasting Wild Plants of Colorado and the Rockies*. Englewood, CO: Westcliffe Publishers, 1998.

Thayer, Samuel. *The Forager's Harvest* and *Nature's Garden*. Birchwood, WI: Forager's Harvest, 2006 and 2010.

U.S. Department of Agriculture, USDA National Nutrient Database for Standard Reference, Release 21 (http://www.ars.usda.gov/nutrientdata).

Young, Kay. *Wild Seasons: Gathering and Cooking Wild Plants of the Great Plains*. Lincoln, NE: University of Nebraska Press, 1993.

INDEX

ABOUT THE AUTHOR

Teresa Marrone has been gathering and preparing wild edibles for more than 20 years. She is the author of *Abundantly Wild: Collecting and Cooking Wild Edibles in the Upper Midwest*, as well as numerous other outdoors-related cookbooks. Teresa also writes magazine articles on wild foods and cooking. *Cooking with Wild Berries & Fruits of the Rocky Mountain States* combines her various skills and interests into a clear, concise, easy-to-use book that helps the reader appreciate the diversity of the various wild berries and fruits that grow in this region. Teresa lives in Minneapolis with husband Bruce and their Senegal parrot, Tuca.